# FUNDAMENTALS
# OF SPEECH

# FUNDAMENTALS OF SPEECH:

## *The Theory and Practice of Oral Communication*

SECOND EDITION

ROY C. McCALL
*College of the Desert*

HERMAN COHEN
*University of Oregon*

*THE MACMILLAN COMPANY, NEW YORK*
*Collier - Macmillan Limited, London*

First Printing

Library of Congress catalog card number: 63-9599

The Macmillan Company, New York

Collier-Macmillan Canada, Ltd., Galt, Ontario

*Divisions of The Crowell-Collier Publishing Company*

PRINTED IN THE UNITED STATES OF AMERICA

# *Preface*

New knowledge produces some changes in rhetorical theory; changes in society require changed practices in communication.

This second edition of *Fundamentals of Speech* is intended essentially to bring up to date the content and treatment of the first edition to make it consistent with the requirements of the modern scene.

We have, in this edition, taken notice of the greatly increased knowledge about oral communication. The writings and research of psychologists, sociologists, linguists, as well as rhetoricians, have given us a new insight into the form of human behavior called *speech*. It is our firm conviction that the speech student will profit as much from an understanding of oral communication as he will from specific instruction in speech improvement.

Other changes have been made primarily to achieve greater clarity and emphasis.

Dr. Herman Cohen joins the original author as full collaborator.

Acknowledgment is made to Dr. Carter Davidson and to the International Business Machines Corporation for use of "The Three R's"; to *Time* magazine for use of "Don't Land"; to Appleton-Century-Crofts for the excerpt from *Interpretative Reading,* by Sara Lowrey and Gertrude Johnson; to McGraw-Hill for the excerpt from *Sturgis Standard Code of Parliamentary Procedure,* by Alice F. Sturgis; and to Dr. John R. Shepherd, Associate Professor of Speech, University of Oregon, for writing the section on radio and television, pages 235-240.

ROY C. MC CALL

HERMAN COHEN

# Contents

CHAPTER I

# A Preface to Speech

I F EVER IN HISTORY man needed to improve his powers of communication and to use them effectively, now is that time. Never before have the individual and the group been in such great need of understanding fully the thoughts others try to convey to them, or the intentions they may design to hide from them.

Some writers of our time are cynically defining history as a record of mistakes from which man has failed to profit, while others are simultaneously and seriously saying that most of the errors of history have arisen through failures of communication. This latter group ascribes our failures in part to our unwillingness to talk things out fully before we begin to shoot, but in large measure to the inability of language to pierce the culture barriers that separate nations and ideologies.

Transportation and communication are making neighbors

today out of those who yesterday were strangers, and thus are giving new importance to using our language systems on common ground. As long as we can negotiate, and, therefore, of necessity communicate, with Russian and Chinese Communists, we can hold the hope of averting war. As long as we can *communicate* the values of freedom and democracy to neutrals, we can hope that they will become our allies. Whereas electronic devices and the development of radio, television, photography, and the numerous other devices and media of communication have opened up new channels and increased the speed of transmission of language and ideas, man still employs the age-old vehicle of words as a basis for conveying thought.

The superabundance of modern inventions has not reduced the importance of speech, either in the life of the individual or in the processes of society, but has increased it. Telephones, movies, radio, and television have all given speech an increasing importance in our lives. Wherever a person may turn, he is reminded that ours is a communicating world.

In thousands of places every day, millions of persons are being judged by others on the basis of how they express themselves. We judge others by dress, appearance, voice, language, and conciseness, readiness, and propriety of speech. We may not consciously judge on all these points; but unconsciously we include them all. Do you not daily judge the intelligence of your associates by the manner in which they express themselves? True, after you get to know them, you may learn to respect certain specialized talents and abilities that manifest themselves in spite of awkward speech; but your first impressions are derived largely from speech, and your latest impressions never omit it.

To the student who aspires to become a liberally educated and cultivated individual, or even to the one who desires only to equip himself with the tools that will enable him to be "successful" in a chosen vocation, it may safely be said that no single mark of distinction or avenue to success stands higher than his ability to express himself accurately, clearly, and forcefully.

Thus, not only has invention increased the opportunity to communicate, and circumstance created the most urgent necessity for it, but the whole world also has experienced a growing consciousness of communication, its inadequacies and pitfalls, and, unfortunately, how to turn our faith in it to the advantage of those mad for power and to the detriment of those who would live in peace and freedom. The advances of semantics, as well as its growing popularity, attest to our awareness that "words are not what they seem," and that sophistication in the realm of symbolic thinking is a natural requirement of the negotiator at the contract table, the political strategist, the diplomat, the salesman, the lawyer, the judge, the teacher, the journalist, the lecturer, the playwright, the poet, and the parent. We need this improved insight not only to avoid being misunderstood and to reduce our propensity for misunderstanding others, but also so that we may be less often duped by those who in recent years have studied and used the technique of deliberate distortion. Hitler and his pernicious propagandists were the first to use the deliberate lie on a large scale, to confuse both their followers and those they designed to conquer. This technique for exploiting the gullible proved surprisingly effective, because it took advantage of long centuries of the careful building of mutual trust, of reliance on an individual's word—in fact, of faith in the essential goodness of humanity.

The Communists have "improved" upon Hitler's use of dishonesty. They have used the rostrum of the United Nations to heap abuse upon their opposition, to impugn the motives of other members, to accuse without justification,

3

reason, or restraint, to vent their venom on all those who oppose them. But even when they are sincere, we find it almost impossible to communicate with the Communists because of the completely different meanings they apply to the same words. We simply do not speak the same language!

In this new age, we must learn to distinguish between the honest intent of communication and the deliberate aim of using it to deceive us. The fact that words may be used both for honest and dishonest purposes places upon us all an onerous obligation to learn the ins and outs of human communication, its intricacies and pitfalls, uses and abuses, refinements and ramifications. All of this is the obligation of those who cannot yet articulately express their thoughts.

If this last sentence applies to you, as it does to most of us in a greater or lesser degree, then open your mind to a very frank discussion of what to do about it. Why are you not, at this advanced stage in your schooling, already highly proficient in communication? There are some very good reasons.

Perhaps the most important cause for whatever degree of ineptitude you possess is that you have never really cared very much whether you spoke well. Oh yes, you have wished in a general way that you could speak easily, accurately, and effectively. But your concerns have been vague, rather than vital, real, immediate, or personal. You have not cared enough about your skill in communication to be willing to pay the price of diligent study, and the determined and consistent effort necessary to bring about a substantial change. You have never had an urge to make a systematic attack upon your deficiencies, to uproot them one after another, replacing them with specific knowledge and competencies.

The second cause is the counterpart of the first: that is, one rarely learns anything until one develops an *active* and *specific* desire to learn. Except when nature presents man with a painful, or frightening or otherwise dramatic experience to "teach him a lesson," he does not learn except as he

4

*desires* to learn. You do not remember the names of persons to whom you are introduced unless you consciously make note of their names with the specific intent of remembering them. You do not remember the telephone number you looked up a few minutes ago unless you "fix it in your mind" by conscious effort. You do not learn to swim by paddling around in the water; you learn by studied attention to the various aspects of posture and action that keep you afloat and propel you in selected directions.

A specific example of the importance of active effort in learning may be helpful:

> When Katherine Cornell was playing the role of Elizabeth Barrett in *The Barretts of Wimpole Street* at Baylor University, Waco, Texas (the home of the largest Browning collection in the world), Miss Cornell wore a topaz brooch from the collection: the one given to Elizabeth by Robert Browning on the first anniversary of their marriage. Dr. Armstrong, who has devoted his life to assembling and preserving the Browning treasures at Baylor, wished Miss Cornell also to use from the collection the first edition of Sordello. This was the poem from which Elizabeth Barrett was supposed to be reading when Robert made the remark, "At the time that was written only God and Robert Browning knew what it meant; now only God knows." Miss Cornell was appreciative of the honor paid her by the Browning scholar but responded, "Dr. Armstrong, I'm afraid to attempt to play with a book different from the one I'm accustomed to. You see, when we were learning the play, I had my secretary type in the lines to be delivered as I held the book. Although I've played the role over two hundred times I've never memorized those lines." Miss Cornell had not spoken those lines with the will to remember them. She could not, therefore, depend upon her memory to repeat them accurately.[1]

[1] S. Lowery and G. E. Johnson, *Interpretative Reading* (New York: Appleton-Century-Crofts, Inc., 1953). Reprinted by permission of the publisher.

Note that Miss Cornell had *read the lines over two hundred times* during performances, and undoubtedly many more times during rehearsals, but had never *learned* them! Note also that she had memorized all the other speeches of the play, by *consciously making up her mind to learn them.*

Until now, you have probably received little instruction in speech as such. On your first day of school you could speak two hundred words a minute, but you probably could not read or write even one. But the beginning of school reverses the process for the child. In the first place, on entering school he begins formal lessons in the necessity of keeping quiet. Second, he also starts his first lesson in the laborious process of written communication. In comparison with his speech, his writing will be so completely inadequate that, for some years, it must receive the lion's share of attention. Even at the high-school level, speech courses tend to stress the superficial aspects of oral communication rather than placing the emphasis on serious discourse about meaningful ideas.

The time has now arrived when you have the maturity to take a long, hard, and thoughtful look at the functions of communication both from the point of view of their social usefulness and the strictly personal view of their importance. The time has come for you to take inventory of your specific skills and shortcomings, so that you may be able to identify the particular problems on which you must work for improvement. Such a procedure is the only intelligent approach to learning.

The approach of this book is to lay before you in systematic order and progressive sequence the fundamental operations, processes, and skills inherent in oral communication, beginning with the most basic aspects, and proceeding step by step toward the more particularized, specialized, and refined features of speech, keeping in mind the psychological factors in learning as well as the logical elements.

More specifically, it is recognized that thought is the *sine qua non* of communication, whether by spoken or written word, gesture, Morse code, Indian drums, smoke puffs, or sign language. Naturally, one does not communicate nothingness; one communicates some kind of *thought*. Beyond this obvious fact lie such considerations as the *quality* of the thought to be conveyed—its originality, validity, depth, consistency, accuracy, relevance, and coherence. Equally important is the motive behind the communication of thought: why is one trying to communicate one's ideas? Third, the environment, or matrix, in which communication is attempted is important, because by its nature it may either assist or prevent communication. Certainly the social environment is significant if the receivers of communication are defined as part of the communication process and not as passive hearers.

Our primary concerns are: (1) to establish certain basic concepts, understandings, and attitudes concerning the nature and importance of oral communication; and (2) to provide a series of steps, explanations, and exercises that will lead the student naturally through the various phases of learning essential to improvement in, if not to mastery of, the various aspects of speech.

# CHAPTER II

# The Oral Communication Process

Ours is a communicating world in the broadest conceivable sense. No one can watch the various species of birds in flight, noting their instantaneous response to the leader, their power to remain in perfect formation even when shifting direction in a fraction of an instant when surprised, and doubt that they have highly refined codes of signals. Neither can one watch a mother bear control her cubs without marveling at the effectiveness of her wordless communication. The animal world has its signs and symbols for communicating danger, for giving directions, even for conveying affection.

Some of these man has, also. He is a gesturing, pointing, frowning, smiling, grimacing, shrugging creature; he is, however, unlike other animals of his kingdom, a creature of words. In addition to the subtle signs he makes with arms and hands and face and body, he has devised, as we are all well aware, systems of sound symbols that we call *words*. By the use of these symbols, he is able to convey complexities of thought of which the lower animals are not capable.

The essential difference between how man communicates and how lower animals communicate is that non-human animals are able to *vocalize* but only man can *verbalize*. Vocalization is a characteristic of almost all lower animals. It consists of a collection of calls, grunts, yelps, and moans that can convey only very limited meanings. Without the symbols necessary for verbalization, however, it is impossible to produce communication about judgments, opinions, or abstract thoughts of any kind.

It is generally agreed that man passed through a vocalization stage early in his development. But not until humans found verbal symbols for their thoughts was man clearly superior to other members of the animal kingdom. If we observe the speech development of children, we are able to see the transition from vocalization to verbalization compressed into a very short period of time. The communication pattern of a crying infant is far removed from the speech of an articulate adult. In no other creatures do we find such wide differences between infants and adults, because only man has been able to make use of words for the communication of his ideations.

The use of words has given to man another distinct advantage. Only human beings are able to transmit information from generation to generation. Indeed, in advanced societies the availability of verbal symbols has made it possible for knowledge to be stored as well as transmitted. The process of *time-binding* is uniquely human. Whatever lower animals learn during their lives is presumably lost when they die. In effect, each generation must acquire knowledge already learned by previous generations. Man, on the other hand, may take advantage of the learning of his ancestors and go on to advance knowledge even further. Examples of time-binding are found at all stages of social development. The wise man of an Indian tribe and the millions of books stored in the Library of Congress are two examples of the range of time-binding. Without words, the development of what we call civilization would probably have been as slow as the "civilizing" of lower animals.

In short, man is a talking and writing creature; he is a communicating animal. Man's high place in the animal kingdom is as much the result of his having developed complex systems of communicating thoughts as of his higher intelligence. All animals communicate in one way or another, but only man has used his skills to make his communication a unique aspect of human behavior.

Since communication is one aspect of human behavior, it may be examined in much the same way as other kinds of human behavior. Just as the sociologist, the psychologist, or the political scientist looks at the forms of human behavior in which he is interested, so does the communication specialist (rhetorician) examine the behavior of persons when they communicate with each other. It may be said that communication specialists are interested in discovering "who says what to whom, in what way, and with what effect." It will be helpful for students of speech to know some of the basic principles of communicative behavior before they devote their attention to improving their skills as oral communicators. Although the principles of communication that we will present are those dealing most directly with oral communication, most of them are equally applicable to written communication.

Many of us think of speech as an innate and almost automatic act. We assume that because almost all human beings talk, speech is much like walking and climbing; at a particular stage in his development a child begins to speak. Such a notion is not only misguided; it may actually be mischievous. Speech is really closer to its related communicative skills of reading and writing than it is to physical skills such as walking and climbing. The act of speech is not a necessary result of physical maturation. Left to himself, the child begins to walk in his own good time. Lessons in walking are of little assistance to him. Furthermore, a child in Norway will walk in very much the same way as does a child in the Congo. But left to himself, a child will not begin to talk in his own good time. He will have to be taught to talk by the stimulation of his environment. Furthermore, the child in Norway and the child in the Congo will talk in ways completely different from each other. Each of them will have learned the verbal symbols agreed upon by his social system. Speech, therefore, is an aspect of behavior that must be learned from others. A child really left to himself will probably never talk, although he may engage in simple communication through vocalization.

Not only is speech learned behavior; it is also a product of social development. Early in his life, a child's needs are satisfied through the use of vocalization. As the child grows older and finds that his needs no longer can be satisfied by the means of communication available to him, he begins to acquire the symbols whereby other human beings in his social system satisfy their needs. Ordinarily, if a child's needs are satisfied without verbal communication, he will be slow in learning to speak. Likewise, as his need for expression becomes greater and his ideas more complex, he will learn more and more words for expressing his ideas.

At first thought, it may appear that speech is a simple act. Disregarding for the moment the extremely complex physiological processes involved in speech, the social and psychological aspects of oral communication are hardly simple. First of all, we must recognize that communication is a process. That is, it is continuous, on-going, and dynamic. The process of communication may be likened to an automobile assembly line. Although it is possible to follow the progress of one automobile on an assembly line as it reaches completion, automobiles are not made one at a time. At any given moment, many automobiles are undergoing various steps in the assembly process. In much the same way, although we may discuss each element in the process of communication individually, we must realize that all of the elements in the process may be occurring simultaneously. With the concept of process in mind, let us now look at the ingredients of the process of communication.

It might, first of all, be well to remind ourselves that communication is never unilateral. Communication does not occur if your message is not received and understood. Ideal communication is the conveying of what is in your mind to the minds of one or more other human beings. It should be clear, therefore, that communication begins not with the act of speaking, but with the act of thinking. The first ingredient in the process of communication is that of *encoding*. In the encoding stage, the communicator first thinks of the material he wishes to convey and then chooses the best possible verbal symbols to express his thoughts. The reason encoding and thinking are combined in one step is that encoding is not simply the translation of thoughts into words. Rather, it is doubtful that abstract thought may occur without the use of words. It would seem, then, that encoding and thinking occur together. Encoding cannot take place without thought; but, on the other hand, thought is very difficult without encoding.

Following the encoding stage, in the process of communication, comes the *transmission* step. Up to this point, the ideas and the language in which they are phrased remain in the mind of the speaker. Not until the communicator finds a means of transmitting his thoughts, can we say that a message exists. In the context of oral communication, transmission ordinarily refers to the vocal mechanisms and muscle systems that produce vocal and physical delivery. In other forms of communication, there are, of course, other forms of transmission. Handwriting, typing, and printing are all examples of varieties of written transmission. Even within oral communication, there are a number of choices available to the transmitter as means of transmission. He may, for example, choose to deliver a formal public address, to engage in informal conversation, to participate in a group discussion, or to conduct an interview. Although, in each instance, use is made of the vocal mechanisms and muscle systems, the media of transmission are quite different, and quite different results are likely.

Once the message has been encoded and transmitted, the receptive aspects of communication begin. Just as a tree falling in the forest makes no sound unless it is heard, so messages transmitted are not communicated until they are received and understood. Therefore, the next stage in the communication process is the *reception* step. From the point of view of oral communication, reception is, to a considerable extent, physiological. Just as the vocal mechanisms and muscle systems are the basis of transmission, so is the auditory system the basis of reception. Without a receiver, any oral communication disappears in thin air.

Reception, however, is not the end of the communication process. In order for communication to take place, the sound waves must be given meaning through *decoding*. In the decoding stage, the sounds received are translated into words, and the words are assigned meanings. The decoding step is, in a sense, the reverse of the encoding step. Where earlier symbols had been chosen to represent ideas, now the receiver must choose those ideas that correspond to the symbols he has received.

It is possible now to list the steps in the process of communication:

(1) encoding
(2) transmitting
(3) receiving
(4) decoding

In discussing the process of communication, we have described it in its ideal state. Actually, there are many barriers to communication that may lessen the fidelity of the communication process. Perhaps the most obvious barrier is that often the receiver and the transmitter do not share the same code. Without a mutually agreed upon code, there can be essentially no understanding and thus, initially, no communication. It is clear that little if any communication occurs when people speak in languages that their listeners do not know. If a Russian speaks to a Japanese, it is obvious that these two persons are using mutually unintelligible codes, but two Americans may also speak to each other and still not share the same code of symbols. If the vocabulary used by the transmitter is more extensive or more technical than that of the receiver, the fidelity of the communication process is certainly reduced. Both the transmitter and the receiver must recognize that the collection of symbols, which we call a message, has no meaning in itself.

Meanings are not contained in words or collections of words, but in persons. The message may have meaning to the speaker when he transmits it, but it has no meaning to his listener unless the latter is able to interpret the symbols. If you were to come upon a newspaper written in Swahili, it would probably have no meaning to you, but if a person who could read Swahili were to look at the newspaper, the message would acquire meaning because he and the newspaper shared a system of symbols. The greater the mutual understanding of symbols, then, the higher the fidelity of the communication process.

Even under the most ideal conditions, however, we are never completely understood. It is highly unlikely that any two human beings attach exactly the same meaning to the same symbols. Although we may use the same code, we do not use it in identical ways. If, for example, two persons were instructed to describe a given event, it is almost a mathematical impossibility that they would use exactly the same symbols. In other words, to express the same thought they would choose different symbols.

This variation in encoding is also found in decoding. The same symbols will never represent the same thought to two persons. Of course, a much higher degree of fidelity in encoding and decoding will result if the receiver and transmitter belong to similar social systems and have had similar experiences.

There is another reason why we never say exactly what we mean. The entire process of communication is one of symbolization and representation. The words we choose are not things or ideas. They are merely symbols or representations of things and ideas. You have perhaps heard the saying, "The word is not the thing." A word is no more the thing than a photograph or painting is the thing. If you are shown a photograph of your home, you may say, "That is my house," but it really is not your house. If the photograph is destroyed, your house remains standing. Only the symbol has been destroyed. Words, too, are only symbols. Thus, even when he is using words with highest fidelity, man can do no more than choose those symbols that come closest to representing his thoughts. Since his thoughts are at least partly non-verbal, man can never say exactly what he means. There are means, however, of attaining close resemblance between thought and symbolization, and those means will be discussed in the chapter dealing with language.

What is potentially a very important communication barrier is the attitude of the receiver and transmitter toward themselves, toward each other, and toward the message. A speaker who lacks confidence in himself, for example, will be less effective in communicating his ideas than a speaker who is sure of himself. A speaker who regards his listeners with contempt, or one who feels himself inferior to his audience, will have difficulty in transmitting his thoughts. Similarly, the amount of interest, enthusiasm, and knowledge a speaker has about his subject will be very significant in determining the efficiency of his communication. The attitudinal barriers of the speaker are matched by those of the listener. For example, a listener who has a favorable attitude toward a speaker is likely to receive with much higher fidelity than he would if his attitude were unfavorable. By the same token, a subject that is interesting and significant to a listener will be received more precisely than a subject that is uninteresting or insignificant. When we browse through a magazine, why do we stop to read certain articles and not others? Is it not often because of our degrees of interest in the subjects? All students are aware of the greater difficulty encountered in reading assignments in subjects they dislike as compared to subjects they like. The same principle is operative in the relation between the listener and the subject.

A further barrier to communicative efficiency is the factor that some writers have called "noise." If anything happens, inside or outside of the communication system, which distracts either the transmitter or the receiver from the intent of the message, the communication process may be said to be "noisy." A quarrel with his wife, or a reprimand from his boss, will affect the receptivity of a listener. News that his car has been damaged, or that relatives are coming for a visit, will affect the ability of a speaker to communicate his message. A wide variety of causes may account for noisy communication processes. Perhaps there is something about the speaker's voice that distracts from the meaning of the message; perhaps there is something about his manner of dress or his gestures that call attention to themselves and not the message. Since human beings cannot give full, undivided attention indefinitely, it may be said that all communication systems are more or less noisy, but some are much noisier than others. It should be the goal of every communicator to develop a communication environment that is as "quiet" as possible.

Earlier in this chapter, we noted that communication cannot be unilateral: it involves both transmission and reception. Communication can, however, be bilateral or multilateral. Most public speaking occasions are bilateral, in that the speaker is the transmitter, and the audience, even though it may number in the millions, is a composite receiver. Such forms of communication as group discussion and parliamentary procedure, on the other hand, are multilateral. In multilateral communication, we find that at any given moment a particular member of the group may be either a receiver or a transmitter. Whereas bilateral communication has one *receiver* and one *transmission source*, multilateral communication may have many transmitters and receivers.

No matter whether communication is bilateral or multilateral, it is dependent upon the relationship between the speaker and his audience. Indeed, there exists a real communicative interdependence between the encoder and the decoder. In order for communication to proceed efficiently, the encoder must have some idea of what kind of response he is eliciting from his receiver. The process of monitoring our communication and evaluating its effect is sometimes called *feedback*. Feedback is actually a prerequisite of human communication. If we were unable to hear ourselves and monitor our own speech, we would be totally unable to engage in verbal communciation. Many deaf persons do not learn to speak because they get no feedback from the sounds they are able to make. They cannot adjust their communication to achieve a desired response. What we are concerned with in the deaf person is physiological feedback; but the social feedback of everyday discourse is closely related.

Feedback in oral communication takes many forms. Certainly a barrage of rotten tomatoes and an outbreak of hisses and catcalls are violent and immediately recognizable forms of feedback; so are applause, cheering, and whistling. Most of the feedback present in oral communication, however, is more subtle. Whether engaged in conversation with one other person or addressing a crowd of thousands, we are, to some degree, able to evaluate the effect of our communication on the receiver. A nod of the head or an understanding expression may indicate that the message is being received. On the other hand, if a receiver seems to be absorbed in his newspaper or gazes absently out the window, there may be some doubt whether any communication is occurring. In many cases, having received such feedback, the speaker will modify the message in an attempt to improve communication. He will, of course, be able to take advantage of feedback to determine further whether the modifications have been beneficial.

In some genuinely communicative situations, there is no immediate feedback. Persons who communicate through the media of radio, television, film, and recordings cannot usually make use of perceived feedback during the time the message is being transmitted. Even here, however, it is worth noting that many television and radio personalities have insisted that a studio audience be present during a broadcast to provide feedback.

Even when a particular communication system is lacking in immediate feedback, delayed feedback is almost invariably present. An instructor reading examinations is able to make some judgments about the effectiveness of his lectures; a newspaper columnist knows something about the reactions of his readers from the letters he gets from them. Even the President of the United States makes use of delayed feedback when he examines the telegrams, letters, and newspaper editorials written in response to a televised speech.

It should be clear by now that the concept of feedback involves an action and a reaction. The speaker, through his act of communication, receives a reaction from his audience. If the reaction seems favorable, the speaker continues, and even accentuates his communicative behavior. If the reaction seems unfavorable, he may make extensive modifications. The speaker's actions are followed by reactions from the audience. The audience's reactions, in turn, become an action to which the speaker reacts.

Although all communicators are somewhat aware of feedback, the person who has studied the process of oral communication can anticipate and rather accurately predict the kind of feedback he will receive. Such a prediction, however, must be based on knowledge of the audience. Some speakers seem to be audience *un*conscious. They think of no particular size, kind, age, intellect, or attitude of audience in advance, and they make no adjustment or adaptation of message, attitude, or delivery to signify awareness of the audience they face. That such speakers are dull is a foregone conclusion. Regardless of the attitude of a speaker toward the actuality and inevitability of an audience of some sort, the important concept is that all speaking is focused on the audience.

What, then, are the characteristics of audiences, knowledge of which will provide the speaker with more reliable feedback? First of all, the speaker must recognize that an audience is composed of one or more listeners. No matter what its size, however, an audience is always a collection of individuals. The greater our knowledge of those individuals, the more dependable our predictions about them will be. Most of us have little difficulty predicting the reaction of a close friend in conversation, and we do not ordinarily come to the conversation with apprehensions. Talking to an audience of a thousand strangers, however, is another matter. Since we have much less knowledge of, and experience with, this larger audience, we are much less certain about feedback predictions, and we may have real concern about our abilities to communicate in such a situation. Thus, we may say that the smaller the audience and the more we have in common with them, the greater the ease of adaptation.

When we talk about the speaker and his listeners having something in common, we are really saying that they share some of the same values, and that they share membership in a social system. Communication within social systems is always easier than communication between social systems. No one would deny that the difficulties between the Western World and the Communist World are real and substantive. Nevertheless, our problems are made even more intense by the differences between the social systems. Under such circumstances, it is extremely difficult for Russian and American statesmen to communicate with each other, even with the aid of expert translators. When we talk about social systems, however, we do not necessarily refer to such elaborate organizations as the governments of the United States and the Soviet Union. All of us are members of many social systems of varying size and complexity. Families, church groups, fraternities and sororities, clubs, political parties, labor unions, professional organizations are all varieties of social systems. In fact, you are probably reading this chapter because of your membership in a social system: namely, a class in speech or a related subject. The most important characteristics of a social system are that all members identify themselves as members of the group and share certain common values. It is group identification and mutual values that make intrasystem communication easier because of the more dependable prediction of feedback.

In the case of communication between social systems, the speaker must ask certain questions about his audience and their values, and he must then attempt to find the most reliable answers to his questions. As his questions are answered, and as more information about his listeners is acquired, the communicator will find that his task is easier. Certain of his questions about the audience will be quite simple: What is the size of the group? What are the ages of its members? What is their educational level? What are their political affiliations? What are their economic positions? What are their religious affiliations? Many more questions could be asked, but these should give you an idea of the kind of information speakers should try to gain about their listeners.

In addition to these relatively simple questions, the speaker will want to ask certain more complex questions about the values and beliefs of the group. These questions are more subtle and less amenable to simple answers than factual questions. In examining the attitude of an audience, the communicator will seek to determine what is important to that social system and what it is that motivates the group. The members of a Rotary Club, for example, place much greater value on individual enterprise and competition than do the members of a Navajo tribe. Personal popularity means more to high school students than to members of a religious order. Punctuality is much more important to an American than it is to a Venezuelan.

It is not our desire to offer here an exhaustive guide to the analysis of audiences. From a practical standpoint, such an analytical approach would probably be both discouraging and confusing to the beginner. The crucial concern, instead, ought to be that the communicator should try to visualize *an* audience, ought to realize that he is speaking *to persons,* and that the whole purpose of his attempt to communicate is to produce an effect upon those persons. This means that, as a matter of plain, good sense, he ought to try to visualize who and what those persons are and how this should affect what he says and how he says it.

Although communication between social systems presents more problems than communication within a social system, we must not assume that intrasystem communication is always simple. We have already noted that all of us are members of a number of social systems. Within each of these social systems we may occupy different positions. Each social system develops an internal arrangement, sometimes called a *status hierarchy* or "pecking order." To put it rather simply, within a given social system, all members of the system may be ranked according to the status given them by the system. It is possible, however, for a particular person to occupy a position of high status in one system and low status in another. The Grand Exalted Noble Knight of his lodge may, during his working hours, be a carpenter's helper. We would not be surprised to find that he speaks to his lodge brethren in a completely different way than he does to his foreman. Ordinarily, the higher a person's position in a status hierarchy, the less anxiety he has about communication. Conversely, the lower his position, the more likely it is that he will be "anxious" about speaking to other members of the system.

The amount of anxiety present is also dependent on the rigidity of the structure of the social system. In social systems where positions are clearly defined and specified, communication is likely to become quite inhibited, especially when subordinates speak to superiors. In societies of an earlier time, the peasant did not speak to a nobleman with the same ease as he did to persons of his own station. In a military organization, a private is well aware that he is speaking to a colonel and his communication shows it. On the other hand, in permissive social systems where status distinctions are not emphasized, communication is usually easier and occurs with less anxiety.

Another of the factors that may account for anxiety is the amount of *threat* present in a communication situation. When the consequences of communication are likely to be serious, the situation may be said to be *high threat*. When there is little possibility of personal danger to the speaker from the effects of his communication, the situation may be described as *low threat*. High threat situations might include reports to supervisors, marriage proposals, and job interviews. Generally speaking, the greater the upward status difference between the communicator and his listener, the greater will be the amount of threat.

Whenever evaluation is present, the amount of threat is likely to be high. Just knowing that their speeches will be criticized and graded is enough to make some beginning speakers feel threatened. In other words, the anticipation of evaluation is more threatening than the evaluation itself. If, however, a speaker is an expert in his field and is confident about his communication skills, he is much less likely to feel threatened.

It is not our intent here to write searchingly about the causes and cures of "stage fright." That natural occurrence will be discussed in the next chapter. Rather, we want to show how communication is affected by the relations between and within social systems.

Before we turn to more specific instructions for the speaker, it will be helpful to list for you some of the major points which you should keep in mind as you read the rest of this book.

(1) Verbal communication is a uniquely human characteristic.
(2) Verbal communication is a complicated process.
(3) Meanings are in people, not in the messages they transmit and receive.
(4) Because of the difficulties of symbolization, we never say exactly what we mean.
(5) All verbal communication is bilateral or multilateral.
(6) All oral communication is dependent on feedback.
(7) Communication within a social system is easier than communication between social systems.
(8) Communication is affected by the relations between the speaker and other members of his social system.
(9) Communication is affected by the amount of threat present in the communication situation.

SUPPLEMENTARY READING:

BERLO, DAVID. *The Process of Communication.* New York: Holt, Rinehart & Winston, Inc., 1960.

CHERRY, COLIN. *On Human Communication.* Cambridge: The Technology Press (Massachusetts Institute of Technology), 1957.

HARTLEY, EUGENE L., AND HARTLEY, RUTH E. *Fundamentals of Social Psychology.* New York: Alfred A. Knopf, Inc., 1952.

LEAVITT, HAROLD J. *Managerial Psychology.* Chicago: The University of Chicago Press, 1958.

WIENER, NORBERT. *The Human Use of Human Beings.* Garden City: Doubleday & Company, Inc., 1956.

CHAPTER III

# Choosing Ideas

ONE OF THE MOST COMMON COMPLAINTS heard from students of speech is, "But I don't know what to talk about." The teacher of oral communication hears such remarks so often that he is sometimes tempted to prepare a list of subjects from which his students might choose. Such a procedure, however, does a disservice both to the student speaker and to the discipline of oral discourse. It is well to remember that speech is the oral communication of ideas from the mind of the speaker to the minds of one or more other human beings. Therefore, if we are to engage in real oral communication, we must deal with subjects that originate in our minds, and not with subjects found on mimeographed sheets of paper.

Stressing the importance of speaker-chosen subjects, however, does not answer the question, "But what will I talk about?" Perhaps the answer to the query may be found in the needlessly low estimate that many student speakers place upon their own preparation. In a sense, such an attitude is understandable. College students are at a stage in their lives when they spend much more of their time acquiring knowledge than they do in dispensing it. They spend a large part of each day in the presence of allegedly superior minds. Many students are not so much impressed with how much they are learning as they are with how little they know. Students also sometimes feel that their short experience in living puts them at a disadvantage. Given these circumstances, it is not difficult to understand the diffidence felt by numerous novice speakers. But in almost all cases, such diffidence is unwarranted.

Nobody expects a beginning speaker to present as learned a discourse on a subject as one who has a Ph.D. degree in that subject. You will find, however, that there are many subjects you can discuss quite competently—more competently, perhaps, than any other member of your immediate social system. You are, after all, a unique person. No one else in the world has exactly the same background, the same inheritance, the same experience. Even a society such as ours, which has sometimes been criticized for being "other-directed," does not produce human beings who are as exactly alike as two new automobiles, or as two cookies formed by the same cookie cutter. As a result of your individuality, you are better informed about some things than are most of your contemporaries. In the seventeen or more years you have been alive, you have developed interests, aptitudes, and hobbies in a pattern that is peculiarly yours.

The most important step a speaker can take in discovering his resources is that of thoughtful introspection. It really is necessary to take mental inventory of your store of information. You need to ask yourself questions about the jobs you have had, the hobbies you have pursued, the localities you have lived in, the places you have visited, the subjects you have studied. In asking such questions, you will discover many communication resources that were unknown to you, or of which you were only dimly aware. Sometimes a student speaker who is unwilling to take inventory, or who lacks confidence in his background, may be prodded into awareness by questions from others. A young lady who professed to have no background from which to draw a subject, revealed to her instructor that her father was a "tree farmer." Since she knew her father's business, the student was able to present a very interesting speech on the subject, but not until her instructor had induced her to examine her own resources.

It would follow, then, that one of the first rules of subject selection is that you should talk about things you know about. You need not be a certified expert in the subject, but you must know something about it. You should have had first-hand experience in your field. You should have seen what you describe with your own eyes. In short, you should be *informed*, and your information should not be hearsay or second-hand. It really makes little sense to go to the library to leaf through reference works in search of a subject. A subject suitable for someone else may not be suitable for you. If you use someone else's resources, not your own, your speech will usually show it. Summarizing a magazine article is also no substitute for using your own resources. Even though no member of the audience may be aware of the source of your subject, you are not engaged in meaningful communication. You are merely serving as the channel for another transmitter. Stressing the personal choice of a subject does not mean that we wish to discourage your using the library. Later in this chapter, we will discuss how the resources of the library may be used to supplement the speaker's own assets.

Possessing first-hand acquaintance with a subject does not fully qualify you to talk about it; you need to feel some enthusiasm for it. If you are not interested in your subject, you will not prepare with originality and zest; you will not speak with conviction; you cannot expect your audience to be interested. Enthusiasm is contagious. If you have it, your listeners will catch it. Therefore, be sure you have a lively interest in the subject on which you are informed.

No matter how well informed you are or how interested you are in your subject, you are not fully prepared to communicate until you have satisfied yourself that your chosen subject is meaningful and significant. To be significant a subject need not deal with matters of earth-shaking magnitude. If you are qualified to discuss matters of international importance, by all means go ahead, but remember that significant subjects may be found at all levels of human endeavor. Significant subject matter may concern itself with the nation, the state, the city, the campus, the family, or the individual. Foremost in your mind should be the consideration of whether any change will occur in your listeners when they have heard your speech, or will you only be wasting their time. You will have profited little from your training in oral communication if you insist on transmitting trivia. As we have pointed out earlier, speech is essentially a mental process, and good oral communication should require some cerebration on the part of both the transmitter and the receiver. Perhaps the most common offense against the law of significance is the choice of a subject that does not take advantage of experience but merely recounts it. Too many speeches have already been presented on "My fishing trip," "My vacation," or "My summer job." That is not to say that speeches about fishing trips, vacations, or summer jobs are inherently trivial. Later in this chapter, when we discuss the purposes of speech, we will show how such subjects may be made significant.

But turn your thoughts now to the audience. What will be their reaction to your subject choice? Is it a subject in which that particular group will be interested? At this point, the speaker must bring into play the kinds of questions suggested in the preceding chapter. If the audience is representative of the same social system as the speaker, the chances that they will be interested in a subject he chooses are much higher than if they represent a different social system.

You need to determine whether your listeners have had the experience necessary to motivate interest in the subject; whether there is some marked bias in the group toward your subject, and whether their age level would indicate receptivity to the subject. Water-skiing may be fascinating to 17-year-olds, but it is questionable whether it would be so enthralling to 7-year-olds or 70-year-olds.

The educational level of your audience is another of the controls that will determine your choice of subject. Such factors as occupations, hobbies, religious backgrounds, political affiliations, income, race, nationality, and special interests need to be considered when choosing a subject. Remember, you are communicating to persons, and you cannot automatically assume that they are necessarily interested in what fascinates you. There are very few subjects that are appropriate to all audiences.

As a speaker, you need to ask yourself whether the subject fits the time, place, and purpose of the meeting. Even though a subject might be well suited to a particular audience, you cannot take for granted that the subject will be interesting to all members of the group under all conditions. Human beings' interests shift with the particular role they are playing at the moment. Imagine a group of men who share membership in a church, the board of directors of a corporation, a bridge club, and a luncheon club. It would be folly to assume that their interests remained constant from the meeting of one organization to that of another. Ordinarily, our own feedback mechanisms will give us a pretty good idea of what kind of subject is suitable for a given occasion. Even so, we need to know all we can about the tone of the occasion. Obviously, solemn occasions call for different kinds of subjects than do joyful occasions.

In choosing your subject, then, ask whether you possess the requisite information and enthusiasm, whether the topic will be within the appreciation and interest of your audience, and whether it is suited to the occasion that brings your listeners together.

## NARROWING

You are not prepared to go before an audience with your speech after having merely chosen your subject. In general, we think of the subject as signifying a very broad field. For example, you might choose to talk about education, philosophy, religion, war, politics, slavery, marriage, or agriculture. These are all subject areas, but no one of them commits the speaker to a given line of thought. It indicates only in a broad and very general way the territory he expects to explore. From each general subject area, there are an almost infinite number of topics that may be extracted. The subject of education, for instance, contains within it such highly diverse topics as a plan for the desegregation of schools, and an explanation of the tutorial system at Oxford. Thus, in order for communication to take place, the speaker must make a decision about which specific aspect of the subject he will discuss. He must narrow his subject so that it represents a package that can be conveniently handled. Obviously, the danger of superficiality is great if the subject is inadequately narrowed. No matter how much time you were given, you could never do justice to such subjects as "Foreign Affairs" or "Education." Even the weightiest tomes deal only with divisions of such broad subjects. Subjects that are too broad are much more common than those that are too narrow.

There are several considerations that may help you determine how far your narrowing should go. Time is an obvious factor that will influence your decision. If you have an hour in which to develop your ideas, you may safely treat a broader area than if you are given only five minutes in which to speak. President Woodrow Wilson was reputed to have said that he could prepare a two-hour address in one day, but that he would need a week to prepare a fifteen-minute speech. Wilson undoubtedly recognized the more intensive narrowing and concentrated work that would be necessary for the shorter speech.

Your audience will also provide a clue to the amount of narrowing that may be necessary. An atomic physicist speaking to members of his profession would concentrate his attention on a much more restricted division of his speech than if he were speaking to an eighth-grade general science class. If your audience already knows something about the subject, you will need to do more narrowing than if the subject is new to them. Generally, the more sophisticated the audience is about the subject, the more narrow the subject must be. In any event, the subject should always be sufficiently narrowed to avoid superficiality and incoherence.

Your own knowledge will also influence how much you should narrow your subject. If you have only a general knowledge of a subject, you are obviously limited in the amount of narrowing you can do. If, on the other hand, you have a specialized knowledge of the subject, it will be possible for you to narrow it considerably.

## PURPOSES

Even after narrowing has taken place, the job of subject selection is still incomplete. The most important step of the process is still ahead of you. Let us suppose that you have chosen education as your general subject and that you have narrowed the general subject to the more specific topic of "Education of Mentally Disturbed Children." You still need to ask yourself, "What about the education of mentally disturbed children? What is it that I want to communicate to my listeners?" In other words, you are asking what is the purpose of your communication.

Since all communication must reach its destination in a receiver, it follows that the purposes of oral communication are audience-centered. Uppermost in the mind of the speaker must be the question of what kind of response he seeks to elicit from his audience. Does he want them to know how emotionally disturbed children are educated? Does he want his audience to give of their time and money to support such education? The great trouble with most speakers is that they do not know where they are trying to go. They may know what their subject is, but they do not know what it is they want to accomplish. And yet, is it not evident that unless a speaker clearly visualizes his own goal, he cannot very well lead an audience to it? He needs, therefore, to be very clear in his mind about the purpose of his discourse.

It is helpful to talk about purposes in two ways: first, about *general purposes;* and, second, about *specific purposes.* General purposes of speech may be conveniently thought of in terms of stimulus and response. If you seek some response from your auditors, you must provide them with the proper stimulus. The general purpose of a given speech, therefore, is the response you expect to receive or the reaction you hope to arouse.

The speaker's purpose may simply be to *inform* his receivers. He merely wishes them to understand the information he transmits to them. He wishes to instruct or reveal. He desires to give them information on how to do something, on how something appears or happened or operates, or on how something is organized. You, as college students, encounter examples of speeches to inform, among other places, in many of the classroom lectures you attend.

Beyond the level of simple explanation lies the desire to persuade: the speaker wants his hearers to believe or act in a certain way.

Some writers have distinguished between the speech *to convince* and the speech *to persuade*. The speech of conviction has been thought of as a speech that seeks as its response the agreement or belief of the audience. The speech of persuasion, on the other hand, has been regarded as having action as its final response. This distinction has been rejected by most modern social scientists on the grounds that man's motives are not so easily divisible. Nevertheless, for the beginning speaker, such a distinction makes sense in determining the response he seeks to elicit from his listeners.

There is, after all, a real difference between securing agreement and securing action from your receivers. A Presidential candidate is by no means satisfied to have his audiences *believe* that he is the best candidate for the office. He wants his listeners to go beyond belief—to *action*—by casting their votes for him. In a court trial, on the other hand, the contesting lawyers may seek only to *convince* the jury that the truth is on one side rather than the other. A defendant is convicted or acquitted only *after* the jury has been convinced that he is guilty or innocent. It is important for the speaker to know in his own mind whether his goal is to secure action or whether he is satisfied with achieving agreement or belief. Often speakers are disappointed in their efforts at persuasion when their messages are designed to elicit only agreement. As one writer put it, "It is one thing to convince an audience that it should be ashamed of itself, but it is quite another to make it feel shame."

There is a subdivision of persuasion that should be noted.

That is the speech to reinforce or stimulate. The real importance of reinforcement, however, is that it has as its purpose
the strengthening of already existent beliefs and actions. The
Nazis in Germany used a group of party orators whose mis-
sion was to travel about the Third Reich strengthening the
belief of Germans in naziism. From a more beneficent point
of view, the minister in his sermons often seeks to reinforce
the beliefs of his flock in the tenets of his church.

Some communication theorists have maintained that all
communication is persuasive in the sense that communication
always effects some change between the speaker and his environment. That is, in every communication situation the
listener is a changed person for having received the communicator's message. As a description of communication as a
social force, this view of communication is probably valid,
but it offers the speech student no useful standard by which
to choose his subject.

Many other general purposes of communication have
been specified by various authors. Writers have spoken of
speeches *to entertain, to interest, to impress, to stir to action.*
It is not so critical that you develop an intricate classification
of general purposes. The important consideration is that a
speaker should think of his goal as an audience response, and
that he should clearly visualize the response he desires in
order to be able to weave his design more effectively to
achieve that reaction.

Although one general purpose may be dominant in a given
speech, we must not make the mistake of thinking that it is
the only general purpose. In a speech to inform, the speaker
may entertain as a means to accomplish the transmission of
information; but informing is his real and inclusive objective.
In a speech to convince, the speaker may entertain and inform as a means of getting his end. In a speech to persuade,
the speaker may entertain, inform, and convince in order to

achieve persuasion. As a matter of fact, from one point of view, conviction cannot take place until a receiver is informed and persuasion always requires that a listener know and believe.

Once the speaker has decided upon his general purpose, he must determine to what specific purpose the general purpose will be applied. It is not enough to say that you plan to persuade, to convince, or to inform—to persuade about what? to convince about what? to inform about what? It is at this point that wise subject selection and careful narrowing are of great benefit to the speaker, for the specific purpose will be derived from the combination of the selected and narrowed subject and the general purpose. Thus, instead of presenting a vague, ill-defined speech about "My Vacation in New York," you will seek to *convince* an audience of the advantages of living in a large city. Instead of presenting a speech about "My Job in the Bakery," you will undertake to *inform* an audience of how bread is baked commercially. Instead of presenting a speech about "My Fishing Trip," you will try to *persuade* an audience to give their assistance in the conservation of salmon.

## THE THESIS

The time has now come to combine the specific and general purposes into an explicit and precise statement of the purpose of the speech. Many names have been given to this statement. Among the more common are: subject sentence, topic sentence, purpose statement, and proposition. The nomenclature is not important. The important consideration is that the student of speech clearly understand that the basic task in preparing any unit of communication is to have a goal that he can describe in a single sentence. The term *thesis*, which we have chosen to denote the statement of purpose, was selected because it implies a central idea around which the message may be developed. The real purpose of the thesis is to give a clear and accurate statement of the speaker's objective in terms of the territory to be discussed and the response desired from the audience. For example:

It is my desire to explain to you what philosophers mean by "logical positivism." (Speech to inform.)

It is my hope to prove to you that intercollegiate athletics are compatible with academic excellence. (Speech to convince.)

I want to enlist your support for Dick Bryan for President of the Student Body. (Speech to persuade.)

Note that each of the sentences designates clearly the scope of the discussion and indicates whether the audience response is to be one of understanding, acceptance of belief, or action. Not only is the subject clear in each case, but the limitations of the subject, the specific purpose, and the general purpose are all quite apparent.

Although the formulation of the thesis is extremely important for the listener, it is even more essential for the speaker. The thesis is the most important single element in the speech. A clearly conceived and well-stated thesis is half the battle of successful communication. If you are certain of your central objective, you can refer all ideas and materials to it for testing to determine whether they belong in the speech or violate the principle of unity. You have at least a beginning toward purposive rather than haphazard procedure. You know what you are trying to accomplish in the time you consume. You *have* something *to* accomplish.

What are the characteristics of a good thesis? Some good tests for appropriateness are the following: Is it brief? Does it contain only one idea? Does it clearly indicate the goal? Can the idea be expressed in a single sentence, even though, for psychological reasons, you may choose to use two or even several to bring it into focus? Will it antagonize the audience, or will it arouse their interest and dispose them to listen favorably? Either an interrogation or an implied question is usually good, for both open the mind of the audience instead of closing it. Both imply investigation rather than the speaker's forcing his own conclusions upon the audience. They suggest a co-operative venture in thinking instead of an "I'm-telling-you" attitude. Instead of saying, "I intend to prove today that capital punishment should be abolished," it would be much better to say, "And so I think it is appropriate to ask, 'Does society have the right to kill its members?'" Or, better still, "I should like you to consider with me whether society has the right to kill its members."

Choose your subject to suit you, your listeners, and the occasion of their meeting; narrow your subject so that it is meaningful for you and your listeners; formulate your objective so that it is clear to you and clear to your receivers, and you will have taken the first important step toward effective communication.

## SPEECH PREPARATION

Once the subject has been selected, properly narrowed and made purposeful, you will find it helpful to consider some of the preliminary steps in speech preparation. Undoubtedly one of the greatest problems that faces beginning speakers is the sense of uneasiness or anxiety that comes upon them as they prepare to face an audience. Although nothing we can say here will cure "stage fright," perhaps we can be of assistance in giving you some insight into the problems you may face. We do, however, wish to avoid reinforcing whatever anxieties you may already have. If we are too graphic in our descriptions, we may find ourselves in the position of a physician who was describing a very unusual disease in which the patient feels fine, shows no signs of distress, but suddenly collapses and dies. "My symptoms exactly," said a hypochondriac.

There seems to be a feeling among beginning speakers that something is abnormal or unnatural about feeling ill at ease in the speech situation. Actually the reverse is true: it would be abnormal or unnatural not to feel some anxiety. A reasonable degree of anxiety is a healthy and desirable state. In fact, it is to be hoped that you will never be entirely free from the nervousness that accompanies the anticipation of speaking. An anxious attitude is a good sign. It means that you will be operating at maximum efficiency; you will be alive, alert, sensitive to feedback, and probably well prepared. Modified fear is a stimulus to good work. When you lose *all* fear of an audience, you will be as dull and lifeless as a block of wood.

We must recognize that anxiety about speaking is in part a result of man's own heritage. In spite of all our learning, refinement, and sophistication, we still have some mechanisms that were perhaps better suited to an earlier age. At moments of anxiety, our bodies undergo certain changes to allow us to deal with emergencies. Depending on whether we are heroes or cowards, our bodies are being prepared to run or to fight. We are certainly aware of the changes that occur in respiration, pulse, and muscular tension. What a pity it is that we are unable to tell our bodies that we plan only to make a speech, not to do battle with or flee from our enemies of the forest. Since the outburst of energy, which will relieve the tension, usually does not occur in the speech situation, many of us come to the platform with our strength still in reserve and thus with our anxiety unrelieved. Few student speakers seem to recognize that they can take advantage of these changes to present their messages with greater enthusiasm and energy.

Young speakers should not be disturbed to find themselves uncomfortable at the prospect of facing an audience. Many of our greatest orators have confessed that they, too, suffer from "stage fright." Harry Emerson Fosdick, who at the height of his preaching was recognized as one of America's leading speakers, confirmed that he had a paralyzing fear of audiences during his student days, which shifted to a distressing "anticipation" in later years when he found the world hungry for his messages. He often had to resort to sedatives in order to sleep on the nights preceding his Sunday sermons.

The very realization that you are not alone in your difficulty should be of some consolation to you. Although you may be aware only of your own problem, you must recognize that most other members of the group are in exactly the same situation as you are. It seems to you, however, that only *your* knees quiver, only *your* voice breaks, only *your* hands tremble. The truth is the same things are happening to your classmates, but you are really aware of only your own symptoms. Why? Because the symptoms that seem so marked to you are really only barely discernible even to a trained observer. Most of your fears are within you; your audience is not aware of them. But your classmates, almost without exception, when in your position, have the same feeling of apprehension and nervousness as you.

Human beings tend to become anxious about public performance because their performance is evaluated. Any speech, including a classroom speech, is an evaluative situation. Even when we do things in which we are experienced and skilled, we feel uneasy when our performance is evaluated. You may have great confidence in your ability to drive a car, but that does not prevent you from feeling uncomfortable about taking your examination for a driver's license. The knowledge that your speaking will be evaluated by your instructor and your classmates can be a real cause of anxiety. It is helpful to remember, however, that all of your classmates will be evaluated just as you are. The very fact that you are all in the same boat should be of some consolation to you. There are undoubtedly many things you do well and with confidence. Yet if you were asked to perform before the watchful eyes of others, you would feel some apprehension. If you were an expert swimmer, you might still feel hesitant about displaying your skill before others. Similarly, the public-performance aspects of oral communication may cause some apprehension. We are, after all, human beings with social egos, and we realize that, in the speaking situation, we are singled out for special observation. All eyes appraise us and evaluate us. We are being tested in the crucible of public opinion. Who would not be somewhat afraid of such a situation?

Another thing—the very newness of the experience is cause for some concern. Imagine yourself trying for the first time to swim while others are looking on, swinging a golf club for the first time, serving your first tennis ball, dancing your first steps while others give their attention exclusively to you. Eventually these activities become of little concern to us whether we are being watched or not; but while new they contain elements of fear. The same is true of speaking; its newness makes it strange and therefore discomforting.

The most soothing word we can give to novice speakers about stage fright is that things will get better. You will overcome most, if not all, of your fears. Improvement will come even more quickly if you follow several suggestions. First, the mere repetition of the act of speaking will be greatly effective in relieving tension. The uncertainty that arises from the newness of the situation is lessened primarily through speaking so frequently that the act seems not a new experience but one of your regular habits. The solution to fear of the water lies partially in careful instruction in how to control oneself in the water, but largely in spending enough time there to develop confidence. Repeating the experience will do much toward removing fear of water—and of speaking. Consequently, the appropriate admonition is to speak at every opportunity. Do not put off the evil day, but plan to speak every time you can. Be among the first to ask for the floor. If your fear is strong, that is all the more reason for summoning courage to speak early.

Perhaps the surest way of reducing anxiety is to develop confidence in yourself and in your subject. Such confidence is best achieved by careful preparation before you begin to speak. If your preparation has been haphazard, if you are unsure of your command of the subject, if you are uncertain what you are going to say next, a speech experience may well be traumatic. If, on the other hand, you have been careful in selecting a subject in which you are competent, if you have delineated a purpose with which you are capable of dealing, if you have given care to the preparation of your message, you will have eliminated much of your uncertainty and replaced it with confidence. You certainly know how much better you feel before an examination if you have studied. You also know the hopeless feeling you have if you have been negligent in studying.

Your feelings about the subject you have chosen also have an important effect on your anxieties. The turning point in the battle against communication tension often comes when the speaker is able to ask himself, "What do they think of my message?" rather than, "What do they think of me?" The sooner the speaker gets his mind off himself and on the subject, the better it is. The easiest way to develop such concentration is by choosing a subject that you find interesting, even engrossing. If you feel strongly, sincerely, and enthusiastically about a subject, your attention will more likely be devoted to the communication of the message than to yourself. You ask for trouble when you come to the speaker's stand with a speech that you have not given your careful preparation, knowledge, and interest.

Up to this point, we have spoken of speech preparation as a means of reducing communication anxiety. But speech preparation has significance that bears on every part of the communication situation. Often the beginning speaker may have a fairly clear notion of where he is going, but he does not have a clear idea of how to start, let alone how to get to the destination. It may be helpful, therefore, to outline the steps in speech preparation and then to offer some suggestions that may make oral communication easier for you.

The very first steps in speech preparation have already been discussed earlier in this chapter. The first and most essential steps, of course, are the selection of a subject, the narrowing of the subject, the assignment of general and specific purposes, and the formulation of a thesis statement.

After a thesis has been formulated, it is your responsibility to make a thorough examination of all the resources available to you. Earlier we spoke of your use of your own internal resources. You can also make valuable use of external resources. With your thesis in mind, you should consult all possible sources that might offer support for the thesis. These will include periodicals, books, consultation with experts and authorities, and material from other college courses. One warning is in order here: you should consult other sources only when you have exhausted your own original storehouse of ideas and materials.

Let us caution you, however, that the extraction of materials and ideas even from a multitude of other sources does not constitute preparation for purposeful communication. Such extraction is really a refined form of plagiarism, since you are communicating a mixture of other men's thoughts, and purposeful communication deals with self-originating thought. Extensive use of library sources should be made, but as a means of developing your own ideas, not as a means of suggesting ideas to you.

After you have gathered material from your internal resources and from external resources, you will very likely have more material than can be used in the time allotted to you. It is a curious fact that many student speakers are very concerned that they will be unable to fill the time assigned to them. Yet student speeches that are too long are much more common than speeches that are too short. One of the reasons some speeches run overtime is that some speakers feel compelled to use all the material they have discovered in their research. In the following chapters, we shall discuss in detail the structure of ideas and the use of materials. Let us say for now, however, that material must be used selectively. Only that material which directly supports your thesis should be assimilated into the speech. If you still have too much material, choose that which supports your thesis best. Do not despair if you find yourself with surplus material. You may make use of it in a future speech, or, if not, it is still new knowledge whose value may well become apparent later.

The best way to marshal your material is to prepare an outline. If the thesis is properly divided, you will be able to see which material belongs with which mainhead, and you will be able to discard irrelevant material. In the next chapter, we will deal with the outline and its organization in much greater detail.

After the outline has been prepared, you will want to rehearse your speech. The basic purpose of rehearsal is not primarily to perfect your vocal delivery and physical action but to give you a chance to talk your speech out. Not until you have attempted to transfer the written symbols of an outline to the oral symbols of speech, will you really know whether you can communicate your ideas. If you insist on appearing before an audience without adequate practice, you are committing a discourtesy to the audience and a disservice to yourself. Lack of sufficient rehearsal can lead to a speech that is wandering, irrelevant, and aimless. Moreover, inadequate practice will invariably lead to a lack of confidence.

During rehearsals, most beginners are tempted to write out their thoughts and commit them to memory. This procedure should be avoided, because to use it is to invite failure. Attempts at memorization only compound the uneasiness that you may have about the speech situation. In addition to the usual fears, you have now added a new and most potent fear—the fear of forgetting. The more concerned you are about forgetting, the more likely you are to forget. Since we normally memorize words rather than ideas, forgetting one sentence may stop a speech and cause needless embarrassment.

Memorization is destructive of wholesome communicative relationships. The beginner is normally so intent on remembering that his feedback mechanisms are put out of order. He is so concerned with getting his words out that he pays little attention to his ideas or the response they engender in his listeners. Once a message has been committed to memory, it is extremely difficult to make even the slightest adjustment to the speech environment.

Besides, your aim should not be to give from memory something you have previously prepared; your goal should be to learn to stand on your own two feet, to think clearly, and to communicate directly, simply, and naturally with people who are thinking with you and in turn stimulating you to thought and expression.

Many of the disadvantages of memorization apply also to writing out a speech and then reading it verbatim. Most student speakers are unskilled in oral reading, and their presentation is likely to inhibit communication seriously. In addition, reading from a manuscript presents a great temptation for the speaker to hide himself in his text and avoid even the most minimal contact with his audience.

If you should neither memorize nor read, what then should you do? If you have really thought your speech through thoroughly, and if you have outlined it carefully, you will be able to prepare notes that will indicate to you the development of your speech. Each speaker must decide for himself what kind of notes he needs and how extensive they should be. Almost any speech you are asked to present can be summarized on a 3 x 5 or a 4 x 6 card, if your preparation has been conscientious. This card can be used as a guide as you deliver your speech. Later, as you gain confidence in yourself, you will be able to transfer your notes to your head.

Finally, give your speech plenty of time to grow. If you sit down during one hour and prepare the whole speech, it probably will be dull, confused, uncertain, and incomplete. But if you allow several days or a week for your imagination and recall to work intermittently upon an idea, you will discover many thoughts and incidents that you could not hope to unearth in a concentrated period. You get inspirations while combing your hair, waiting to go to sleep, or walking about the campus; you meet ideas and examples at the dinner table, in the classroom, on the street.

It is often a good idea to plan a general outline early and then to let it grow and change and refine itself as time passes. You may modify it so drastically that the original idea and plan disappear; but if this happens, you will probably improve upon the original. If you will lay a sketchy outline on your desk on one Tuesday, and from time to time add to, change, and review the pattern until the next Tuesday, you will have a much better product than if you depend upon a single hour of concentrated preparation.

SUPPLEMENTARY READING:

BRIGANCE, WILLIAM NORWOOD. *Speech: Its Techniques and Disciplines in a Free Society,* 2nd ed. New York: Appleton-Century-Crofts, Inc. 1961, Chapters 8-10.

McBURNEY, JAMES H., AND WRAGE, ERNEST J. *The Art of Good Speech,* Englewood Cliffs, N. J.: Prentice-Hall, Inc., 1953, Chapters V-VII.

OLIVER, ROBERT T., AND CORTRIGHT, RUPERT L. *Effective Speech,* 4th ed., New York: Holt, Rinehart and Winston, 1961, Chapters 8, 9, 10.

CHAPTER IV

# The Structure of Ideas

IF YOU HAVE CHOSEN your general subject, and have limited the broad field to a specific phase that you have clearly identified and delineated by an appropriate thesis statement or purpose sentence, you are ready to take further steps in preparation. The most important problem now facing you is how to organize your material into the pattern that will give greatest force to your ideas.

We must be very clear that when we use the terms *structure* and *organization,* we are not talking about the mere shuffling of materials until some sort of pattern emerges. Rather, we are talking about an element in the communication process that is second only to thought in its importance. As a matter of fact, one is sometimes hard put to draw a clear distinction between the process of thinking and the process of organizing. It is doubtful whether real thinking occurs without organization. Random thoughts may occur, but unless they are organized, unless the relationship between the thoughts is made clear, it is almost impossible to reach any kind of conclusion. Organization is man's way of relating his thoughts to each other in a meaningful pattern. It is his way of indicating the relationship between his ideas. It is his way of distinguishing between main ideas and supporting ideas. In short, organization is a picture of the way man thinks.

Organization of ideas is by no means restricted to oral communication, but it is central to the communication process. No matter how we communicate, whether by letter, report, conversation, or public speaking, we need to structure our ideas to give them form and meaning. We learn rudimentary lessons about organization early in our lives. The 4-year old who gives you a breathless description of "his day" is making use of a simple chronological structure to communicate what is on his mind.

The fact that we have learned a little about structure does not mean that we are adequate organizers of communicable thoughts, even for everyday use. One of the most serious defects of beginning, and even advanced, speakers is that the force of their message is blunted by their deficiencies in organizational skills. The frustration of speakers who feel that they have not said what they want to say, in the way they want to say it, is often due to their failure to organize their ideas so as to communicate them most effectively. We must remember that clear communication structure is not a goal in itself. The structure of a speech is good or bad only to the degree to which it reveals or obscures the thought of the speaker.

It hardly need be said that it is most important that rhetorical structure be clear to the speaker before it is communicated to an audience. Unless the speaker has developed a pattern of organization that orders his thoughts in some logical and coherent pattern, it is useless to hope that receivers will be able to discern relationships that a speaker neither sees nor communicates.

If the objective of serious discourse is to transmit thoughts, then the speaker must be conscious of the mental and organizational processes of receivers. As the speaker transmits thoughts, he is thinking thoughts. As the listener receives thoughts, he is also thinking thoughts. If communication is to take place, it is important that the receiver be able to think in the same way as the speaker. The structural patterns of the listener must correspond to those of the speaker. The encoding and decoding of structure, the transmission and reception of the mental symbols of communication, must be clear. You can be certain that organization that is unclear to the speaker will not be clear to the listener. On rare occasions, a very perceptive receiver will be able to reorganize materials mentally so that they make more sense to him than they do to the speaker.

There is, of course, no single best way of organizing materials to give them the highest possible amount of meaning.

As we will discover in Chapter 5, we have available a wide variety of structural patterns suitable for various subjects, purposes, and audiences. For the present, however, we will concentrate our attention on a rather simple and very flexible plan for ordering thoughts. This pattern we shall designate the *four-part speech*. It consists of *introduction, thesis, discussion,* and *conclusion.* As a general order of procedure, it has been consistently advocated for nearly twenty-five hundred years. Other patterns are sometimes more desirable, but all are variants of this basic structure and best understood in terms of it. Consequently, this basic plan should be mastered before you attempt more complicated structural systems.

## *INTRODUCTION*

The first step in the presentation of the speech is the *introduction*. The introduction is, of course, not the first step in organizational analysis. We have already discussed the formulation of the thesis as the first step in organizing discourse. The importance of the introduction is that it provides an entryway to the thesis and from there to the general development. We must not conclude, however, that the introduction is merely an appendage to the serious development of a speech. Actually, the introduction is both logically and psychologically necessary to any meaningful speech. One of the most important functions of the introduction is that it provides a framework within which the subject may be better understood. It is at this point that necessary background to the subject is furnished by the speaker. Here, any terms or concepts that are unclear or confusing are defined or explained. Moreover, it is in the introduction that the audience often becomes aware of the process of narrowing. Here they are shown how the thesis relates to the broader subject area from which it is drawn. In short, the introduction bears the very important responsibility of providing orientation for the listener.

Securing the audience's attention is another important task performed by the introduction. No matter how significant and interesting your subject may be, some of its force is bound to be lost unless you have engaged the attention and interest of your audience before you state your thesis. If the attention of the receivers is not captured early, you have no assurance that they will attend to the development of the subject. An important rule to remember about attention is this: receivers will focus their interest on your remarks more intensively if you relate your introduction directly to them. You must give the subject some personal and immediate meaning to your receivers. In other words, the introduction should make the audience feel that the subject is of consequence to them. For example, a recovered mental patient accomplished this when she chose to speak on the value of electric-shock therapy in her treatment. Therefore, in the introduction to her speech, she simply pointed out that, based on present statistical expectations, one of every ten class members could expect to spend some time in a mental institution.

The introduction provides the first, and sometimes the strongest, opportunity for the operation of feedback in the speech. It is often in the first few minutes that the speaker and the audience make mutual appraisals. The speaker is able to make some predictions about the kind of response he and his speech will receive, and the receivers are able to make some preliminary judgments about the speaker and his subject. Unfortunately, an unfavorable impression created in the introduction will frequently persist throughout the speech. The student speaker, therefore, is well advised to avoid doing anything that might antagonize the audience, either toward himself or toward his thesis. The speaker should take pains to be as fair, as moderate, and as thoughtful as possible in order to create confidence in his judgment and intentions.

Another value of the introduction is that it is of some use in reducing feelings of anxiety. A few minutes are provided in which the speaker may become accustomed to the audience and to the speaking situation before he begins the full treatment of his subject.

Even if the functions we have just described were not valid, there would still be one very important reason for the inclusion of an introduction. If a speaker launched immediately into his subject, his audience would very likely find themselves adrift and confused. This would happen not only because they would lack the necessary background to follow his main point, but also because they probably would not hear all of his opening material because a few moments will elapse before the receivers give their full attention to the speech situation. During that time, they are making themselves comfortable, sizing up the speaker, and accustoming themselves to their surroundings.

In preparing an introduction, the speaker should make use of whatever knowledge he can acquire about the audience and the social systems from which they come. The more information a speaker has about the interests, the motivations, and needs of his listeners, the easier he will find his task of securing attention and interest and providing orientation. Very often, such information will determine the kind of introduction that should be prepared and even its length. If, for example, your subject is one with which your receivers have some acquaintance or interest, it may not be necessary to develop a very detailed introduction. If, on the other hand, the receivers are relatively uninformed or have a bias toward your subject, you may find it necessary to develop a rather extensive introduction. Thus the introduction may be only two or three sentences in length, or it may be two or three minutes, depending on how difficult it is to develop attention and orientation.

The nature and function of the thesis have already been discussed. It should be evident that the thesis is a natural outgrowth of the introductory process, and thus naturally occurs at the end of the introduction. Even though it is only a single sentence, it is nevertheless designated as a separate unit in the organizational process because of its importance in determining the unity and form of all that precedes and follows. Brief though it may be, the thesis may very probably be the most important unit of the speech, since all other units of the speech are directly related to the thesis.

## DISCUSSION

The real development of the thesis occurs in the *discussion*. In a sense, the discussion *is* the speech. Since its purpose is to develop the thesis, or to elaborate upon it and to fulfill its prophecy, it naturally contains the leading ideas and materials of the speech. It is both the bulk and substance of a discourse. It contains the argument and evidence, the ideas and examples of a speech.

Although all materials in the discussion occasionally develop the thesis directly in what is called a one-point speech, the thesis is usually broken down into two or more divisions, commonly called *mainheads,* to facilitate comprehension or evaluation by the listeners. It is in the development and formulation of the mainheads that the speaker is called upon to use all the powers of analysis, insight, and judgment available to him, for it is here that he must make a determination about the natural divisions of the thesis. That is, it is here that he must decide what units or divisions should be used in unfolding his subject. This decision must be made in terms of the particular subject. There are no easy formulas that a speaker may apply readily to all subjects. Certain kinds of subjects, however, are more amenable to certain patterns of development than others, and we will discuss a number of those patterns in the next chapter.

If a speech is somewhat long or complex, it may be necessary to make use of *subheads* in developing the thesis. The subheads bear exactly the same relationship to the mainhead as the mainheads do to the thesis, and the same criteria for acceptance and rejection apply.

The following set of standards will be helpful to the speaker in evaluating the mainhead development of any speech. The first is simply whether each of the mainheads directly supports and develops the thesis. Or, to put it another way, is each of the mainheads a subthesis of the main thesis? If a mainhead does not lend direct support to the thesis, it must either be rejected or rephrased so that it is a natural division of the thesis. It is difficult, of course, to discard the products of our own mental invention, but rejection comes easier if one recognizes that irrelevant mainheads really constitute noise and are thus disruptive of the communication process.

Another standard is that the mainheads must really be mutually independent divisions of the thesis. All mainheads may be in direct support of the thesis, and yet the structure of the speech may inhibit the communication of your message because of confusing overlapping. Attention must be given to the relationship between the mainheads. You should ask yourself whether the mainheads are really independent divisions of the thesis. When such a question is put, it is often advisable to make use of the test of mutual exclusivity. The speaker must ask himself whether each of the mainheads treats a separate division of the subject, or whether, as a matter of fact, some mainheads overlap each other and treat, at least in part, the same division of the subject. A speech dealing with the distribution of trees in the United States, for example, ought not to include the following mainheads:

I. The Trees of New England
II. The Distribution of Pine Trees

It is clear that these two mainheads are not really independent of each other. Since pine trees are found in New England, both mainheads would concern themselves with New England, and both would concern themselves with pine trees. Such structural patterns should be rejected, not simply because they are illogical, but also because they are extremely difficult for listeners to follow.

Some speakers do not properly distinguish between mainheads and subheads in formulating a structural pattern for their ideas. We must be certain that each mainhead is a distinct division, and not merely part of another mainhead. Look at the following mainheads drawn from a speech stressing the advantages of owning a foreign automobile:

I. Foreign cars are more economical to operate
II. Foreign cars use less gasoline

Since gasoline consumption is only one aspect of automobile economy, it is quite apparent that the second mainhead is really a sub-division of the first.

The student speaker must also exercise caution to see that the mainheads are not merely repetitions of each other or of the thesis. If such repetitions occur, it is obvious that the speaker has not perceived the natural divisions of his subject. It is immediately evident that the following mainheads drawn from a speech extolling the benefits of studying a foreign language really say the same thing:

I. You will learn about other cultures
II. You will learn about other peoples and how they live

The same error would be committed if the thesis were, "The United States should oppose the seating of Communist China in the United Nations," and if one of the mainheads were, "We should resist any attempts to replace the present Chinese delegation with one representing Peiping."

All of the above criteria of mutual exclusivity are discussed not merely because they are sacred rules that must not be violated. In terms of the fidelity of the communication process, there are good and proper reasons for checking the mainheads against the thesis and against each other. Without such examination, whatever logical unity your speech has may very well be destroyed. Since the audience will probably be unable to grasp any logical and perceivable pattern of development, they may very well have the feeling that your speech "wanders" or "drifts." When patterns and relationships are difficult to see, receivers lose attention and the communication process becomes noisier.

## CONCLUSION

When a speaker has discussed a theme to the point that no further elaboration is necessary, or until audience fatigue or the pressure of time makes necessary the termination of the discussion, he arrives at the very important final part of the pattern known as the *conclusion*. It is at this point in the co-operative venture in thinking when the complex thought of the speech is reviewed and simplified, is brought to a final focus.

Ordinarily, a normal function of the conclusion is to summarize the thought developed, to restate in some form the thesis and the mainheads, so that the audience has an outline of the whole message and can see it in perspective. In the case of conclusions of persuasive speeches, the speaker may appeal for action, attempt to arouse the emotions of his listeners, or ask for a fair appraisal of his reasoning. He may do no more than review and simplify for purposes of clarity, or he may strive to motivate. In no case should he be satisfied with a bare summary; he should make an effort to achieve even a higher degree of interest and friendliness from the audience than in the introduction.

A warning or two about the conclusion is in order at this point. Once the audience is psychologically prepared for the speech to end, the speaker should see to it that it does. The conclusion should be brief enough so that it does not destroy its intended effect. All irrelevant materials should be rigorously excluded; only those materials that contribute purposefully should be included. Above all, the speaker should be careful not to introduce new ideas and arguments. The audience is no longer prepared to accept and listen to new ideas in the conclusion, and thus the logical unity of the discussion is easily destroyed through unnecessary additions. All materials that are in direct support of the thesis should be found in the discussion and not in the conclusion.

There is danger also that the conclusion may be too brief to accomplish its purpose. The audience must be prepared for the end of the discourse. The speaker who comes to the close of his discussion and concludes with, "I guess that's about all," leaves his audience with a feeling not unlike that of applying the brakes in a sudden stop of a car. It is far better for both the speaker and his receivers to allow the speech to coast to a more comfortable stop.

The basic organizational pattern of a speech, then, consists of four parts: *introduction, thesis, discussion, conclusion.*

## TRANSITIONS

As road-signs are necessary to guide the motorist in his travel from one point to another, so are signs of a new movement or unit in the structure of communication necessary to carry the audience along the road of development. Such signposts, or processes of connection, are known as *transitions.* They are the glue that holds the parts of a speech together. They are the net that catches the wandering attention of members of an audience and brings it safely home to the central trend of discussion. They are the stepping-stones by which your listeners are able to move along the stream of thought.

Because oral communication, by its very nature, contains so many opportunities for loss of understanding, careful transition is requisite to clear speaking. When a person sits down to read, he may choose his own pace; he may move at whatever rate enables him to follow the thought of the writer. If he loses the movement of thought momentarily, he may go back to whatever point is necessary to put him on the track again. He can rely on the visual picture of the paragraph, too, to help him follow the writer's outline. But words uttered by a speaker do not visibly paragraph themselves, and they do not remain in the hearer's memory long enough to enable him to go back and study those he did not quite comprehend. Furthermore, the listener must move at the rate of the speaker, giving his attention to utterance at the moment; if he pauses to look back, the speaker will have moved on ahead and the hearer will have lost the thought.

Another important reason for the use of transitional devices is that the speaker must make clear to his listeners where the divisons between the structural units occur. At the same time, however, he must not make these divisions so baldly evident that the movement from one to another is abrupt or mechanical. Rather, he must lead receivers from one unit, or subunit, to the other with clarity but with smoothness.

The need for transition lies chiefly between the introduction and the thesis, between the thesis and the discussion, between the mainheads, and between the discussion and the conclusion. Since the purpose of transition is connection, or demonstration of relationship, it follows that some form and degree of transition is necessary from the beginning to the end of the speech if it is to be a connected, coherent whole. However, actual transition in thought is psychological rather than mechanical. It is something to be *felt* by both speaker and listener rather than merely observed.

You have all perceived and used transitions in communication, whether in conversation, public speaking, letters, or themes. It may be worthwhile, however, to remind you of some of the more common transitional devices. A transition leading to the thesis may very well take this form:

> "It seems to me appropriate, then, that we consider together what makes criminals."

Note that this statement is much smoother and carries the audience along better than:

"It is my purpose to discuss the causes of crime."

A transition between the thesis and the first mainhead might be:

"I would place first on the list of causes of criminality the factor of poverty."

Between two mainheads, a transition might be worded along these lines:

"Poverty, then, makes an enormous contribution annually to criminal forces; but I would place almost as high parental neglect and poor home training."

Between the discussion and conclusion, one might find such a statement as:

"We should now be able to formulate a list of the major reasons why men become criminals."

Note that these transitions not only show the receivers where they have been, but also indicate to them where they will go next.

Important as transitions are, poor transitions or the overuse of transitions may, on occasion, inhibit good communication when their goal should be to promote it. Good judgment not only allows, but also demands, that when transitions begin to intrude and encumber rather than to assist thought, we may use abbreviated transitions at some points. The important consideration is always whether the audience feels the movement from one unit to another and senses the relationship between divisions.

# CHAPTER V

# Structural Patterns

S o far, we have discussed oral communication in terms of only one structural pattern. Although the four-part speech represents the most basic and most common of all patterns of organization, it is obviously not the only way to order materials to achieve effective communication. Since structure is a symbolization of the thought process, we cannot assume that all human beings think about all subjects at all times within this pattern. Neither can we assume that clear communication of ideas cannot take place without the use of the four-part pattern described in the preceding chapter. It is true, however, that most structural patterns are variations and developments of the four-part speech. If we look carefully, we will almost always find, in any pattern, an introduction, a thesis, a discussion, and a conclusion, although they may be arranged somewhat differently. Since the patterns of organization are, for the most part, descended from the four-part speech, the simple four-part pattern should be mastered before more complex patterns are attempted. You will also find that the four-part pattern, because of its simplicity, is easier for beginning speakers.

If the four-part speech is so basic and so easy to use, why should any other structural patterns be presented at all? First, the four-part speech is really a very broad and generic concept. There are, in truth, a number of patterns that are subvarieties of the four-part speech. They contain the same four divisions in the same order, but they make use of more specific patterning of the development of the discussion. The mainheads are related to each other in a very particular way. Such patterns as *chronological, topical,* and *spatial,* which we shall discuss later in this chapter, are examples of subspecies of the four-part speech. You may well discover that the speeches you have already presented are refinements of the basic four-part speech.

Another reason for making use of different patterns of organization is that the four-part speech may not necessarily be the best form for communicating your ideas. The four-part speech may be thought of as a kind of general-purpose vehicle. It will probably work quite satisfactorily in most situations, even superbly in some circumstances, but there are occasions when other structural patterns will do the job better. A station-wagon is a pretty versatile vehicle too, but at times a pick-up truck, a sports car, or a limousine may be more satisfactory in accomplishing a particular purpose.

What, then, are the factors that suggest which kind of pattern should be used? Without spelling out the particular patterns, let us discuss the considerations that might affect your decision in choosing a pattern. After these reasons have been presented, the examples of patterns, included later in this chapter, may be more useful to you.

Perhaps the strongest determinant of structural choice is

the subject of the speech. Certain kinds of subjects divide themselves naturally into certain patterns of organization. Subjects dealing with structure and form, for example, are naturally partitioned into patterns that are *spatial*. Subjects that are historical find their divisions along *chronological* lines. The speaker, in exploring his subject, must make a basic decision about what kind of pattern will best fit his subject. Or, to put it another way, which pattern will be most effective in communicating ideas. The reverse of this process must be avoided. If a speaker decides in advance what kind of pattern he will use and then finds a subject to fit the pattern, he is really perverting the process of communication. Content should always dominate form. The speaker should never allow form to determine the ideas of communication. Instead, form should be shaped and adapted to content. It is possible, of course, to cram and shove almost any subject into any pattern, but such tricks invariably obscure the message and rob it of its force.

In many cases, the decision about relation of pattern to subject may not be as easy as we have made it seem. Often a subject may be developed in more than one way without abusing the integrity of communication. World War II, for example, might be discussed from either a chronological perspective or from a geographical one. In these instances, the speaker must rely on his own judgment as to which pattern will reveal his own thinking most clearly.

In addition to the subject, the speaker must also keep his purpose in mind as he seeks the best form for the communication of his ideas. Again, certain patterns are better adapted to some purposes than they are to others. A chronological pattern, for example, may be exceptionally well-suited to informative discourse, but it may not be as adaptable as another pattern to persuasive communication. In such speeches, a *problem-solution* or *motivated-sequence* pattern may be more satisfactory.

The audience also has a voice in the choice of structural patterns. An audience with little background, for instance, may require a relatively simple pattern of organization, whereas a more sophisticated audience may respond to a more complex arrangement. Human beings are more comfortable doing things the way they have been accustomed to doing them. They are more likely to receive your communication if you use a pattern of reasoning with which they are familiar. The attitude of the audience toward you and your subject may also be influential in your choice. If they are antagonistic toward you, your subject, or your thesis, it may be desirable to delay the thesis until the end of the speech, as in an *inductive* pattern, or to make use of a *problem-solution* or *causal* pattern.

The speaker himself will obviously play an important role in the choice of patterns. Although we hope that you will master all of the fairly simple patterns in this chapter, you will find that some patterns better fit your mode of thinking and are more comfortable than others. If the choice of patterns does no disservice to the subject, the purpose, or the audience, the speaker should ordinarily make use of the patterns that seem to suit him best.

It should be clear now that the determination of a structural pattern must not be a random choice. The organization of communication is too important a matter to be decided by hit-or-miss guesses. The communicator must be as conscientious as possible in deciding whether the pattern he has chosen is best adapted to his subject, his purpose, his audience, and to himself. He must also understand that subject, purpose, audience, and speaker are not independent elements in the communication process. As we have indicated earlier in this work, the attitude of the receivers toward the transmitter and the message are of critical importance. Hence the communicator must not only keep all of these elements in mind; he must also understand the relationship between them and the way such relationships may affect the choice of pattern. A given pattern may be well suited for a particular subject, but it may not do to use that pattern before a specific audience.

With this background in mind, let us now turn to an examination of some of the more frequently used structural patterns. It should be noted, however, that the patterns discussed do not represent the complete range of possibility. Since there are a great number of variations in the processes of reasoning, there are a corresponding number of patterns of arranging thoughts. As you become more sophisticated in the preparation of materials for oral communication, you will undoubtedly come to use perfectly satisfactory patterns that are perhaps more complex or more subtle than those described in this chapter.

If you are to understand variations in structure, it may be advisable to provide you with a very simple explanation of the two most significant modes of reasoning: *deduction* and *induction.* Within certain limits, which we shall indicate later, almost any pattern may make use of deduction or induction, either as the form for the entire speech, or as the form for one or more of the component units.

Whether you know it or not, the four-part organizational pattern is really a simple deductive pattern in that the reasoning and development of discourse, particularly in the discussion, moves consistently from the *general to the specific.* With the exception of the introduction and conclusion, the thesis is the most general statement in the entire speech. Since the mainheads are divisions of the thesis, they are more specific than the thesis. The subheads are subdivisions of the thesis and hence are more specific than the mainheads. The materials of speech, which will be discussed in the next chapter, are still more specific than the subheads. If we extend our examination beyond the thesis and discussion, we will find that the introduction is normally even more general than the thesis, since the process of narrowing to the thesis ordinarily occurs in the introduction. The conclusion returns from the specific to the general, since it normally covers the scope of the entire deductive communiation. It is possible to picture the form of a deductive speech in the approximate shape of an inverted triangle.

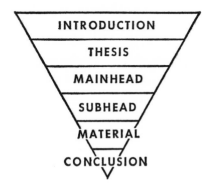

The whole arrangement of a deductive speech is a descending order. Its order is from hypothesis through verification. It is in part this conformity to accepted scientific method that gives rise to our belief that the four-part form is basic, and that all other forms are variants of it.

The distinguishing characteristic of deductive structure is its clarity; and clarity itself conditions the acceptability of thought. Theodore Parker said of Daniel Webster that his power of inimitable clarity constituted his greatest force in persuasion. The fact that in this form you can see the objective before illustrations and other materials are offered, is in itself like having someone point toward an object before he begins to describe it; whereby merely describing something without indicating its whereabouts would increase the difficulty of your locating it.

Furthermore, the unfolding of the deductive structure enables the speaker to keep his materials more clearly in mind than when using other forms, so that a certain power is gained from mere self-possession and ease of forward movement.

There is, however, one marked shortcoming of the deductive pattern, particularly when it is used for persuasive purposes. Deductive speakers always state conclusions before offering proof, which allows hostile or antagonistic receivers to build up resistance to arguments even while the arguments are being offered.

Whereas in deductive reasoning the thought unfolds by moving from the general to the particular, *induction* moves in the opposite direction. In induction, the thought is developed by consistent movement from the *specific to the general.* Although the inductive speech makes use of all of the units of the four-part structure, they appear in quite different order than in a deductive pattern. In a sense, an inductive speech is a deductive speech standing on its head.

When induction is used in oral communication, it involves the presentation of materials before revealing the mainheads, completion of all mainheads before statement of the thesis, which is really a combination of thesis and conclusion. The introduction of such a plan is quite different from that of a deductive speech. It is really not an introduction at all, but material that leads to the development of a conclusion, which is, in reality, a mainhead. In deduction, a premise is stated that is supported by material. In induction, on the other hand, a conclusion is derived from material.

After the mainhead-conclusion has been stated, a new movement of materials is then started toward another mainhead, then a third movement toward still another mainhead, and so on until all mainheads are developed and stated. They are then summed up as a thesis that receives some elaboration as a conclusion. It is possible to symbolize the form of inductive communication in the shape of a "right-side-up" triangle.

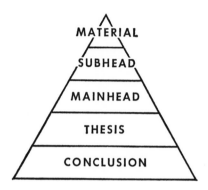

It must not be assumed that inductive reasoning or inductive structures are mere tricks. Induction is much more than simply turning a normal four-part speech upside down. Indeed, it is a basic form of human thought. As a matter of fact, a good case can be made that it is *the* basic form of reasoning. Much of our learning comes about through our ability to draw conclusions from specific examples or experiences. Children learn to recognize dogs and to distinguish them from rhinoceroses only after they have seen enough dogs to draw conclusions that enable them to know that only certain quadrupeds are dogs. Similarly, we know that dogs have four legs because all dogs we have seen have four legs. To put the matter simply, inductive reasoning would take this form:

1. Spot is a dog and has four legs.
2. Fido is a dog and has four legs.
3. Rover is a dog and has four legs.
4. Prince is a dog and has four legs.

*Conclusion:* Therefore all dogs have four legs.

In deduction the conclusion would appear first as a premise and the reasoning would take this form:

*Premise:* All dogs have four legs since:

1. Spot is a dog and has four legs.
2. Fido is a dog and has four legs.
3. Rover is a dog and has four legs.
4. Prince is a dog and has four legs.

Many experts maintain that deduction must always be preceded by induction, since we cannot possibly arrive at the premise that all dogs have four legs without examining all the dogs we know inductively. The saying, "Experience is the best teacher," is really a tribute to induction.

The inductive structure in communication is best suited for persuasive speeches in that it avoids audience resistance. Not knowing what belief or action you propose, your receivers have little opportunity to set up mental objections. You lead them so gradually toward a reasonable conclusion that its validity is upon them before they can find excuses for refusing it. In a good inductive development, the speaker and his audience should seem to come to the same conclusion at the same time.

Therein lies one of the perils of the inductive form. The speaker must tread a narrow line between revealing his thesis too soon and being so obtuse that his listeners cannot follow the development of the ideas. It is sometimes difficult to avoid statement or implication of the thesis while stating mainheads. If the thesis becomes apparent, then psychologically the procedure ceases to be inductive, for listeners are, from that point on, testing the premise.

At the same time, inductive communication must be so clearly developed that the receivers are able to comprehend and follow each step. They should reason together with the speaker. If they are unable to participate in the joint reasoning process, they will become lost, their interest will diminish, and so will their attention. In case they are still listening when the thesis is stated, it may come as a complete surprise to them. It is admittedly more difficult for the student speaker to achieve clearer development inductively than deductively. In deduction, the conclusion is stated first and the listener has a reference point for all subsequent development, no matter how illogical. If deductive and inductive speeches are equally well developed, however, they should be equally clear.

There is no reason why inductive and deductive forms may not be combined within a single speech, provided there is a reason for mixed development and provided the speaker undertakes such a procedure deliberately and not indiscriminately. There are a number of ways in which semi-inductive development may be approached. The over-all development of the speech may be deductive with one or more inductive mainheads. Or an essentially inductive speech may have one or more divisions that are developed deductively. A speaker, for example, may have no objection to revealing his purpose, but he may wish to treat a particularly sensitive mainhead inductively to gain greater audience acceptance.

Within the general inductive and deductive schemes of development, there are a variety of patterns that the speaker may use. His choice of pattern will, of course, depend on such factors as the subject, the audience, and the purpose. Some of these patterns may be developed better inductively, some deductively, and in other cases they may make use of either mode of reasoning.

## CHRONOLOGICAL

One of the most commonly used patterns of ordering materials and ideas is the *chronological* pattern. Whenever messages divide themselves naturally in terms of time order, the chronological pattern is suitable. This pattern is used not only in public discourse, but in private conversation as well. The description of experiences, the telling of stories, make use of some kind of chronological pattern. Many humans find it helpful in their communication to move from the past to the present, or the present to the future. Unfortunately, many of these patterns are only randomly chronological. The development follows a time progression, but no attempt is made to divide the progression into its significant portions. One might use the following division in discussing the armaments race between the United States and the Soviet Union, but it has the merit only of convenient separation; it does not reveal the real meaning of the armaments race.

A. 1945–1949
B. 1950–1954
C. 1955–1959
D. 1960 to the present

Note how the development below, which uses more logical time divisions, separates itself into more logical and meaningful units.

I. The United States the only atomic power
II. Russia gets the atomic bomb
III. The Russians pull ahead of the United States

These units may be unequal in years covered, but they more nearly represent the natural divisions of the subject.

## SPATIAL

*Spatial* divisions are those which divide a thesis on the basis of the arrangement of its parts in space. For example, if you were explaining how to lay out a football field, your divisions would perhaps be: the boundaries of the playing field; the yard markers; the end zones. These divisions are chosen on the basis of spatial characteristics. A description of a floor plan for a house is also spatial, as may be a discussion of the beauties of Yosemite Park. Sometimes the division of a speech may contain aspects of both spatial and chronological development, as in the following example dealing with an automobile assembly line:

A. Motor Assembly
B. Body Assembly
C. Interior Assembly

Although each of these divisions deals with a separate part of the automobile, the assembly process occurs in time order. Such paterns are sometimes called *spatial-chronological.*

## TOPICAL

A *topical* pattern is one in which the thesis is divided into its natural components. In a real sense, chronological and spatial patterns are also topical, since they, too, are natural divisions. But they are more than topical, since they possess in addition a quality of temporal or spatial significance. The more simple topical pattern consists of mainheads that are direct subdivisions of a thesis, as in the following development:

*Thesis:* What Are the Benefits of a College Education?
A. Intellectual Benefits
B. Social Benefits
C. Economic Benefits
D. Aesthetic Benefits

As you can easily see, each mainhead in the preceding development is a clear and natural subdivision of the thesis. In other words, the thesis has been broken down into its component parts or topics.

Just as in the chronological and spatial patterns of development, it is important that you be sure that the mainheads of a topical speech are actually the natural units of division. In making such a decision, you will have to use your powers of judgment, insight, and analysis, since no easy formulas are available. The criteria of mainhead development outlined in Chapter 4 will be helpful, however.

## CAUSAL

Another type of organization which you may find very helpful in speeches of explanation is the *causal* pattern. There are, in reality, two important kinds of causal structure: *cause-to-effect* and *effect-to-cause*.

In the cause-to-effect pattern, the speaker first describes an event or phenomenon and then asks, "What will be the effect?" The effect-to-cause order, on the other hand, involves first describing a state of affairs and then discussing, "How did we get there?" Either form may deal with the past, the present, or the future in one or both of their divisions. A speech, for example, dealing with the effects of the 1960 Presidential election might very well have a causal section, dealing with the past, in which the results of the election are described. The effects division in which the immediate and long-range effects of the election are discussed might very well deal with the present and future. A speech that treats the causes of racial segregation in the South may have an effect division, with its orientation in the present where current practices are discussed. The causes of current practices obviously are rooted in the past. Thus the cause division would deal with the past.

It will be helpful, then, to think of causal developments as having only two mainheads: one dealing with cause and the other with effects. These mainheads, of course, may be further subdivided. It should be stressed that a causal pattern of organization *always* has two divisions. A speech dealing merely with causes or merely with effects may be very worthwhile, but it likely is topical rather than causal in its development. The following examples may help illustrate the difference.

CAUSAL

*Thesis:* Where Are We Headed in Intercollegiate Athletics?
A. The Present Situation (The Cause)
   1. Subsidization of Athletes
   2. Recruiting of Athletes
   3. Exploitation of Athletes for Profit
B. Results Which Will Develop from Present Situation (The Effect)
   1. Athletes regarded as separate from other students
   2. Athletics become more important than scholastic activities
   3. The athlete's sense of values becomes distorted

TOPICAL

*Thesis:* What Will Be the Effects of Our Intercollegiate Athletic Policies?
A. Athletes regarded as separate from other students
B. Athletics become more important than scholastic activities
C. The athlete's sense of values becomes distorted.

In the second development, it is assumed that the causes are clear to the audience. Therefore, the speaker need not dwell on causes but may proceed directly to the effects.

In Chapter 6, we will discuss, in some detail, the tests that should be applied to causal reasoning. At this point, it should be sufficient to point out that the cause and effect must be directly related to each other. The effect must be caused by the cause described, and the cause must result in the effect described.

## *PROBLEM-SOLUTION*

Another structural pattern that always has two mainheads is the *problem-solution* pattern. In all problem-solution developments there is always a first division that states a problem and a second division that presents a solution. In contrast to causal patterns, however, the order of these sections cannot be reversed. Human beings reason in order to find solutions for problems. It is almost ludicrous, however, to imagine a person with a solution for which he is trying to find a problem.

Problem-solution speeches may also have their orientation in the past, the present, or the future; and different time-sequences may be treated in each mainhead. A description of the means by which the Royal Air Force combatted the German air raids deals entirely in the past. In a speech about the elimination of water pollution, the problem mainhead concerns itself with the present, and the solution mainhead with the future.

At this point, it is worth noting that the same close relationship that applies to causal development is also applicable to problem-solution development. The solution presented must actually solve the problems described in the problem mainhead.

There is no reason why a speech may not limit itself to either a problem or a solution. In that case, however, the structure will probably be some variety of topical development.

## *MOTIVATED-SEQUENCE*

If you have listened or watched radio and television commercials, you are probably familiar with a simple form of *motivated-sequence* pattern. Let us examine a fictional example to discover the basic steps in such a pattern.

1. *Attention*        Ladies!
2. *Need*             Do you suffer from dishpan hands?
3. *Satisfaction*     If so, use Sudsy for dishes.
4. *Visualization*    In days, your hands will be soft and
                      smooth.
5. *Action*           Next time you're shopping, pick up a
                      package of Sudsy.

The motivated-sequence has its basis in the psychological rather than the logical nature of man. That is not to say that the pattern is illogical; it is not. But it is based on the steps that are particularly potent in affecting the behavior or response of a listener. It is its adaptation to the stages a listener goes through in being persuaded that has made the motivated-sequence so attractive to advertisers.

The *attention* step of the motivated-sequence is comparable to the introduction in the usual deductive pattern. Perhaps the term "attention" is somewhat misleading, for it suggests that such is the only value of the opening movement of the speech. However, the term arises from the attempt to give statement to the parts of the outline in terms of psychological factors in human behavior.

The *need* phase is very closely related to the problem phase of the problem-solution speech. The psychological term, however, gives sharper focus to the behavioral basis of this pattern. The intent is to focus on unsatisfied needs rather than on unsolved problems. In this section, the need or problem is described, the problem is divided into its various aspects, and the reasons why the problem is a problem are discussed.

Once a need is presented to an audience and they are made aware of that need, some means must be found to satisfy the need. Thus, the third step in the motivated sequence is the *satisfaction* step. The satisfaction step is closely related to the solution step of the problem-solution speech except that it has a behavioral orienation. That is, it is concerned with *how* human beings act, not necessarily with how they *should* act. Nonetheless, its presentation is very similar to the solution step. Its thesis is, "How may this need be satisfied?" If there are subheads, they deal with methods of satisfaction.

After the completion of the satisfaction step, we have, in essence, a problem-solution speech, but the motivated sequence goes beyond the problem-solution pattern in presenting a *visualization* step. The function of the visualization step is to show the listeners the consequences of acceptance or rejection of the satisfaction step. The visualization step may be either negative or positive or both. A negative visualization step would demonstrate what would happen if the proposed solution were not accepted: "If you do not vote for Ezra Dogooder, the Reform candidate for mayor, crime and corruption will run rampant in our city." A positive visualization, on the other hand, will point out the benefits of acceptance of the satisfaction step: "When Dogooder is mayor, there will be prosperity and jobs for all." The visualization step, of course, presents positive and negative aspects in some detail.

The *action* step is not unlike the conclusion of many persuasive speeches. It may be a simple exhortation for the individual to make these matters his concern; it may be an appeal to speak his mind freely and to use his vote thoughtfully; or it may be an outline of specific means by which the individual may make his concern felt more forcibly in the proper places.

The motivated sequence is a valid attempt to express a logical concept in psychological terms. Since communication aims at influencing human behavior, it is a useful way of organizing persuasive communication.

Patterns of organization thus have to do with the order in which the thought and materials of a speech are unfolded to the listener. This order should be determined on the basis of both logical and psychological considerations. The two are neither separate nor incompatible; they are, rather, two aspects of the same process, and the student should make every effort to understand them in that light. He should understand the deductive pattern and the inductive pattern as logical opposites, with many variations growing out of each. *Chronological, spatial, topical, causal, problem-solution,* and *motivated-sequence* are ways of arranging thought and materials on the basis of audience response and natural divisions of subject matter.

*Remember, organization is the distinctive characteristic of intelligently purposive thought and action. A speech, to be effective, need not follow any particular pattern of logical or psychological sequence. But it should adhere to some pattern of which the speaker is consciously aware, and one that he has chosen because he thinks it best suited to himself, to his subject matter, to his purpose, and to his audience on the particular occasion of his oral effort.*

SUPPLEMENTARY READING

BAIRD, A. CRAIG AND KNOWER, FRANKLIN H. *General Speech,* 2nd ed. New York: McGraw Hill Book Company, Inc., 1957, Chapter 5.

BRYANT, DONALD C. AND WALLACE, KARL R. *Fundamentals of Public Speaking,* 3rd ed. New York: Appleton-Century-Crofts, Inc., 1960, Chapters 9, 10, 23.

GRAY, GILES WILKESON, AND BRADEN, WALDO W. *Public Speaking Principles and Practice.* New York: Harper and Brothers, 1951, Chapters XIII-XV.

MONROE, ALAN H. *Principles and Types of Speech,* 5th ed. Chicago: Scott, Foresman and Company, 1962, Chapters 14-17.

WHITE, EUGENE E. *Practical Speech Fundamentals.* New York: The Macmillan Company, 1960, Chapters 12, 14.

CHAPTER **VI**

# The Materials of Speech

W E HAVE THUS far emphasized the following concepts as of prime importance in getting the beginning student of speech off to a good start: first, recognition of the unique nature and significance of communication through the medium of language; second, the place of the receiver, or audience, in determining the communicator's attitudes and methods and purposes; third, the crucial importance of discovering, identifying, and clearly stating the purpose or objective that the speaker or writer wishes to accomplish with his audience; fourth, the importance of structure not only in achieving coherence in discourse, but also in testing the relationship of ideas during the process of preparation so that the speaker may be sure that he has a logical and inherently consistent outline of thought.

The concept of *developmental materials*, which we shall strive to convey to you now, will probably be more directly helpful to you than anything else we say to you in this text-book. Strangely it has long been neglected by rhetoricians, and has emerged as a useful rhetorical concept only in the current century. If the beginner, however, has grasped the concepts thus far elucidated, he is ready now to add one that will do more to make speaking and writing easy for him and to insure his effectiveness than anything else that can happen to him.

## "THOUGHT" AND "MATERIAL"

The distinction between thought and material is difficult but basic. Briefly, thought structure is generalization; material is composed of specifics. The mainheads of the body are general and inclusive statements; they are the result of analysis of the thesis, a larger generalization. They are in large measure abstract. But examples are more nearly *material* and tangible substance, for we can almost touch and feel them. Any generalization is a thesis, or *hypo*-thesis. Any example, on the other hand, is a unit of experience from our lives that verifies or confutes the hypothesis. The four major parts of your speech, together with the mainheads, and any subheads, of the body are structure, or outline; that with which you *develop,* or fill up, the introduction, body, and conclusion is a combination of *materials.*

Perhaps an example in the form of a comparison will assist in clarifying this important distinction. If you have ever planned a building or have tried to read a blueprint, you know that your first drawings, or even the final blueprint, only mark off space according to scale or in a graphic manner. It is the architect's (or imaginer's or conceiver's) way of trying to visualize for himself and to convey to others the over-all dimensions and the dimensional relationships of a building that might eventually become a reality. Nevertheless, the building is still an *abstraction;* it exists only in *thought.* Only when a contractor begins to move earth, pour concrete, nail wood together, lay bricks, set in glass, put on paint and paper does the building take form in the *concrete.*

A story is told of two Stanford University students on the day after the great earthquake and San Francisco fire of 1906, who, walking across campus, came upon a toppled statue of the French philosopher Agassiz, its head jutting through the broken sidewalk. One of them said, "Well, often have I studied Agassiz in the abstract, but never before in the concrete."

Although the distinction between abstract thought and concrete material is only a relative and necessarily arbitrary one in the realm of rhetoric, it is, nevertheless, an eminently practical and useful one for our purposes. If you can make the distinction, and make use of it, you will find it wonderfully helpful in both the structure and detail of written and spoken composition.

A further application of this concept is found in outlining. An outline has, first of all, two aspects: form and content. Its form alone indicates the general pattern that thought may follow. For example, the following is strictly a form outline:

Introduction
    General Statements
    Example

Thesis

Body
    A. Mainhead
       Example
    B. Mainhead
       1. subhead
       2. subhead
          Example
Conclusion

If the student expresses the thesis and mainheads in the form of sentences, and also the subheads if he employs any, he has added the first phase of content to the bare outline: *thought.* If he goes further and indicates the content of examples, paraphrases his general statements, and records his statistics, he has added the second element of content: *material.* In the latter instance, he has completed what is usually known as a content outline. However, most outlines are in reality a combination of form and content—as they should be.

Regardless of whether the student is in the process of developing his outline or of writing or speaking from it, the distinction between thought and material will be useful to him; and the further knowledge of how materials may be classified, and what their relative uses and values are, will be still further helpful.

Before we turn to classifying and explaining the various types of materials, attention should be directed to the ways in which material enhances the communication process. An extremely effective function of material is to secure the attention and interest of the receivers. If you think not only of interesting speeches you have heard but of interesting writing and interesting conversation, you will recall that those specimens of communication were rich in material that illustrated, exemplified, explained, and pointed up the thought of the message. It is interesting to observe that publications that depend upon securing the attention of receivers make extensive use of materials. You should not be surprised to find that an article in *The Saturday Evening Post* or *The Reader's Digest* contains proportionately more material than one in *The Yale Review* or *Foreign Affairs.*

Still another important function of material is that it provides proof. An outline or speech consisting only of thought is nothing more than a series of assertions. You have no reason to expect your receivers to accept what you have to say until you have substantiated, documented, and supported your thought. In short, greater proof or probability is given to your assertions by the material that lends direct support to thought.

Clarity is also increased through the use of materials. Ideas that are unclear or vague or confusing may often be easily clarified through the use of material. In our everyday conduct, we often find that when our messages are not being received, we use examples and other forms of material to increase the clarity of our ideas. Similarly, when we have difficulty in understanding others, we often say, "Give me an example," or, "What do you mean by that?" In reality, we are asking the communicator to increase his clarity through the more extensive use of supporting material.

## VISUAL AIDS

Both writers and speakers should consider the potential of visual presentation. No textbook writer of history could tell his story without resorting to maps; no physicist could discuss the laws of physics without numerous kinds of drawings; no biologist could give a meaningful discussion of the countless forms of animal life or the life cycle of any life form without numerous drawings or photographs. The use of pictorial and graphic aids in writing has long been taken for granted. But speakers far, far too often either do not realize the assistance visual aids could give them, or else they do not take the trouble to avail themselves of such resources. The use of maps, pictures, rough sketches, models, objects of all sorts, has values both unique and basic.

Compulsion of attention is first, if not most important, in this list of values. We attend to that which we can see, rather than to that which we must imagine through the difficult avenue of words. But when word-pictures and visual demonstrations simultaneously supplement each other, we have communication at its maximum efficiency.

Clarity, or comprehension, is next. We are inclined to ignore the fact that a rough sketch upon the blackboard, an object that can be easily displayed, a chart or graph, a picture, is often much more effective than description or explanation. This in spite of the fact that advertisers have long been telling us that one picture is worth a thousand words. They base their slogan partly on the attention value of pictures, but partly also on their power of telling a story, and of making a long explanation or argument clear in an instant. Sometimes a sketch will fully clarify what could not have been made clear in words in any length of time.

Third in this list of values is that visual aids are a strong assistance to memory. That which is fully clarified is longest remembered; that which leaves a vivid image also remains long in our minds. The speeches that stand out most vividly in a teacher's thoughts as he looks back over a period of years are those in which an unusual object or effective sketching was employed: a Chinese girl explaining the operation of a Chinese adding machine; a premedical student dissecting a frog; a music student demonstrating the use of the metronome; an engineering student sketching the construction of a bridge; an aviation enthusiast exhibiting charts to explain faults of the radio beam; a physical-education major flourishing a tennis racquet; an art student demonstrating examples of art development. Such speeches command a maximum of attention and clarity and remain long in the memory.

Visual aids have the advantage also of placing the speaker at ease. They give him something to do with his hands, some reason and purpose for moving about. They relieve the awkward stiffness that prevails when one must stand in the vast expanse of a bare platform with his fidgety or leaden feet under him, his huge hands attached to suddenly conspicuous arms, and a mouth suddenly overly full of dry and awkward tongue.

In using such devices, it is sometimes desirable to build

a whole speech around a single sketch or object. Again, it may be better to introduce separate sketches or objects as means of developing one or all of the various divisions of the body. No one way is right and any other wrong; all depends upon circumstance.

If you are sketching on the board, be sure to draw while you speak, rather than drawing in silence and then speaking, or vice versa. Make large figures that *suggest* the idea, rather than taking time to draw meticulously and in detail a picture that is too small for the audience to see. The sketch is an *aid* to your spoken words, not an end in itself. Be sure to move from one side to the other of your drawing, so that the audience can see what you have drawn. In fact, stand to one side as you draw, if possible. Move toward your audience and then back again to the sketch when you are free to do so. Otherwise the process of sketching may destroy your audience contact. If possible, practice your speech while sketching before you present it. In this way, you will gain ease and assurance, you will sketch more effectively, and you will be better able to co-ordinate the acts of speech and drawing.

If you are demonstrating an object, be sure it is large enough to be easily seen by the audience. Select objects that are not too complicated in structure to be readily understood, but are easily visible in all their parts. Do not neglect to lift and turn and otherwise manipulate the object so that the audience can see all of it. If possible, it is a good idea to take the object apart, provided you can talk purposively at the same time and do not have to lose time putting it together again. Charts, pictures, and detailed drawings all belong in the object group and are subject to the same caution for use. Rarely pass objects among the members of the audience; they will not be able to pay attention to you and such objects at the same time. Once attention is distracted, it is difficult to regain it. Whenever feasible, reveal your object at the time when it will best accomplish its purpose. If your audience can see it before you are ready to use it, it may divert attention from other important materials that precede it. Also, just as you should refrain from drawing before you begin to speak, be careful not to consume time in preparing or unwrapping an object before you start to talk. Finally, avoid using dangerous materials, such as firearms or explosives, or anything that might place some of the group ill at ease.

## GENERAL PROCESSES

Whereas objects and sketches constitute tangible and visible materials of elucidation and proof, a great body of verbal materials is also at everyone's disposal. Classification of them is difficult, for all of them ultimately overlap and combine and sometimes fuse. However, some form of classification of complex and heterogeneous groups is necessary if we are to recognize the constituent elements; and recognition of types of materials is necessary if we are to use them intelligently.

A builder no more needs to know the differences between wood, steel, glass, brick, and mortar to insure developing an architectural framework into a strong and artistic structure than a speaker or writer needs to understand the distinctive nature and value of the various materials that he uses to round out the framework of a rhetorical outline.

The first materials of the verbal group that usually follow immediately the statement of a mainhead perhaps deserve the name of *general processes,* for their purpose is to construct a general base upon which to rest more specific materials. These processes may be divided into *restatement, explanation,* and *definition.*

*Restatement* consists essentially of restating the sense of the mainhead in a variety of ways. One may occasionally repeat the statement verbatim, speaking it more slowly and with emphasis so that the individual words may sink fully into the hearer's consciousness. Far more often, one will seek to express the thought of the mainhead through a different combination of words, hoping by the use of new language symbols to arouse additional images in the imagination of his hearers and so to bring them nearer the desired concept or belief. For example:

> *The first cause of crime is poverty.* The mere condition of being insufferably poor may be the sole cause of criminality. It is the lack of food and clothing and shelter that makes men cheat and murder and steal. It is the inability to meet monthly obligations that often drives a normally honest man to commit his first minor infraction of the law.

In this instance, restatement has contributed to both clarification and emphasis, for it has enhanced the concept of the influence of poverty, while at the same time it has, by implication, emphasized its importance as a causal agent.

The following paragraphs are further examples of restatement.

> *The primary incentive to fear is uncertainty.* It is the dread of things unknown and unseen that frightens man. The inability to determine what lies ahead, to know what forces for good and evil surround him, to know what tomorrow may hold in store for his body and soul sometimes panics him, though the same man might face real danger unflinchingly if he could but see his enemy. It is not danger that he dreads, but uncertainty.

> *In our attempt to define sound we have thus far considered it only as a physical phenomenon; but our definition would be less than half complete if we did not consider its nature as an experience.* Sound is not simply a physical condition of the atmosphere, or even a physical movement of the parts of the ear; it is a human *reaction* to such a condition, a conscious experience of the organism, a psychological

phenomenon. It is a sensation, or a pattern of sensation, which has *meaning*. It exists in the mind as well as in the atmosphere. Let me illustrate more specifically what I mean by sound as an experience.

> *An instinct is an urge.* It is a basic human drive. It is a mysterious and indefinable force within us that impels us to a certain pattern of behavior. It is a "leaning toward"; it is an inclination; it is a power.

Note that in each case all sentences following the topic sentence (or mainhead) are simply other ways of saying the same thing. They are only additional generalizations. Nevertheless, they clarify and enforce.

Although the implication throughout the discussion and illustration of restatement, that its only proper place is immediately following the statement of the mainhead, is in part justified, this is not wholly true. If its design is clarity, such is almost exclusively its position. If its purpose is emphasis, however, it may be as extensively used at the conclusion of a unit as at the beginning. In practice, it is usually employed in both positions, the pattern of movement being from general to particular and back to general again.

Whereas *explanation* may be accomplished by restatement, it usually requires more specific means. It more often describes, narrates, enumerates, "shows how." It accomplishes for the topic sentence what exposition as a major purpose does for a thesis. It may explain the significance of the topical statement before going on to prove it, or it may show the manner of operation of something before discussing the principle. For example:

> *Another reason why you should buy a Sunbeam electric razor is that its principle of operation insures a closer shave.* Before I can demonstrate this point, perhaps I will need to explain the movements of the cutting parts. The first part . . . etc.

> *Besides the widely recognized method of fingerprinting as a means of identifying the criminal with his crime is the use of the law of probability.* But before emphasizing the effectiveness of this method, I should like you to understand the theory of the law. The whole idea is based upon the assumption . . . etc.

In a sense, explanation is what John Quincy Adams would have called *digression.* That is, the forward progress of thought seems to be held up while one takes time out, as it were, to explain some circumstance or condition necessary to the continuation of thought.

*Definition,* on the other hand, is employed to make clear the meaning of a *term* employed in the topic statement. It concerns itself, not with the whole statement, but with a single word. For example:

> *Poverty is the second major cause of crime.* By poverty I do not mean lack of wealth in appreciation and morality and philanthropy and enterprise. I mean the utter lack of food and shelter and clothing. I mean the sheer need of economic goods.

> *The first value to be derived from psychology is an understanding of the behavior of others.* But let us take time to define the word "behavior" as the psychologist uses it, or we will not properly understand its meaning. To him it signifies . . . etc.

Definition may be accomplished through the specific devices of categorical statement, etymology, history, description, enumeration, analogy, comparison, contrast, negation; but its function is to give specific meaning to a *term.*

Although definition is specific in the sense of confining its intent to a single term, it is nevertheless a part of the *general process* of laying the groundwork for proceeding forward. It prepares the way for more specific materials. It is a necessary preliminary before one can proceed directly to unfolding of the major thought.

Although the beginning student may not wish to labor over the arbitrary distinctions of these three phases of general processes, it is well for him to have some appreciation of the differences between this general group and those which follow. It is well to realize that this group is the type that he would most likely employ if not made aware of other forms. Yet such procedures are so general that they very soon become uninteresting and confusing to the audience, and they are exceedingly difficult for a speaker to remember in any coherent arrangement. They cause him to try to memorize, and so to forget, to fail and to fear. They are thoroughly legitimate and proper materials in their appropriate place and proportion; but the true craftsman will know what these places and poportions are.

## EXAMPLE

*Example,* in contrast to general processes, is nearly always specific in nature.

One advantage of the example is that it is so easy to use. If you have followed the suggestion of choosing subject matter from your own personal observation and experience, you will readily have at hand a number of actual situations that you can relate as a means of depicting your thought. Because you have seen these things with your own eyes, heard them with your own ears, felt, tasted, or smelled them, they have a vivid place in your memory. They are known as memory images, because they are like pictures in your mind. In relating such incidents, you often forget yourself as a person and lose yourself in the narrative. You do not usually have to search for words to narrate such happenings; the images you have supply you with words. Furthermore, such things are easy to remember. A series of examples is far easier to remember than a page of abstract statements. In the one case, all you need to recall is the incident; in the other, you will probably feel the urge to try to remember the words themselves.

Examples are not only easy for speakers to remember, to describe, or to narrate; they are also an audience's delight. When a speaker says, "for example," an audience prepares itself to listen. If the example enjoys some elaboration, if it is in the form of a little story or exciting incident, it will capture and hold the attention of all age groups and all intellectual levels.

If your theme were a discussion of the causes of traffic fatalities, and a subthesis averred that a major contributor was the incompetent driver, you might well offer an example from an accident that you had witnessed or experienced. Who would not be interested in such a narrative? If you describe the accident vividly, and clearly reveal the incompetence of one of the drivers as the cause, you have enabled the audience to experience the same situation and to develop the same awareness. It is like showing them a picture. And they, like the speaker and writer, can clearly see and vividly remember.

For example, the following is a slightly revised version of a true incident reported in several morning newspapers in central California:

> Patrolman Nickerson, observing traffic from a side-road off Highway 99 near the little town of Atwater just after dawn on July 17, was suddenly aware that a sleek, new station wagon was weaving from lane to lane and proceeding not only at excessive speed but apparently also still accelerating. He knew from experience that a weaving car is most likely to be driven by either a drunk driver or a sleepy one. The fleeting glimpse of other heads, some apparently of children, leaning against cushions and window glass as the car

sped by, told him that the driver was a family man who had been driving all night and had been overtaken quite firmly by the kind of sleep that creeps upon one so easily in the first hour or so of daylight. Quickly he moved onto the highway, siren shrieking, in a desperate effort to arouse the sleeper before the inevitable should occur. But the distance was too great for his siren to be heard through the closed windows of the car, which had traveled a full quarter of a mile while Nickerson was making his quick decision. He was just in time to see it mount unsteadily a beautifully engineered overpass, leap through the railing, and spiral gracefully out of sight. When he arrived, he found the car at full rest, upside down, on the railroad tracks below, its speedometer jammed at 90 miles per hour, its family of five all dead. A sleepy driver is not as foolish as a drunk one; but he can be just as dangerous.

To illustrate acquired intolerance, a college student one day offered this example:

Yesterday evening, as I boarded a bus in Modesto, I noted that several Negroes occupied the rear seat, and that white persons had taken almost all of the others. I took a seat approximately half way toward the rear. In a few moments, I noticed a good-looking and well-dressed Negro gentleman enter the bus. He hesitated for a few moments as his eyes searched the rear of the bus for a seat, then he sat down in the only unoccupied double seat remaining, which was well toward the front. Finally, all the seats were filled except that beside him. The last person to enter the bus was a well-dressed and apparently educated woman. When she realized that the only seat available to her was that beside the Negro, she spoke indignantly to the driver, and insisted that the Negro be made to stand in order that she might have a seat without the necessity of sitting beside him. I quickly rose and told the woman she might have my seat and I sat beside the Negro. He had been greatly embarrassed by the incident but seemed pleased that I felt as I did. Personally, I had no

compunction whatsoever about sitting beside him, for I felt
that he was as much one of God's own creations as I, and
certainly as human and full of feeling as I. But an intelligent
and educated woman had *learned* intolerance of her fellow
man.

*Time* magazine, at the time of the Battle of Attu in World
War II, printed the following news item:

Don't Land[1]

*Said the wing commander: "It was a brave and gallant
and heart-breaking thing."*

Two Catalina patrol bombers had been circling for hours
over a pair of bright yellow rafts in the freezing, gale-
whipped sea 90 miles off Attu. On the rafts were six young
naval airmen who had crashed. It was dusk and still no surface craft had answered radio calls for help. Now the fuel
was beginning to run low in the Catalina's tanks.

The pilot, Lieut. Commander Frank R. Moore of Sun-
bury, Pa., made up his mind. He lowered his floats, eased
down through tatters of fog toward the rafts. It was certain
disaster to land in the thundering sea, but the white faces
of the men below had made him decide to try.

On one of the rafts, Lieut. Newel Putnam Wyman of
Canandaigua, N.Y., weak with cold and exhaustion, saw
what was coming. He made up his mind too. As the Catalina, with sparks winnowing from her pipes, drew near, he
gave the signal all Navy pilots know: the wave of the arms
that means "Don't land."

Frank More accepted the decision. With one last circle
over the rafts, he and his fellow pilot thundered off to their
home base.

For three days the storm raged. Then planes found the
rafts, and a ship picked up the men. They were all dead.

Example has the sanction of centuries, and the psychologist has proved its value by testing it in the laboratory of hu-

[1] *Time* magazine, May 8, 1944. Vol. XLIII No. 19, p. 21. Reprinted by
courtesy of the publisher.

man experience. It serves both speaker and hearer, both writer and reader. It interests, it clarifies, it persuades, it stamps indelibly. By all means, develop the technique and the habit of using it.

Essentially, there are four bases of differentiation between the forms, or characters, that examples may assume: length, actuality, specificity, and dramatic value.

Longer examples, frequently called illustrations, we shall designate *detailed illustrations*. Every example illustrates to some degree, and all illustrations are in a sense examples. But the rhetorical illustration has long carried the connotation of length or detail, as well as personal and dramatic character. However, for our purpose, the distinguishing feature of the detailed illustration will be the completeness of detail. It should be a *complete* picture, one in which we see not only a general outline but many individual parts also. For example:

As I stood on the corner of Main and Broadway one hot, sticky afternoon last week, a tall, thin man approached me. He was buttoned all the way from knees to chin in a heavy, black overcoat, and peered out at me from under a heavy, fur cap and big, bushy eyebrows. When he spoke, his voice seemed to come from the very bottom of his coat, and rolled like so much thunder out of the biggest mouth I have ever seen. He asked if I would lend him a postage stamp. I happened to have several in my pocket, and gave him one, a four-cent denomination, without even asking what kind he desired. He took it, put it into a pocket of his coat, smiled vacantly at me, and walked on. Stamp collector? No. Crazy? Possibly. But certainly a character. And the point I have been trying to make is that a "character" is uniquely different from other people.

The first contribution to criminality is what I would call *inherent waywardness*. It is true that circumstances of one's environment may combine to make a potentially law-abiding citizen into a leading criminal, but I insist that, in other cases, even the most favorable environment fails to direct growing young persons in the straight and narrow path because of their inherent inclinations to evil. For example, I well remember a handsome fellow who occupied the seat next to mine when we were in the eighth grade together. He was as intelligent as he was good looking. He was athletic, popular, friendly, but he had a strong determination to do things his own way, and frequently these were not the accepted ways of doing things. This behavior was something more than ordinary mischief; it was a kind of rebellion against the natural laws of society, an inclination to move into the unaccepted forms of conduct. Yet this boy's father held an office of honor in his community, and was generally looked upon as one of its most honest and kindly citizens. His mother was a lady of geniality, grace, and generosity. This boy had every opportunity and every incentive to become a useful, well-educated citizen. Nonetheless, he died in California's electric chair at the age of 21 because he had killed a man in order that he might have his automobile.

The first cornerstone of true religion is *faith*. By faith, I mean one's inherent and unwavering belief in the reality and actuality of a God he cannot reach through the senses of this world. Tennyson says:

> "We have but faith: we cannot know,
> For knowledge is of things we see; . . .
> A beam in darkness . . ."

Theodore Parker expressed it as "being able to feel farther than he could see." At least faith arises from some mysterious force or bond between God and man, and it exists as undeniably as many other forces that operate to determine the nature of our thought and action. Perhaps an illustration will make my point more clear. I was riding in an airplane high above a bank of clouds and fog one day, and I wondered how the pilot would ever be able to land safely. But to my amazement he observed certain instruments on the panel, moved confidently down into and through the fog, and landed safely on the ground that none of us had been able to see. Through space had come a silent and unseen force to direct our flight—but nonetheless a force of guidance. To say that no force exists between God and man to make man sense His presence is to deny both the possibilities and the facts of the universe in which we live.

Note that *faith* is the key word of the topic sentence. The succeeding sentence is a *general process of definition,* or possibly more properly of explanation. The writer then resorts to quotation, to be explained later, and then again to a *general* statement before moving into the *example,* which qualifies as a *detailed illustration,* but, because of its brevity, is hardly more than an *instance* in the form of a *comparison.* Following the *illustration,* the writer returns to a *general* statement to close his discussion of the *topic.*

Your assigned reading will introduce you to many detailed illustrations. Watch for their elements of completeness.

Shorter, undeveloped examples we shall term *instances.* The phrase "specific instance" has wide use in rhetorical literature, but it is somewhat misleading. An instance need not be specific, as we shall shortly see, but may be very general. At the same time, it is ordinarily not considered to be lengthy or detailed, though certainly the term "instance" does not preclude the concept of length. All such divisions and choices of terms are largely arbitrary. The preference in this case has been based on facility. "Undeveloped example" is an awkward phrase for everyday use, so *instance* has been chosen as its synonym, whereas simply *illustration* will usually be intended to imply *detailed illustration.*

An example of a series of instances, as distinguished from the detailed illustrations offered earlier, might be:

On Fifth and Main, I met a very large woman carrying a small poodle and whistling "Ah, Sweet Mystery of Life."

My neighbor puts on a bathing suit and mows his lawn just at daylight every Sunday.

I have a friend who is always broke, incessantly eating popcorn, and always expecting through some miracle to become suddenly very rich.

One of the West's successful speakers used the following series of instances one day in an inductive development of the mainhead of *eccentricity*.

Robert Browning could not sit still. The constant shuffling of his feet wore holes in the carpet.

Zola would never accept an invitation to dinner.

F. Marion Crawford carried his own stationery, pen, and ink, and never wrote with any other. He wrote every word of his long *Saracineso* series with the same penholder.

Edmund Clarence Stedman had his favorite cat sit in a high chair at the table every day for dinner.

Ernest Renan wore his fingernails abnormally long.

Count Tolstoy went barefoot the year round. He was fond of French perfumes, and kept his linen scented with sachet powder. He never wrote without a flower on his desk.

Alexander Dumas, the younger, bought a new painting every time he published a new book.

Edgar Allan Poe slept with his cat. He was inordinately proud of his feet.

Disraeli wore corsets. He had a pen stuck behind each ear when writing.

Thomas Wentworth Higginson possessed a singular power over wild birds, and could easily tame them.

Oliver Wendell Holmes used to carry a horse chestnut in one pocket and a potato in the other to ward off rheumatism.

Hawthorne always washed his hands before reading a letter from his wife.

Thackeray lifted his hat every time he passed the house in which he had written *Vanity Fair*.

Washington Irving never mentioned the name of his fiancée after her death, and if any one else did so, he immediately left the room.

Keats ate red pepper on his toast.

Obviously there is no hard and fast line between specific instance and illustration. Their relationship is largely quantitative. Either may become the other by a process of expansion or shrinkage. The primary purpose of the instance is to add weight, to support the illustration. The illustration gives a complete picture, so that the mind fully understands; the instance names a similar circumstance as an indication that the illustration given was not an isolated case. For that reason, it is used most effectively in series—that is, numerous instances are offered to establish the prevalence or universality of the truth illustrated.

Since general processes, illustrations, and instances bear the functional relationship explained, it follows that if all three are used in a given case they would normally assume the order listed. For example:

One form of symbolic dysfunction is what is known as simple delay—that is, the individual just does not learn to talk. He may have all the potentialities of speech—intelligence, co-ordination, hearing, symbolic power—but through some strange quirk of environment or inherent nature, he just does not follow the usual pattern. For example, some six years ago a brilliant electrical engineer, his well-educated wife and little 3-year-old boy moved next door to us. At his third birthday, the child had not yet uttered a single intelligible sound. He would come into your presence and point and motion and pull your sleeve to try to convey his thoughts, but no semblance of speech had as yet manifested itself. He appeared healthy in every way, obviously understood what others said to him, and exhibited every aspect of intelligence save the expected human behavior of spoken language. One does not speak of such matters to parents, but waits upon their overtures. One day, the father happened to be working near where a graduate student and I were discussing some of the speech problems at the clinic. He eventually approached us, apologized for having overheard our remarks, but raised the question of why his son was not yet able to speak. We assured him that the normal condition would be for him to be saying hundreds of words and chattering more or less incessantly. "And why doesn't he talk?" he asked. I assured him that there were numerous possible explanations, and that we would be glad to study the problem if he wished to bring his son to the clinic. His response was, "Well, don't you think that when he gets to school and sees other children of his age talking, he will realize how foolish it is not to talk and pick it up then?" I assured him I did not think so, but you hardly argue with someone who holds such bizarre views. So he went his way. A bit later, however, his work brought him near us again and he approached us once more and said he had been thinking about the matter and would be happy for us to experiment with his son. Experiment! As though we did not know what we were doing! (As a matter of fact we didn't, but you don't tell all the things you don't know.)

The next day Johnny was brought to my office. Knowing something of his home situation, and thus having my own ideas of what was wrong, I simply locked the door on the two of us and sat down to read. Johnny walked around the office and pointed at many things for almost half an hour, while I gave no evidence of being aware of his presence. Finally he scrutinized me speculatively, looked me in the eye and said "Buah." I looked back at him and said, "Buah." A few moments later he came back, and this time said, "Booblah." I replied as graciously as I knew how, "Booblah"! And so we began to talk to each other. We didn't know what we were saying, but many people talk without being sure of that. For the next half hour we talked vigorously in these barbaric forms, and gradually I began to take the lead, to form more definite words in relation to specific objects. Before we left the office that day he had definitely said the word "key" in connection with having the door opened. That simple beginning constituted the "key" to the whole problem.

The end of the story is that a few months later the father said in a disgruntled tone over the back fence one day, "I'm going to sue you, neighbor." To my amazed "Why?" he laughingly said, "I can't stop Johnny from talking!" And what he said was literally true. Johnny talked incessantly, and constantly coaxed his father to play the "say game." The boy who at three had not said a word, and about whose mental proficiency neighbors were asking concerned questions, is now two grades ahead of his expected place in school, and has as perfect speech as one could ask.

A young mother brought her mute 3-year-old son to our clinic. The last admonition the father had given before he went overseas was that the boy should be taken to a brain specialist to learn why he did not talk. In ten weeks' time this boy was talking fluently, because his only obstacle had been failure of his environment to stimulate speech. A 6-year-old lad who had not spoken at all learned enough speech in ten weeks so that he entered school. A 7-year-old girl who knew only a half dozen words was able in one summer period to take her normal place in school.

In this case, the key words of the topic sentence are *symbolic dysfunction,* which obviously refer to an earlier thesis or subthesis; and *delay,* which is a specific kind of symbolic dysfunction. One sentence of *general process* is used before entering into a very lengthy *detailed illustration* consuming three paragraphs. This is followed by three *instances,* all compressed into one paragraph, the first one a little longer than the second and third.

Another basis on which examples may be classified is their actual as opposed to their imaginary quality. As a rule, examples are and should be from true occurrences. They may be actual happenings from one's own personal experience;

they may be actual incidents from the experiences of others; or they may be the depicting of actual conditions or occurrences that involve little of the personal element. On the other hand, they may, instead of being actual, assume the form of *hypothetical* occurrences. That is, they do not presume to be true, but ask the audience to imagine a possible situation. The fictitious incident or condition may be depicted graphically and vividly, and may be eminently forceful and effective; but it must not presume to be actual. To insure that the audience realizes the fictitious nature of an incident, it may be told as follows: "Suppose you are standing on a street corner, and a tall, thin man approaches you . . . etc." Or, "Let us imagine, for example, that you have just come in out of the rain (fortunately, you had sense enough for that). You are wet and cold. There is no fire in the house, and the house is cold . . . etc."

In order to prevent confusion, it may be well for us to stamp these classes of examples as *actual* and *hypothetical*.

Thirdly, examples differ from each other in that some are *specific* whereas others are *general*. The specific illustration, whether long or short, real or imagined, sets the incident in time and place, names or characterizes the people who are a part of it. For example, "Last night at about eight o'clock I bumped into a little Mexican newsboy as I walked around the corner of the Bank of Commerce building." The general illustration, by contrast, might read, "A man walked around a corner and bumped into a newsboy." The specific illustration has the advantage of arousing more specific images in the minds of listeners, and so is usually more powerful in every way than the general example. Since once again it must be said that specificity and generality are purely relative terms, the guiding principle is to make your illustrations consciously specific.

Finally, examples may be highly dramatic or factual and

dry. Support that demonstrates the nature of something directly has no opportunity to be interesting. For example, if you were offering an illustration of dry abstraction in literary style, you would naturally select the most uninteresting and involved passage of abstract generalizations you could find. The example might be an excellent illustration, but hardly a dramatic one. On the other hand, if you were illustrating the nature of suspense, you would either select a highly dramatic passage or search your mind for the most exciting or gripping occurrence you had ever witnessed.

The point is that, whenever the opportunity occurs, the speaker should strive to employ interesting and compelling illustrations. Those factors that make an example dramatic are: narrative, or story, element; vivid description of specific elements; action; suspense; climax; inclusion of detail; clear and easy unfolding; personal elements; actuality.

Note the detail of the first example below, and the human interest of the second. Both are descriptions of actual happenings.

> Early one fall morning, I was riding through the rolling hills of southwestern Washington with six young men of a college debate team. It was one of those mornings following a prolonged rain, with clouds still lying in the hollows, when the sun rises into a clear and clean sky and brings the raindrops on trees and grass into a sparkling profusion of diamond-like brilliance. Here and there birds' shrill songs pierced the atmosphere. As often happens in such circumstances, when nature seems to bring God nearer, our discussion turned to the subject of religion. I had heard many college "bull-sessions" of this sort, and so was not interested or concerned especially until one six-foot, one-hundred-ninety-pound, intelligent fellow of good Presbyterian stock startled me by asking, "Don't you think that in another two thousand years Christianity will be a matter of history?" I was amazed, yes. But on second thought, I realized that if

people continue to learn and to practice their religion with the same lack of enthusiasm as now prevails, Christianity may well die in far less than two thousand years.

My plane was grounded by enemy fire during the battle of Normandy, and as soon as I realized that I had not been killed in the crash, and was able to extricate myself and look around, I quickly perceived that I was just within the enemy lines, but that no one appeared to have noticed my fall. I noted a farmhouse some three-hundred yards distant, and I thought I might enlist the aid of the French occupants, should there be any. Knowing the danger of allowing myself to be seen, I promptly jumped into a ditch full of icy water and waded along with only my head showing until I was able to approach the house from the rear. To say that the water made me uncomfortable would be to minimize the facts. But I was not thinking of my comfort—I was thinking of my life! Once out of the ditch, I crawled some fifty yards through very cold mud until I finally reached the back portion of the dwelling. Then I raised myself carefully, peered through the windows, but saw no one. Cautiously I worked my way to the door, and opened it ever so carefully, until finally I was inside and had opportunity to explore. Just as I was convinced that no one was there, and that I might be safe for a time, the door suddenly opened and I found myself looking straight into the muzzle of a bayonet-tipped German rifle. I could never know why that German didn't shoot; but for some reason he lunged at me instead, attempting to bayonet me. I admit I was scared. And I don't know how I ever reached my gun. But I did, and I shot him— squarely between the eyes. My bullet stopped him and threw him over backwards . . .

An example, then, may be at once long, specific, actual, dramatic. It may be long, but general, hypothetical, dull. It may be short, actual, general, dull. Usually, length and actuality give opportunity for interest and power that brevity, supposition, and generality do not. The lesson is that examples possess these numerous characteristics, some generally more desirable than others, some holding preference for particular circumstances. But in most cases, the illustration is rhetoric's sharpest tool, and should be always on hand and freely used.

*Comparison* and *contrast* are special types of examples. Their function is also to illustrate. Although they may exhibit any of the four contrasting features of other examples, they are given special place because they involve also the placing of two things or persons or conditions side by side for purposes of noting their points of likeness or difference. Comparison stresses resemblance; contrast emphasizes dissimilarity. For example, "Let us *compare*, by way of illustration, the pressure of water on a man on the ocean's floor and the pressure of the atmosphere on another man standing on the floor of an inland valley." Or, "Our point may be made more clear if we *contrast* the manner in which science arrives at conclusions and that by which barbarians reach theirs." Again, one may accomplish a vivid comparison or contrast by citing two groups of statistics. The relative likeness or difference of conditions becomes immediately and clearly evident when actual figures are given. Blackboard sketches and objects also offer excellent opportunity for comparison and contrast.

*Analogy* is also a form of example, except when so reduced in size as to constitute a figure of speech. Like comparison, it is based upon resemblance between phenomena. In fact, comparison and analogy are in the larger sense synonymous in meaning. However, analogy may perhaps more properly be thought of as an *implied* comparison, rather than a *direct process of* comparison. For example, "Simply because people consistently violate one law is no indication that such violation has bred contempt for laws in general. Many people exceed the speed limit; but very few of them would break into your house and steal." Or again, "The flow of electricity through the wiring of an automobile to its various parts may be likened to the flow of nervous impulses to and through the machinery of the human body."

## STATISTICS

Quite different from examples are statistics. Examples are spice; statistics are stale bread. They are universally looked upon as dry and uninteresting. However, there are times when listeners are eager for the quotation of actual figures. In such instances, statistical data may be more effective than any other type of material. They are usually most fitting after general processes and examples have developed an idea to the point where the listener automatically begins to wonder about actual numerical values or differences. The wise speaker will supply statistics sparingly at this point. He will give them in round numbers unless there is good reason for being more accurate. He will be sure they are valid; he will be sure their connection with the point of discussion is perfectly clear.

Note the meaningful character of the following groups of statistics:

Consider the problem of the stammerer. In the United States alone are 1,800,000 persons who stammer, or about 1 in each 100 persons. For each girl who stammers, there are four stammering boys. Ninety per cent of stammering, or stuttering (there is no difference), begins between the ages of 2 and 7, and the age of highest onset is 4.

Crime is a youth problem. In the United States alone, 1,300,000 crimes are committed annually, or 1 every 22 seconds. One person is murdered every 53 minutes. And 80 per cent of those who commit these crimes are between the ages of 17 and 27.

Our relative spending for war prosecution and war prevention is indicative of our extreme folly. In 25 years, the whole world spent $45,000,000 to make the League of Nations an effective instrument of peace. During our years of participation in World War II, the United States alone spent $270,000,000 each 24-hour period, or 6 times as much daily on war as the whole world had spent in a quarter of a century on peace. In almost 4 years of war, we spent enough to give every child in America a college education, to build every family a new home, and to put a new car in every garage. While this was going on, 100,000,000 people in India and China experienced not a single hour free from hunger; 1 in 10 of the people of the world were driven from their homes by this war; 14,000,000 soldiers were killed, and uncounted millions of civilians died from sword and bomb, disease and starvation.

## QUOTATIONS

It is not only permissible but frequently also wise to quote from other sources. Some persons rarely resort to quotation; others quote to excess. The whole value of quotation depends upon a proper appreciation of the function of such material and sound taste and judgment in its use.

Sometimes the quotation is used because it so forcibly or clearly or beautifully expresses the desired thought. Due to unusual skill or happy accident, someone has expressed a thought so well that it far exceeds the speaker's power to convey it in his own words; so he acknowledges the source and quotes directly. Many times such passages are from prose, but far more frequently from poetry. For example, Clarence Darrow, in his famous defense of Leopold and Loeb, turns to the mystic Omar Khayyám for poetic quotation. Darrow admits the guilt of his clients, but tries to show that capital punishment is no solution to the crime they have committed. Their death, he says, will not bring little Bobby Franks back to life. If it would, he too would favor their punishment; but:

THE MOVING FINGER writes, and having writ,
Moves on; nor all your piety nor wit
Shall lure it back to cancel half a line,
Nor all your tears wash out a word of it.

Sometimes quotations from historical writings or letters carry effective impact. For example, the following from a letter written by the Reverend Cotton Mather to his minister friend John Higginson in 1682 becomes particularly meaningful as a sample of religious bigotry when it is realized that, although Mather had been educated at Harvard, he nevertheless is listed by historians as a "prejudiced investigator" in the famous Salem witchcraft trials:

"To Ye aged and Beloved, Mr. John Higginson:

There be now at sea a ship called Welcome, which has on Board one hundred or more of the heretics and malignants called Quakers, with W. Penn, who is the chief scamp, at the head of them. The General Court has accordingly given secret orders to Master Malachi Huscott, of the brig Porpoise to waylay the said Welcome slyly as near the Cape of Cod as may be, and make captive the said Penn and his ungodly crew, so that the Lord may be glorified and not mocked on the soil of this new country with the heathen worship of these people. Much spoil can be made by selling the whole lot to Barbadoes, where slaves fetch good prices in rum and sugar, and we shall not only do the Lord great service by punishing the wicked, but we shall make great good for his minister and people."

From that same New England that provided its portion of intolerance for which its heirs are ashamed, and so much of humble heroism in which all America takes pride, comes an imaginary picture drawn nearly two centuries later by the meek and mild Quaker poet (the antithesis of "heretic and malignant"), John Greenleaf Whittier, who pictures a Connecticut farmer leading his frightened colleagues of the

Legislature. A speaker discussing modern superstitions might well refer to the occasion when unaccountably darkening skies caused the highly superstitious lawmakers to panic until brought to their senses by the practical and devout farmer:

> Meanwhile in the old State House, dim as ghosts
> Sat the law givers of Connecticut,
> Trembling beneath their legislative robes.
> "It is the Lord's Great Day! Let us adjourn,"
> Some said, and then, as if with one accord,
> All eyes were turned to Abraham Davenport.
> He rose, slow cleaving with his steady voice
> The intolerable hush, "This well may be
> The day of Judgment which the world awaits;
> But be it so or not, I only know
> My present duty, and my Lord's command
> To occupy it till He come. So, at the post
> Where He hath set me in His providence,
> I choose for one to meet Him face to face
> No faithless servant frightened from his task,
> But ready when the Lord of the harvest calls;
> And, therefore, with all reverence, I would say
> Let God do His work, we will see to ours,
> Bring in the candles." And they brought them in!

Some authors include a separate division of quotation that they call *authority*. Whereas quotations are most frequently used because of their beauty, their impressiveness, or their clarity, authority is more often used to furnish proof, to engender greater belief on the part of the receivers. Often a speaker will quote directly from an individual or group in whom the audience has confidence. The use of authority may be noticed in a wide variety of oral communication situations. The attorney who cites previous court decisions makes use of authority. The college debater who reads from reports by government commissions makes use of authority. The political speaker who quotes the words of his party leader makes use of authority.

Authority is properly material and not thought. Through the use of authority, a speaker and his listeners may come closer to truth, but authority in itself does not provide truth. For each authority on one side, there is very likely at least one authority on the other side. The real force of authority lies in its power to make thought more probable and more credible. To the average person, the word of a prominent man is often little less than law. Authority is undeniably a strong rhetorical weapon.

All good quotations are excellent developmental devices.

## PSYCHOLOGICAL TESTS OF MATERIALS

Thus far emphasis has been placed upon identifying and classifying the possible materials that may be marshaled to develop a theme. Some indication has been given of the relative significance of each type. But no standard measure has been suggested by which one may test the materials he contemplates using to determine whether they are the best he can select in the given case. Such a measure might well contain the items of amount, relevancy, reliability, and suitability to audience and occasion.

In determining the appropriateness of *amount*, suitable check questions would be: Have I chosen an amount of material that will allow me to stay within the time-limit set by the occasion? Will the amount I plan to use be sufficient to permit me to use all the time allotted to me? Will this amount tire the audience? Will it be sufficient to secure the desired response of understanding or belief? If the amount seems too great or too small, does the fault lie in choice of material or in too broad or too narrow a theme, or in too many divisions of the discussion?

Ordinarily, one is obligated to cover his assigned or selected subject regardless of the time or space allotted to him. Frequently he will employ as many mainheads for a short discourse as for a long one, for certain ideas, parts, or elements, are inherent in the subject, and none must be ignored. Length, therefore, is dependent largely, in most circumstances, upon the *amount of material* employed for each heading developed.

It has been the privilege of one of the authors to discuss one particular subject with hundreds of groups varying widely in character and number, but the obligation to discuss four basic phases of the topic has always been unavoidable. In some instances, as much as two hours has been available. The usual privilege has been thirty or forty minutes. On occasion, the chairman of a meeting has allowed other business to defy control, until sometimes as little as fifteen minutes remained. In few instances, except in radio broadcasting, does one know how much time he may speak until the chairman actually has presented him. He must then look at his watch, make his calculations, and then, as he moves through the speech, make his decisions on which material to include, which to omit, and which to shorten. He will reduce general processes, omit some examples and shorten others, and omit quotations or parts thereof, all in accordance with the passing of time, the obvious fatigue of the audience, or his sense of his listeners' acceptance or understanding of the idea.

One of the authors has also faced, week after week, an expressionless microphone, and through the control-room glass a grimacing operator who expected him not only to begin exactly on the pointing of a finger but also to talk glibly for exactly 13 minutes and 38 seconds. This type of restriction would seem to some, not only foolish and inhumane, but virtually impossible of achievement as well. Actually, such exact timing is not difficult. In fact, it is easier to achieve in extemporaneous address than in reading from manuscript. In reading fifteen minutes of material aloud, even experienced readers may vary as much as a minute or more per reading. Thus, making the closing match the clock becomes exceedingly difficult, and one's only insurance lies in the preparation of short paragraphs that may be included or omitted at will. In extemporaneous broadcast, a speaker will similarly omit or include contemplated units, either illustrations or general processes, as circumstances require. The final adjustment in his timing is made by the degree of summary, rounding out and dismissing he gives his topic. A speaker's success or failure often is determined by his selection of an amount of material consistent with the time allotted and with the special needs of the audience he faces.

*Relevancy* is dependent solely on whether the material bears a direct relation to the thesis. It is a fundamental determinant of unity. One may violate the law of unity by inclusion of either extraneous thought or material. If he selects an incongruous mainhead, then certain material may be relevant to it but still not consistent with the thesis. By the same token, material may be included in a particular mainhead that does not support the mainhead. It may, as a matter of fact, support the thesis or another mainhead, but material is not relevant if it is not directly related to the mainhead to which it is assigned.

Regardless of the point at which inconsistency occurs, irrelevancy is nonetheless wasted effort. Lawyers complain about certain matters as "irrelevant and inconsequential"; audiences may not complain, but consciously and unconsciously they segregate, reject, deplore, and condemn.

The famous incident of the four chaplains of different religious faiths who gave their lifebelts to servicemen leaving their sinking ship in the icy North Atlantic, then turned and put their arms about each others' shoulders, lifted their faces in prayer to their one God, and went calmly down with the foundering vessel, is a remarkable example of *something;* but its legitimate use is a matter of discriminating judgment. It illustrates courage, faith, devotion, greatness even in obscurity, and many other things, perhaps. It does not illustrate selfishness, cruelty, barbarism, vandalism, truth, honesty, or fear. Whether it illustrates tolerance, beauty, humility, kindness, and patience is debatable.

*Suitability of material to audience and occasion* is basically a matter of taste and judgment. Keen audience analysis and a sense of the probable spirit of the occasion are prerequisite to effective choice. In general, tired and unintellectual groups need a preponderance of illustrative materials; for all groups, the speech should represent a kind of rough scene-painting, done with broad strokes and vivid splashes. Thus one must weigh the proportion of general processes, illustrations, and statistics, measure it against the ages, occupations, and intellectual levels of his audience; then view it in the light of the occasion upon which his listeners meet. In addition, the political or religious inclination of an audience may determine whether it is wise to quote a given authority, include a certain proverb, cite a particular incident, or make an intended assertion. What some people delight to hear will quickly offend and prejudice others. What would be effective to use at a serious club meeting might be quite out of place at a rally. The important consideration is that audiences do differ, and the same audience will be different from time to time in its attitudes and moods. The speaker must ask himself about the desires, fears, hates, the physiological and psychological states of his hearers, and choose his materials accordingly.

## LOGICAL TESTS OF MATERIAL

There are at least two important reasons why the serious student of oral communication should be able to apply certain simple tests to determine the logical integrity of the materials of communication. First, the student speaker should be able to avoid, in his own speeches, the most common fallacies in the use of materials in order that he not mislead himself and his receivers. Second, in listening to oral communication, he should be able to detect those fallacies so that he does not become the victim of reasoning that is fallacious or erroneous.

It is not the intention of the authors to offer even the most elementary introduction to logic at this point; far from it. Rather, it is our hope to point out some of the most common errors that are made in the use of materials. Admittedly, our approach here is negative. We do not tell you "how to reason"; instead, we offer you some suggestions on "how *not* to reason." Moreover, our discussion will be limited to those fallacies that are products of the improper use of materials.

You will recall our discussion of induction and deduction in the previous chapter. You will also recall that induction proceeds from particulars to generalizations and that deduction proceeds from premises to particulars. At this point it is worth-while to note the way in which we make use of these forms of reasoning in developing thought. It is valuable also to observe the ways in which the two forms relate to each other and the ways in which errors might occur.

As we have indicated earlier, much of our learning has made use of inductive reasoning. As we acquire more and more particulars, we are increasingly able to make generalizations about those particulars. The generalizations we make about the particulars, however, may range from the wildest guess to almost absolute certainty, depending on how well the inductive chain of reasoning is used. Since the sun has risen every day of your life, and, as far as you know, every day in the past, the generalization that the sun will rise tomorrow is certain almost beyond any doubt. After you have seen several thousands Douglas firs, you may be quite certain about your generalization that Douglas firs do not lose their leaves in winter. Often, however, our generalizations are based on much less information and fewer observations. When generalizations are based on increasingly less information, the danger of committing the fallacy of the *hasty generalization* becomes increasingly greater. Generalizations are hasty in the sense that conclusions are drawn based on material which is insufficient, not representative, or ignores contrary examples. A particularly apt synonym sometimes used for the hasty generalization is the *inductive leap*. Most induction involves some leaping from particulars to generalizations, but the speaker must be sure that he has an adequate basis for his conclusion. He should choose the very shortest possible distance in jumping to conclusions.

Full certainty in induction can be symbolized by an unbroken triangle in which all the particulars of a given case are known:

If your aim is to determine the age range of the student body and you have interviewed every student, there would be no leap at all. If you have interviewed 90 per cent of the student body, the inductive leap would be very short and the triangle would be slightly broken:

If you spoke to 50 per cent, the generalization would be more hasty and the leap would be longer:

If you stationed yourself in the Student Union and spoke to the first ten students who came along, the generalization would be hasty indeed and the leap would be very long:

It is, of course, obvious that the longer the leap the more hasty the generalization. As the generalization process becomes more hasty, the conclusions become increasingly uncertain.

We cannot tell you how much material you must have before you can draw a reliable conclusion. You must, however, be aware of the possibility that you may generalize from too few instances. Many of our unfavorable impressions of people, places, and groups is based on the use of insufficient instances. If there are two football players in a class and both of them are poor students, you cannot conclude that all members of the football team are poor students. Even if all members of the Mafia are Italian, it would be an extremely hasty generalization to conclude that all Italians, or even many Italians, are criminals.

If the instances from which the generalizations are drawn are highly representative of the group as a whole, you may actually use a relatively small number of instances. Dr. George Gallup, in determining the opinions of 180,000,000 Americans, often interviews no more than 1500 persons. His sample, however, is a miniature model of the entire United States. It is highly representative of the opinions of all Americans. In the group of 1500, ethnic, political, religious, professional, educational, geographic, and other characteristics are represented in direct proportion to the population as a whole.

Most of us, of course, are not able to use the rigid statistical controls of professional pollsters. Therefore, we are often guilty of drawing generalizations from situations, events, and persons that are unrepresentative. If you have traveled on a train, you know that the railroads normally go through the most unattractive parts of cities. They pass through slums and industrial and warehouse areas. If a Russian were placed on a train and traveled coast to coast and back without getting off the train, it might seem to him that the United States is a land of blighted and impoverished cities. His generalization would be based on observations that are hardly representative of American cities.

If a survey were taken at a motion-picture theatre to determine opinions about reducing the Federal entertainment tax, you might suspect that the group was not very representative. You would hardly expect to draw any reliable conclusions about the general desire for elimination of the Federal liquor tax by interviewing the inhabitants of a cocktail lounge. Yet a student speaker attempted to prove that the student body was opposed to restrictions on fraternities by quoting a poll he had made of his fraternity brothers.

The hasty generalization as the principal fallacy of induction can lead to serious abuse of developmental materials. It is no more mischievous, however, than faulty deduction. In handling materials deductively, it often happens that an inductive generalization arrived at hastily becomes the premise for a fallacious deductive argument. Thus, if you reason—

> Mary Smith is a blonde and she is dumb.
> Jane Jones is a blonde and she is dumb.
> Susan Brown is a blonde and she is dumb.
> Therefore, all blondes are dumb.

—you are committing a quite obvious hasty generalization. If you accept the generalization, however, and reason in this fashion—

**1 1 5**

All blondes are dumb.
Therefore, Barbara Green is dumb.

—you are committing a fallacy of deduction which we shall call the *biased premise*. If you begin the deductive development of materials with a premise or assumption that is biased, doubtful, or uncertain, the conclusion of your development is also biased, doubtful, and uncertain, no matter how impeccable the reasoning process may be. If you accept the premise that all dogs have seven legs, it must follow that your dog, Spot, has seven legs. The difficulty with such a development is that the premise in this case is obviously false.

Many of our stereotypes and prejudices are the result of biased premises that we have acquired, one way or another, in our years of living. If you believe that Negroes are shiftless, doctors are wealthy, Jews are mercenary, artists are immoral, your views about individual members of these groups will be almost predetermined. In making use of deductive development, you must be constantly alert to avoid the use of premises that are false, biased, or doubtful. The principal form of developmental material involved in hasty generalizations and biased premises is the example.

The analogy is a frequently used form of developmental material. It is also a form that is subject to misuse. One of the prime functions of the analogy is to provide comparisons between highly similar events or phenomena; to show that if something is true in one case it must also be true in another highly similar case. A difficulty in using analogies, however, is that the cases compared may not be very similar, or they may not be similar where it really makes a difference. A student speaker, for example, attempted to prove that football is not a dangerous sport by pointing out that the death rate among high school, college, and professional football players is much less than the death rate among the total population. It should be clear to you that a fair comparison cannot be made between a group that includes only young, healthy males and a group that includes old and young, sick and healthy, females and males.

Similarly, a speaker who proposes that a forty-hour week be instituted in agriculture because of its success in industry, ignores the essential differences between agriculture and industry. The student who argues that midterm examinations not be required at Podunk Sub-Normal College because they are not required at Oxford University is making use of the false analogy in much the same way. So is the speaker who laments that he cannot purchase a new automobile today for $750 as he could in 1937. This year cannot be compared to the year 1937, nor can automobiles of today be compared to those of 1937.

Actually, we have been aware of false analogy since we were children. When you demanded a new toy because Johnny had one, your parents may have responded, "But we are not Johnny's parents." In effect, they were telling you that you were guilty of the fallacy of false analogy because your family and Johnny's family were too dissimilar for a fair comparison.

Authority is another form of developmental material that requires careful testing. The need to examine the use of authority in communication we receive and transmit is increased by human tendencies to rely on authorities. There are several questions you should ask about the use of authority in communication. First of all, you will probably want to know whether the authority quoted is an authority in the field in which he claims authority. Major-league baseball players may know a good deal about their sport, but we are not obligated to accept their views about juvenile delinquency.

You will also want to ask whether the authority is relatively unbiased. We recognize that few persons are completely impartial about controversial issues, but we must be careful of the authority who quite obviously has an axe to grind. We are extremely naive if we accept, at face value, the appraisal of political prospects by the National Democratic and Republican Chairmen. Perhaps the question that needs to be asked is whether the authority's biases prevent him from making honest statements.

It is also helpful to discover whether the authority has first-hand information or is merely relying upon information that he acquired elsewhere. Other factors being equal, we will give greatest credence to the authority who is able to report the facts from his own observations.

We must be careful to avoid using or believing vague and uncertain uses of authority. When you hear or read such statements as, "usually reliable sources report . . ."; "according to 500 New York doctors . . ."; "it is widely reported . . ."; "they say . . . ," then you must recognize that the usual tests of authority cannot be applied. Therefore, such vague attributions of authority are of practically no value.

Any fallacious use of authority is generally designated as *misuse of authority*.

The dangers in the use of statistics are so widespread and so numerous that it would require some fairly complicated mathematics to explain most of them. Nevertheless, it will be helpful for you to know and recognize one or two of the simpler *statistical errors*. Most human beings are willing to accept "the average" as an extremely reliable measurement of the central tendencies of an entire group. Yet the average, under certain conditions, can be a most undependable measurement.

If, for example, you hear that a group of five families has an average annual income of $12,000, you do not know whether the distribution is:

| Family 1 | $12,000 | | Family 1 | $56,000 |
|----------|---------|------|----------|---------|
| Family 2 | 12,000 | | Family 2 | 2,000 |
| Family 3 | 12,000 | or | Family 3 | 1,000 |
| Family 4 | 12,000 | | Family 4 | 500 |
| Family 5 | 12,000 | | Family 5 | 500 |

In either case, the average annual income is $12,000. In the second distribution, however, 80 per cent of the families have incomes of less than $12,000, and 40 per cent have incomes of less than $1,000. Probably a more representative figure is the median, or midpoint, of $1,000. A distorted average is particularly likely to result when you deal with small groups of figures.

Many of us have a disturbing tendency to assume that what is true of the average must be true of the whole. If, for example, we know that physicians have an average annual income of $19,000, some of us are likely to reason that all, or at least most, physicians are prosperous. Actually, a case can be made for their being rich or poor, since there are probably as many physicians with incomes below $19,000 as those with incomes above $19,000.

We must also be careful to see that the statistics really say what they seem to say. A few years ago, a critic of secondary education announced that not a single course in physics was available in 40 per cent of American high schools. On closer examination, it developed that only 2 per cent of American high school students attended those high schools. The 40 per cent represented high schools that were almost entirely rural and small. For the past 25 years, the number of persons killed in automobile accidents has been increasing somewhat. When this death toll is measured against the greatly increased number of automobiles and against the many more miles driven, it becomes clear that, in terms of miles driven, the highways have become more safe rather than more dangerous. In these cases, the statistics cited do not give us the real information we need in order to come to reasonable conclusions.

Since causal reasoning is a common method of developing the thought of a speech, it is worth-while to note that fallacies may often occur in *mistaken cause*. Some of the possible causal errors have been suggested in Chapter V, but it

may not be amiss to extend our discussion. We are often mis-
led into thinking that when two events occur simultaneously,
or in immediate chronological order, that there must be some
causal relation between them. It was once pointed out, for
example, that as the asphalt pavements in New York City
became softer, the rate of infant mortality increased. Therefore, there must be something in the melting asphalt that
caused babies to die. The error in this kind of causal reasoning is that the speaker has confused a cause and effect with
two effects. Actually, infant mortality and melting asphalt
are both probably effects of summer heat.

A study of successful executives showed that large vocabularies was a characteristic common to the group. Therefore, said the author, a large vocabulary must be a cause of
success, and future executives would be well advised to develop their vocabularies. What the author probably failed to
see was that large vocabularies *and* success are much more
likely to be effects of education and intelligence than causes
of each other.

A very mischievous error in causal reasoning is the fallacy
of the *single cause*. This fallacy is troublesome because many
human beings would like to find a simple answer to complex
problems. Thus, Hitler told the German people that *the single
cause* of many of their troubles was the Jews. Senator Mc-
Carthy announced that *the single cause* for American problems in the 1950's was Communist infiltration. In both of
these cases, the causes were exceedingly complex but it was
easier and more comforting to blame a single cause. We must
be extremely cautious, both as transmitters and receivers,
about advancing single causes when multiple causes are more
likely to be involved.

Many of our superstitions are probably the result of *faulty
cause*. The unknown man who broke a mirror, encountered a
black cat, or walked under a ladder before he suffered misfor-

tune, assumed that these phenomena were the causes of his difficulty. We may laugh at his primitive errors of causality; but how far removed is he from the man who blames our unusual weather on the testing of atomic bombs?

If the speaker selects an amount of material suited to time he should consume, and adequate to the full development of his subject; if he makes sure of its relevance and reliability; if he applies to it tests of simple logic; if he evaluates it for suitability to the audience and the occasion, he is then ready to give thought to other problems of making the speech effective.

SUPPLEMENTARY READING:

---

BRIGANCE, WILLIAM NORWOOD. *Speech: Its Techniques and Disciplines in a Free Society* (2nd ed.). New York: Appleton-Century-Crofts, Inc., 1961, Chapter 13.

CROCKER, LIONEL. *Public Speaking for College Students* (3rd ed.). New York: American Book Company, 1956, Chapter 13.

SARETT, LEW, FOSTER, WILLIAM TRUFANT, AND SARETT, ALMA JOHNSON. *Basic Principles of Speech* (3rd ed.). Boston: Houghton Mifflin Company, 1958, Chapter 12.

SOPER, PAUL L. *Basic Public Speaking* (2nd ed.). New York: Oxford University Press, 1956, Chapter 6.

## *SAMPLE SPEECH* (*Didactic Pattern*)

### "Stop That Man"[2]

[HYPOTHETICAL ILLUSTRATION IN INTRODUCTION] I have no intention of murdering anyone in this room this morning—

[2] This speech is only slightly modified from the form which it assumed when given by student Philip Hood.

though I may seem to follow the example of our instructor
and force upon you a torture-of-words worse than death.
But, assuming that I were of a disposition to deal with you
in the more humane fashion of outright murder, and should
pull a gun from my pocket and shoot the most beautiful
lady or the most handsome man present, through the heart,
and then should run quickly out of the room and make my
escape in some rich college student's car, what do you suppose are the chances that I would be apprehended and
brought to full justice?

[GENERAL PROCESSES IN INTRODUCTION] I have made some
slight study of criminology, and one of the things that im-
presses me most in that study is the sharpness of insight
which criminal lawyers have into loopholes in the law, and
the cleverness with which they can juggle evidence so that
many times a guilty man is allowed to go unpunished, and
you and I as laymen wonder if justice be done or not. However, criminologists are constantly at work devising means
by which they can outsmart the cleverest of criminals and
their lawyers; and through this research they have now developed methods whereby a given criminal can be identified
positively with a given crime, so that no amount of juggling
of the evidence by his lawyer can set him free.

[THESIS] I think it important that we as citizens be informed
upon advancements in the solution of problems that affect
us; and so I shall use the time allotted to me this morning to
explain what these methods are.

[MAINHEAD] [GENERAL PROCESSES] The first of these methods,
the one that is probably familiar to you all, is that of *fingerprinting*. You are all aware of the small ridges on the skin of
the hands and feet, probably developed to enable one better
to grasp an object. These ridges tend to form a definite pattern; and on no two individuals is this pattern the same.
Now, if the fingerprint is found at the scene of a crime, and

that fingerprint corresponds with the fingerprint of a given suspect, then there is no doubt that the suspect has a connection with the crime, because no two people have the same fingerprints.

[DETAILED ILLUSTRATION] For example, George Bremer, a wealthy St. Paul manufacturer, was kidnapped. The authorities called on the case were able to find Mr. Bremer, but they were unable to find any trace of his abductors. Persistent search failed to unearth any clue, until finally an old gasoline can was found, which was thought to have some connection with the crime. Nothing was visible on it; but, when it was treated with certain chemicals, a fingerprint was indistinctly revealed. This fingerprint, when checked with fingerprints on file at the Federal Bureau of Investigation in Washington, was found to belong to Doc Barker, a leader of a very ruthless gang of criminals. Well, Doc Barker was traced, his mother was traced, his brother was traced, and several members of his gang were traced, until the kidnappers were found. In all, 36 convictions resulted from this single fingerprint, which wasn't even visible until it was treated chemically.

[SERIES OF INSTANCES] Many examples of the use of fingerprinting could be cited. Leroy Sumter of New Orleans was convicted for the murder of a woman by means of the fingerprints found on a revolver at the scene of the crime. Marcus Paul of Chicago was captured for a very daring theatre hold-up by means of a fingerprint left on the counter of a box office. Farol Clyde of Los Angeles was convicted for the murder of his wife, and an innocent man was freed, by means of a fingerprint found on a club with which he had beaten her to death.

[STATISTICS] [QUOTATION] So useful is this method to the police that 63 per cent of all crimes solved in San Joaquin County are solved with the aid of fingerprinting in one way or another. The Chief of the Bureau of Identification in San Joaquin County says that "the method of fingerprinting is so effective that were we suddenly deprived of its use, the department could scarcely operate."

[TRANSITION] [MAINHEAD] [GENERAL PROCESSES] But besides this method of fingerprinting as a means of identifying a given criminal with a given crime, there is also another method equally effective, and that is the use of the *law of probability.* If I toss a coin into the air, it has an equal chance of coming down either heads or tails. The probability that it will come down either heads or tails is one chance that it will to one chance that it won't. However, if I ask what is the probability that the sun will rise tomorrow, the answer is quite different. It's possible that the sun won't rise; but there are so many things in favor of its rising that the probability that it will rise is many hundreds of thousands of millions of billions to one that it won't. When the probability that a thing is true is so great, we can accept it as a fact that it is true, even though there is a small chance that it isn't true. If the probability that a given criminal committed a given crime is one to one, then we haven't much on that criminal. But if the probability that it was committed is millions to one, then, just as in the case of the rising sun, you may state as fact that he did, and the jury will accept the evidence.

[DETAILED ILLUSTRATION] For example, two families in the mountains of Tennessee were feuding. Mr. Green of one family, in order to gain revenge, stood behind a bush in the woods; and as his neighbor's young son came whistling down the path on his way home from school, Mr. Green stepped out from behind the bush and clubbed him to death. Then he tossed the club away and walked calmly home. Of course he was suspected, but no evidence could be found—no fingerprints or anything else to prove him guilty. But one of the investigators, while at the scene of the crime, found some wood shavings evidently whittled by the murderer while waiting for the lad to come by. Mr. Green was apprehended. On him was found a pocket knife, and with it some shavings were made. The minute striations in the wood caused by microscopic imperfections in the blade of the knife were found to coincide exactly with those on the wood shavings found at the scene of the crime. Now it's possible that two different knives could have made the same markings, but the probability that they could is so small that in order to find another knife that would make the same markings as the one Mr. Green had, every man, woman, and child in the United States would each have to own over 5,000 knives. The jury accepted the evidence as valid and Mr. Green was punished by the law.

[INSTANCE] The manager of the Sweet Clover Dairy Company in New York opened his plant one morning and found nothing left of his safe but the knob and a handle. But on the knob was a mark made by a pair of pincers. A suspect was found; and the mark made by the pincers found in the back of his car was identical with the one found on the safe knob. The probability that the two marks could have been made with different pincers was too small to prove the suspect anything but guilty.

[INSTANCE] A board was missing in Hauptmann's attic, and four nail holes where it had been nailed to the cross-beam corresponded exactly with four nail holes in one of the boards found in the ladder used to kidnap Lindbergh's baby. The probability that two different carpenters could have driven four nails exactly in the same position was too small to allow, and the jury accepted it as a fact that the board in the ladder came from Hauptmann's attic.

[INSTANCE] An old prospector was found in a remote region of Alaska, dead from a rifle wound. Near the scene was found a former convict and an Eskimo both carrying rifles of the same bore as the one used to kill the prospector. The convict was suspected but an examinaton showed that the minute grooves in the bullets from the Eskimo's gun caused by imperfections in the barrel of the gun corresponded with the bullet found in the dead prospector's body, thereby proving his guilt.

[STATISTICS] [QUOTATION] So effective is the law of probability in crime solving that over two thousand cases were solved last year in the United States by this method alone. J. Edgar Hoover, Chief of the Federal Bureau of Investigation, says that in his laboratory, where the law of probability is so much used, "it offers the greatest efficiency to crime solution of any agency in the world."

[SUMMARY] [INTEREST] This will give you an idea, then, of how the law of probability as well as the method of fingerprinting aids the criminologist in definitely connecting a given criminal with a given crime. And, while the criminal is getting more and more clever in his ability to evade the law, those who are working against him are getting clever too—clever to the extent that the general public is coming more and more to feel that justice is being done.

## SAMPLE SPEECH

### "THREE R'S FOR A NEW DAY"[3]

#### I

My subject may seem elementary, but it is the elementary things, after all, that are the most important. I am going to talk on the three R's—not the old three R's that you are acquainted with, because the old is constantly being changed

[3] An address by Carter Davidson, at commencement exercises for graduate professional classes of the Division of Business Education, International Business Machines Corporation.

into the new, as I am sure any one acquainted with the way in which IBM has revolutionized the business world will not deny.

Diogenes, as you recall, spent his days in a tub—perhaps because he was facing a housing shortage of his day. On an occasion when Alexander the Great, one of his pupils, talked to him, Diogenes remarked: "When I die, please bury me with my face down; because I am very sure when the truth is known, everything that we now think is true will be upside down, and I will be the only person who is right side up!"

Those of us in the educational field feel somewhat that way about what we are teaching. As one teacher remarked the other day, "I am teaching you fellows both sides of every question. I am teaching you twice as much as you will ever need to know, but the trouble is that only half of what I am teaching you is true—I don't know which half." So if any of you feel that you have had it "laid on thick" while you were here and that you had more to absorb than you have been capable of absorbing, just remember that half of that, if it sticks, is all that is required.

The old three R's are reading, 'riting, and 'rithmetic. We used to think them very important indeed, but in your factory I saw a machine that does reading, 'riting, and 'rithmetic, and it may be that you have created robots to take the place of human beings in the world of the future. What do we mean by the new three R's for the adult citizens of America facing the civilization of the future? I suggest a new three R's which I believe Americans need very much and which the trained businessman of the future is going to need in every aspect of his daily work.

## II

The first of these is the R of Reason. For a long time in American life we supposed that literacy was enough, that if we merely taught people to read they would acquire all the knowledge necessary and would become highly educated, highly sensible, and highly effective citizens. But we made a discovery, now that we have taught ninety-nine per cent of our Americans and a good many other people throughout the world to read. What do they read? Here our hearts begin to sink and our whole conception of civilization begins to crumble, because the most popular reading in America has very few ideas in it. It consists mostly of picture magazines and comic books, materials which fill our newsstands and apparently fill the hearts and minds of most of our population. The greatest heroes of America are the Dick Tracy's and the Supermen, rather than the heroes of the novels or of the drama or of history we hoped they would be.

There are a good many people who do not like to reason, do not like to think. As a matter of fact, I fear that Dr. Charles W. Eliot of Harvard was optimistic when he said that fifteen minutes each day would be enough to give a complete education. Most people can't think for ten minutes a day; that is a terrific strain to place upon the mentality of the average citizen. Most of us feel very much like the old Southern uncle who remarked, "When I works, I works hard. When I sits, I sits loose. When I thinks, I falls asleep." I am sure we sympathize with him; therefore, we ask: Why is it necessary for us to learn the first R, the R of reasoning? The best answer is that the ability to reason makes us better persons; there is one person in this life with whom one has to live from the start to the end, and that is oneself. The person I feel sorry for is the individual who doesn't like himself, who can't stand himself, who is bored with himself, and who seeks to get away from himself at every opportunity. We have to live with ourselves; therefore, let's be reasoning people in order that we will be interesting people for ourselves to enjoy. The Greeks had a word for it; over the Oracle of Delphi, you recall, there were just two Greek words, which meant a great deal in the lives of the Greeks, "Know Thyself." That is essentially what I meant by the term "reasoning."

There is another good answer which the war and all of its

attendant circumstances have forced upon us—that reasoning will enable us to protect ourselves against unreasoning or against propaganda or against falsehood. If we cultivate the powers of reasoning, we are to that extent protected and armed against a host of foes.

Reason, however, is a broad field. It consists of a great deal more than what we used to think of as a study of formal logic, with analogies and syllogisms and all the other devices and forms of logic listed and arranged for our memorization. At the bottom of the scale of reason lies what might be called attention or concentration, really a difficult accomplishment. There are many people who cannot concentrate. They find themselves constantly wandering away from the topic that is under discussion. Frequently their eyes wander off the page, and they can't keep their attention centered. Concentration is needed to prepare a mind to think.

Next in the scale of reason is the power of observation. Very few people, apparently, have that power. All you need for proof is to get four or five witnesses to come to a court case to testify as to what they saw. All of them saw the same thing happen, yet all five witnesses will tell entirely different stories as to what they observed. The power of observation is carelessly used. All of us admire the powers of Sherlock Holmes and the whole tribe of detectives, not so much because they always get their man, but primarily because they are able in two seconds to observe everything that could possibly be observed. They then draw their conclusions, tell the results—spending at least an hour and a half telling you how they arrived at those deductions. It is the power of observation that makes a great detective and a great thinker.

The third step, going up the scale of reason, is the power of memory. I am not suggesting that all of us need to cultivate the remarkable power of memory which makes John Kieran or other members of the "Information Please" program famous. But there is something to the ability to remember. Although you may have recordings made of everything said, the power of the human memory is worth developing.

On the fourth step we must put logic. It isn't enough

merely to remember what somebody else said; you must be able to think for yourself. We have the power of logic to test every possibility that is put before us. The trouble is that too many people take logic as an automatic formula. Logic will not supply everything for the mind. It must have something more than formula behind it.

Even higher than logic is the power of judgment. We much admire judgment and the related ability to wait until all the evidence is in. My, but that is a hard thing for us to do! We want to jump at conclusions, we want to get things done in a hurry, without waiting for all the evidence. We like the man who arrives at a sound judgment so much that we put him on the bench and call him a judge, and we allow him to decide on life and death for us.

So judgment in the human estimate is one of the highest qualities of reason; but even above judgment, sitting at the top of the mental table, is the power of imagination. Imagination is the power that enables us to get something out of nothing or, as Shakespeare put it, "to give to airy nothing a local habitation and a name." That is the quality that all education should try most to cultivate—the power of imagination. That is the sort of thing that led Thomas J. Watson to organize the new IBM. It has given inspiration to the greatest things that have come into our lives.

Many of you are collectors of one sort or another. I think the most important kind of collection we need in this world is not the collecting of etchings or of any other art objects, but the collecting of ourselves. Because we spend so much time gathering up things, we never find time to gather ourselves together. And there is no opportunity in life that should be grasped with more avidity than the opportunity to gather ourselves, even if for only a moment.

### III

The R of Reason means that you must know why; but you also need the second R which is the "know-how." It isn't sufficient merely to know why something is—you must know how something can be done; so we will call that R the R of Resourcefulness, which I nominate as the second of the new R's.

The American ideal, which all of us agree to, is that a person should know how to do something, should have some skill, should have some dexterity, should have some real ability. There are many people who don't want to do anything: they always want George to do it. But let me say to those people that, although they may have enjoyed being problem children, we don't need problem adults in America. The trouble with too many who want to be in that class is that they imagine that everyone who was so tolerant, so kind toward the problem children, is going to be similarly friendly and tolerant to the problem grownup. We need people who have some answers and know how to put those answers into effect. Even those who are born to wealth in America feel that they have to pull their share of the load. It is an American tradition that every individual must be able to do something with his talents.

That doing may be of two entirely different types. It may be just a routine task, a turning of a wheel or nut, or it may require an education. The difference between education and training is that in training, a person learns to do a task by imitating some other person who is doing it, by watching the various performances of that person, and then by doing the same thing himself until he finally reaches the point where he can do it as perfectly as the teacher. But education is something entirely different. It is seeing through the processes by which a task is done or by which a problem is solved, so that when a problem no one has ever seen before is placed before that person, he can, through the processes of know-how, work out a way in which that problem can be solved. That is the difference between education and mere training.

G. K. Chesterton, one of the cleverest of all twentieth-century writers and who loved paradox, said: "Whatever is worth doing is worth doing poorly." That isn't what you thought I was going to say, and that isn't what most people thought Chesterton meant. Understand, if a thing is worth doing at all we ought to try to do it, even though we can't do it with the best in the world. We ought to be able to do it a little. I can hunt and peck on the typewriter, and maybe I do two or three words a minute. Even that, according to Chesterton, is worth doing, if I really sit down and learn to do that much.

There is a tombstone in Arizona upon which a very wise man wrote his own epitaph. He wrote it for the special benefit of his son, but since it was on the tombstone, anybody else who came along could look at it; apparently it was there for public consumption. He had written, "My son, if you would preserve the heritage which I leave to you, you must build it anew yourself." We must have the resourcefulness in each generation not to leave to the past the determination of the life we are leading, but in our own generation we must find the resourcefulness to build our own heritage, to build the kind of life we want to live.

## IV

The third R, I believe, ought to be emphasized more now than at any other time in the history of the world; the R which I feel must be added to the others is the R of Responsibility. Why do we need to cultivate a sense of responsibility or a social conscience? Primarily because we have to live not only with ourselves, or as workers, but also we have to live with others. We are part of a great human family, a society, and in order to live with others, we must be better members of that society.

The education of the reasoning individual is largely the education of the mind. The education of the resourceful individual is to a considerable extent the education of the hands and of the body as a whole to perform certain acts. But the education of the responsible individual is neither of these. It is the education of the human emotions, and those are the elements hardest to control.

If you are going to be a well-rounded, responsible individual you have to respond; you have to feel emotions. If you are going to be completely developed, you must give love, joy, and admiration. But you must do more than that; you have to sympathize. In other words, you should understand the emotions that are surging within the hearts of other people. If you don't understand their emotions, if you don't sympathize with their emotions, if you don't put yourself in the other fellow's heart as well as in his shoes, then you are likely to make gross errors in judgment. In the third place, we need to control our emotions—because if we don't, our hatreds and our anger and our sorrow may become so great that they will destroy our judgment, destroy our reasoning, and destroy our whole sense of responsibility.

One interesting fact about this responsibility is that it seems to be more characteristic of democratic peoples than of any other kind, because Hitler and other people who have set up non-democratic societies around the world are not so much interested in responsibility as they are in obedience. There is all the difference in the world between a society that is obedient and a society that is responsible. Freedom demands responsibility, but mere obedience is a denial of freedom. That is significant about our republican form of government; it is republican because it allocates responsibility. It says that the citizens individually have certain responsibilities. They elect certain officers who in turn have delegated to them certain responsibilities. Our society as a republican form of government will function effectively only if all of us accept the responsibilities and carry them out to the ultimate degree.

When I was beginning my teaching career years ago, I was told that it was no longer wise to educate leaders; that there were already too many leaders in the world and too many people had been educated with the idea that they were ready to step in at the top of the ladder. Therefore, there was a great demand for followers, not for leaders; we were to concentrate our education on the training of followers. My years of experience have taught me that we were in error. The only way a person can be a satisfactory follower of a good leader is to know how to lead himself, and the only way in which good leaders are going to be produced for this particular task is to have good leaders for all the tasks; everyone must train himself to be a leader in some aspect of life. We won't all move into the White House. Maybe we won't all be given this or that particular position of leadership, but somewhere along the line we will have to exercise leadership. That is what democracy means—every man, every woman, a leader within the realm of his or her own responsibilities.

Recently I met an engaging and influential newspaper editor and publisher who said: "I feel this is the most important idea we need to give America today. Therefore, I would like to establish at your institution a professorship of loyalties, a professorship of American democratic loyalties. I want this professor to lecture three times a week to the student body upon the things in America of which they should be proud, the things to which they should be devoted, the things which they should believe, heart and soul, and be willing to give their lives to maintain. I don't care whether or not you have to have any textbooks for them. I don't want them to have any final examinations. But I want that teacher to be so filled with inspiration, so filled with enthusiasm, that it will carry over to the students in that class in such a way that they will go out thrilled and determined to be better citizens because of it." That is a great idea. I wish more colleges had professorships of American democratic loyalties.

What are we trying to do, anyway? What are all teachers trying to do in America, but to inculcate these enthusiasms, these loyalties, for democratic American ideals? Some of us do it in one way and others in another, but that is what we should all be aiming at eventually. Certainly that is what the teachers of religion or preachers in the pulpit would say is their objective.

We have at Union College a faculty member who is using an IBM machine to determine what elements of human character are educable. Over the last ten or fifteen years he has assembled a vast amount of material which he is using as a basis for a study of character development, and now he has arrived at a point where he is willing to set up what he feels are correct methods for inculcating character into American youth. I am all in favor of it. I am going to give him all the support I can, because character is what the world needs in addition to reasoning individuals, in addition to resourceful individuals, in addition to clever and responsible individuals.

V

In the business world we need people who have these three R's deeply engraved in their consciousness. They have reasoning minds; they think things through. They are resourceful; they aren't baffled by problems; they don't give up. In the third place, they accept the responsibilities which their job involves. Apply that test to yourselves. Ask yourselves whether the education you have received and the ideals inculcated in you meet the test of the three R's. If they do, then you have the kind of education that will be valuable in the years ahead.

You remember another Greek figure, Archimedes, and how he became excited over the law of levers after working with the levers and discovering that the longer the lever and the shorter the distance from the fulcrum to the object to be moved, the more force exerted on the end of it, the more could be moved. Finally, in a moment of inspiration, he said: "Give me a place where I can stand and I will move the world."

I feel that with these R's—a reasoning mind, a resourceful ability to face problems, and a responsible willingness to accept the duties that are placed upon you as a citizen and a member of our human society—education can move the world.

CHAPTER **VII**

*Language*

THE INTRODUCTORY SECTIONS of this book stressed that all verbal communication deals with words. We have pointed out that communication does not take place unless there is mutual agreement between the receiver and the transmitter as to the code they plan to use. Encoding a message means that the mental activities of a transmitter are translated into symbols that are so familiar to the receiver that he can decode them and translate them into ideas again. If the transmitter makes use of a code that is not familiar to his receiver, decoding does not take place and the communication process ceases to operate.

Although there are many other kinds of communicative codes, including writing, gestures, signals, facial expressions, we are primarily concerned with the symbolic code of oral communication. That code is the language we speak, presumably English. The basic ingredients of our oral code are words and combinations of words.

In discussing, earlier in this book, the general theory of oral communication, we described language as one of the most important factors in the process of communication. Much of what we had to say in Chapter 2 will be amplified here and treated somewhat more systematically. In addition, we will examine the unique characteristics of the code that is used for the transmission of oral messages. We will also devote some attention to the code common to most of us— the English language. Finally, we will offer you some suggestions as to how you can improve your own use of language.

To understand the importance of language as the basic code of verbal communication, we need to remind ourselves that when we use language we are not dealing with actual things but with symbols. The word "dog" is only the symbol we have chosen to represent a particular object; in this case, a canine quadruped. A dog does not become a different animal for being called "chien" by a Frenchman or "hund" by a German. Thus the dog has no inherent name. It has merely the name assigned to it by a particular social system at a particular time. What we are really saying is that the words or symbols we use to represent our ideas are purely arbitrary. A person or a group of persons, if they so desired, could devise an entirely new set of symbols to replace those they now use. As a matter of fact, this is the process that occurs when you master a foreign language, except that you retain the older code. If we decided to call a hat a dog and a head a table, I could say, "I put my dog on my table," and it would be perfectly clear to you provided we agreed on the meaning assigned to the symbols.

In short, we are saying that all linguistic symbols are arbitrary, but as long as we have reached some agreement about the meaning of the symbols, communication can take place.

This characteristic of language is the basis for the creation of the so-called international or synthetic languages such as Esperanto. We can, if we agree, assign any symbol to any thing. Similarly, with agreement, we can make any word mean whatever we want it to mean. Thus, all Swedes use one general code of communication, and all Koreans another; not because the codes are inherently Swedish or Korean, but because their societies have arbitrarily chosen those languages as their codes of communication. The individual really has no choice about his code of communication; his language has been chosen for him. If a Korean child is taken to Sweden as an infant, however, he learns Swedish, the language of his new culture.

Within any culture, there is a general code of communication that all members of the culture learn. There are, at the same time, however, many subcodes used by segments of the culture. To some extent, the use of subcodes is determined by the social status, the educational level, the place of residence, and the occupation of the user of the code. A person with a college education, for example, may habitually use a more extensive code than would a person who had only eight years of schooling. A large portion of his language would be understandable to a person of less education, but some of it would be outside the shared symbols and could thus not be communicated. Similarly, a person from the city and a person from the farm may both speak English, but each may use some symbols that are not mutually understandable. Even in a nation like ours, strongly bound by the ties of mass communication and rapid transportation, there are some symbols commonly used by Southerners that are not readily understood in the North. Certain words spoken by New Englanders are decoded with great difficulty, if at all, by residents of other sections of the United States. Each occupation, whether it be heavy construction or medicine, has its own language. Some teenagers use a code that is well-nigh incomprehensible to their elders. The esoteric jargon of jazz musicians is so distinct as to have become a source of much humor.

It should be clear then that the fidelity of process of communication increases as the agreement between receiver and transmitter about the meaning of symbols becomes stronger. Two persons of highly similar backgrounds will very likely have a much higher degree of understanding than two persons of dissimilar backgrounds, because they probably use language with very similar meanings. In effect we are saying that the meanings we assign to symbols, and the symbols we assign to ideas, are learned. The culture in which we are reared determines the general code of communication we use, but all of our experiences contribute to the development of code that is uniquely ours. Because no two people have had exactly the same background and exactly the same experiences, no two people use exactly the same code of communication.

Language, then, is not only a product of culture; it is also the product of the total sum of human experience. As long ago as the eighteenth century, the view was held that oral style is "the peculiar manner in which a man expresses his conceptions, by means of language." Even earlier, the idea was expressed that "style is the man." What these statements mean is that each human being develops a language code that is uniquely his. As we pointed out earlier, it is almost mathematically impossible for any two human beings to use exactly the same words to express even the simplest kind of organized communication.

Since each person has his own private code, it follows that we never *completely* understand each other. We do *not* mean to say that all communication is therefore Greek to your listeners. We *do* mean to say that your message will never be received with the exact meaning you assigned to the symbols.

If you understand the symbolic nature of language, you will appreciate why messages that seem perfectly clear are misunderstood or distorted by receivers.

We must also understand that the symbolic process itself prevents us from saying *exactly* what we mean. If you think of "table," you cannot transmit a "table" to your listeners. All you can do is to communicate the mutually agreed-upon symbol for that object. Sometimes the symbol will bear a very close resemblance to the thought. At other times the resemblance will be very vague. Let us look for a moment at the word "table." The word "table" alone may convey a variety of meanings, ranging from multiplication tables to dining room tables to operating tables. We have no assurance when we use the word "table" that we are conveying anything like the exact meaning we have in mind. We may, of course, say, "Mahogany, Chippendale dining table." This symbol would be much clearer, provided the receiver also understands the words "Chippendale" and "Mahogany" as we understand them. Thus, by specifying which table we have in mind, we may communicate a much more specific symbol of our mental conceptions. If we point to a table and say "this table," the message begins to attain high fidelity. The practical lesson to be derived from this discussion of tables is that the greater the specificity of language, the closer is the relationship between the symbol and the idea.

If what we have said is true, it should be clear to you that there is absolutely no inherent meaning in what is said. There are no meanings in words. There are only meanings within people. Words have only the meanings assigned to them by people. A dictionary does not give us the real meanings of words. It only reveals the meaning that our society has agreed to give words. If our society chooses to modify, expand, remove, or change the meaning of a word, then in time the dictionary will reflect the changes man has made. It is the transmitter's responsibility to see to it that the words he uses are those that will elicit a meaning in the receiver very similar to the meaning in the mind of the transmitter.

It might be helpful, at this point, to recall the times when we have had difficulty in making ourselves understood. Our temptation is to blame the receivers for their lack of intelligence. More frequently, however, the fault lies with us as transmitters: we have not been successful in translating our ideas into words that elicit meanings in receivers. We must not assume that if we understand what we are saying it will automatically be clear to those who listen.

In our discussion of language, we have alluded to its personal qualities; but the bulk of our discussion has been devoted to its social aspects. It is helpful, however, to note that, in addition to the meanings assigned by a social system, words also have private and personal meanings. A definition found in a dictionary may be termed a *denotative meaning*. The individual meaning given to a word is called the *connotative meaning*. Connotative meanings grow out of our experiences, our backgrounds, our values, and our prejudices. Words that seem cold on a dictionary page may engender heated reactions when used in purposeful communication. The term "Communist" is one to which Russians and Americans, for example, attach quite different connotative meanings. A Russian assigns a meaning to "Communist" that is favorable, whereas an American assigns an unfavorable meaning. To call a Russian a Communist may be flattery; to call an American a Communist is to insult him. These differences exist even though a Russian dictionary and an American dictionary may not differ substantially in their definitions of "Communist."

The same kind of connotative differences that exist between societies also exist between persons. Since connotative meanings are highly individual, we can never know exactly what meanings all receivers assign to certain symbols. Moreover, it is impossible for a person to tell you what his personal meaning is for a term. He may tell you whether a word is good or bad, favorable or unfavorable, but not exactly what the word means to *him.* Think for a moment of the meanings beyond denotation that we attach to such words as: "Negro," "fraternity," "liberal," "Catholic," "Jew," "politician," "farmer," "mother," "Christian." It may properly be said that each reader assigns to each of these words a personal meaning that is beyond the dictionary meaning. Considering also that the readers of these words are the products of different environments, there will be a wide range of connotative meanings.

Although part of the connotative meaning will always remain hidden, some communication of connotative meanings is nonetheless possible. If the receiver and the transmitter are the products of the same or of similar social systems, their connotations will very likely be quite similar. Where there is considerable difference or variation in background, the task becomes more difficult. Nevertheless, the important point is that the speaker be aware that many of his symbols may convey meanings different from those he assigns to the symbols.

Much of what we have said up to this point is equally applicable to oral *and* written language. There are, however, some significant differences between the subcodes of written language and oral language. If there were not differences, all of us would write exactly as we talk and vice versa. We all know that this is not the case. Written language is actually a step beyond oral language in the cultural development of communication. As we have pointed out earlier, all human societies make use of oral communication. Some cultures have not yet developed to the point where they feel the need to preserve their communications, or the need to communicate with persons some distance away. Be that as it may, the point to be made is that, in the history of mankind, the use of an oral code precedes the introduction of a written code. From one point of view, then, written language involves the translation of oral symbols into written symbols, just as oral language involves the translation of ideas into oral symbols. Although it is not the direct concern of this book, it is interesting to note that the same process occurs in reverse in the receptive phase of written communication. Have you not noticed that when you read, you often hear the words sounded in your "mind's ear"? This is further evidence of the relationship between oral and written communication.

If there are differences in the development of oral and written language, there must be some characteristic differences in the forms of the two subcodes. The differences grow out of the dissimilar circumstances under which oral and written communication are assimilated. Generally speaking, a receiver may choose the time, the place, and the circumstance to read, but listening takes place here and now. If you want to read this book at 3 A.M. while soaking in a bathtub, that is your own business. If you choose to set this book aside and pick up another, so be it. If you decide to take a month to read a novel, that is your choice. If you want to read a paragraph several times to be sure about its meaning, you are free to do so.

Oral communication, on the other hand, must be absorbed at a time, a place, and an occasion that are not necessarily those you would yourself select if you had your choice. In oral communication, you must accept the conditions under which the message is received. You cannot, ordinarily, say to yourself, "I will listen to this later, when I am in the mood." You cannot listen later, because words once spoken disappear never to be heard again, unless you make a tape recording of the words. Written communication may be preserved almost permanently.

Because of the immediacy of oral communication, oral language must be immediately intelligible to the receiver. The listener does not have time to go back over the message in the hope of finding there some trace of intended meaning. The receiver must understand as soon as words are uttered by a speaker. He must follow the pace set for him by the speaker. This difference calls for oral language that is immediately clear, instantaneously intelligible, and free from ambiguity. Although there may be, at times, artistic justification for deliberate obscurity in writing, there is never such an excuse in speaking. There is no place for "abstractionists" in oral communication. The conditions of oral communication demand "representationalism."

The need for instantaneous intelligibility demands that the form and structure of sentences be somewhat different from those ordinarily used in written communication. The sentences of oral communication are generally briefer than those used in writing, so that their sense may be absorbed immediately. The receiver must remember every word until the very end of a sentence, and he remembers short sentences better than long ones.

Since oral language is used much more often in informal communication than is written language, we should not be surprised to find that the usage of oral language is generally less formal. Contractions such as "it's," "don't," "can't," "won't," are more often used in speaking than in writing. Simple oral words are more frequently used than more unusual literary words. A speaker will likely use the simple word "but" rather than "however" or "nevertheless."

Because of the need for immediate understanding, the level of usage of oral language is somewhat lower than written language. You undoubtedly know that we all possess several vocabularies that vary considerably in size. Our speaking vocabularies are usually smaller than our writing vocabularies, and our writing vocabularies are usually smaller than our reading vocabularies. Thus the words that are used in speaking tend to be the simpler, more common words in our vocabularies, not only because they come to mind more readily, but also because they are more quickly recognized and identified by receivers. Thus, a speaker is likely to say "house" rather than "residence," "have" rather than "possess," "pay" rather than "remuneration," "ended" rather than "terminated." In oral communication, some judicious use of colloquialisms and slang may even be sanctioned, provided they contribute to the communication of ideas.

There is in oral communication also less adherence to strict grammatical and syntactical rules. Speakers faced with a typed transcript of a speech are often appalled at what seems to be linguistic chaos. Yet when the speech was given, it apparently was received with some meaning by the audience. The explanation here will probably be found in the inherent differences between oral and written language. The reader of a speech expects it to conform to the standards of literary usage, whereas intelligibility in listening may require somewhat different standards. The presence of sentence fragments, comma splices, and even an occasional split infinitive or dangling participle, may be not nearly so serious in speaking as in writing. After all, the sentence itself is a fairly arbitrary unit of written language. The speaker who cannot erase or scratch out his utterances, may sometimes use words quite differently than he does in writing. This discussion should not be thought of as a justification for grammatical and syntactical carelessness in oral communication. Speech should, of course, conform to the accepted rules of our language. We intend merely to point out that oral communication tends, in use, to be less observant of those rules that are devised primarily for written language.

Earlier in this book, we advised beginning speakers not

to write out and read their speeches. One of the reasons we frown on such a practice is that the speaker's language is likely to be literary rather than oral, and thus not so well suited to reception by listeners. A speech is not "an essay on its hind legs." Rather, it is live thoughts communicated to an alive audience in a particular place at a particular time. In order to meet his communicative responsibilities, the speaker should understand some of the basic characteristics of oral language and the ways in which it differs from written language.

Before we turn to some suggestions about how you may improve your use of oral language, it will be useful to examine briefly the medium that most of you will use in communicating your ideas. We speak here of the English language. It is not our intention to present a systematic treatment of the development of English or of its structure. Instead, we want to present some of the characteristics of the language we use. Knowing these characteristics may help you to make better use of the tools available to you.

If you use English as your code of communication, you are fortunate in that you have probably more symbols available to you than do the speakers of most other languages. English has a larger vocabulary and greater resources than most other languages; certainly more than any other Western language. The primary reason for the resourcefulness of English is that it is not really one language but a combination of languages. The basic vocabulary of English has been derived from many other languages, including Old English, Celtic, Scandinavian, French, Latin, and Greek. Minor contributions to our stock of words have been made by Italian, Spanish, Persian, Hungarian, Turkish, Arabic, Malay, Polynesian, Australian, Mexican, German, Hindi, Dutch, and American Indian. English has not shown the reluctance to absorb words from other languages as have other European languages. As a result, the speaker of English has more choices available to him when he selects symbols to represent his thoughts. In many instances, the communicator who encodes his messages in English is able to transmit finer nuances of meaning than speakers of other languages.

Although English has borrowed liberally from many languages, it is fundamentally two languages. English is at the same time a Germanic language and a Romance language. Our basic language, which is ordinarily used for simpler ideas and concepts, is Anglo-Saxon and is related to Dutch and German. Such common words as "man," "finger," "house," "coat," "dog," "watch," "tell," "cold," "alike," are Germanic in origin. Synonyms, derived from Latinate sources, may be found for each of these words. "Human being," "digit," "residence," "garment," "canine," "witness," "testify," "frigid," and "similar" are all terms that came into English through French or Latin. Almost any expression may be translated from Germanic English to Latinate English. We may say "neighborhood drugstore" or "local apothecary establishment"; "I neared the street" or "I approached the avenue"; "turn out the light" or "extinguish the illumination"; "a great crowd came to see" or "a vast concourse was assembled to witness"; "the owner is dead" or "the entrepreneur is deceased."

It is probably evident to you that Latinate English is more commonly used in written communication than in oral communication. Almost any page of this book, which has much Latinate English in it, could be paraphrased into Germanic English. That such paraphrases are possible should, however, not be considered an injunction against using Latinate English. Often there are shades of difference in meaning between words as they are received by listeners. "Fatherly" and "paternal" certainly do not carry exactly the same meaning to all persons. "Juvenile" ordinarily conveys a connotation quite different from "youthful."

Latinate English is ordinarily more learned than is Germanic English and is more easily received and understood by educated audiences. The speaker should choose those symbols, Latinate or Germanic, that convey *his* meaning best to *his* listeners. He should be aware, however, of the resources available to him if he needs to use them.

Another characteristic of English that should be noticed is its simplicity. English grammar is simpler than that of most languages. Contrary to a popular notion, English does not have the complex structure that people suppose it has. If you have studied a modern foreign language, you may be aware of the greater number of cases, tenses, moods, gender differentiations, formal and informal modes of address than in English. Perhaps the one area of grammar where English is rather rigid is in word-order. The meaning of English is conveyed more through word-order than through inflection and case endings. English is not only a versatile linguistic tool; it is also a flexible one.

The preceding sections have been written in the hope of providing you with some background that will assist you in making better use of language in transmitting your ideas. With that background in mind, let us turn to some suggestions about using language. Much of our advice will be derived from material presented earlier in this chapter.

Perhaps the most important suggestion we can make to you is—be specific. The user of words must develop the practice of searching not for *a* word but for *the* word that comes closest to expressing the conception he has in his mind. Specific language conveys a clearer image to receivers than does general language. A friend once wrote that on her vacation she had seen the Grand Canyon, the Mormon Temple, and Marilyn Monroe. She described them all as "beautiful." Perhaps they are; but surely she could have chosen more specific terms to describe the qualities of a wonder of nature, a religious

**1 4 9**

edifice, and a movie queen. Try for yourself to see if you can discover other words that more appropriately describe these objects of beauty. Our earlier example of "table" is illustrative of the principle of specificity. "Table" conveys much less meaning than "Mahogany Chippendale dining room table." "A girl I know" is less meaningful than "Mary Jones." "When I was in a certain Midwestern city" lacks the specific image of, "When I was in Omaha."

Unfortunately, many of the words we use have become so general in the meanings attached to them that they can convey almost nothing but a general impression. "Beautiful" is an example of this kind of word. So are "good," "bad," and "interesting." Some words that once possessed specificity are now used in a way that allows them to communicate generally favorable or unfavorable impressions. There is no terror in a "terribly nice time." There is no awe in "awfully good cake." There is no divinity in a "divine dress." There is no marvel in a "marvelous toothpaste." It must, lamentably, be said that no person can speak more specifically than he thinks.

Ideally, language should transmit a maximum degree of meaning. Unfortunately, vague and general language may be used to obscure meaning or to transmit no meaning at all. Look at this widely publicized "Speech for All Occasions."

"Mr. Chairman, Ladies and Gentlemen: It is indeed a great and undeserved privilege to address such an audience as I see before me. At no previous time in the history of human civilization have greater problems confronted and challenged the ingenuity of man's intellect than now. Let us look around us. What do we see on the horizon? What forces are at work? Whither are we drifting? Under what mist of clouds does the future stand obscured? My friends, casting aside the raiment of all human speech, the crucial test for the solution of all these intricate problems to which I have just alluded is the sheer and forceful application of those immutable laws which down the corridor of time have always guided the hand of man, groping, as it were, for some faint beacon-light for his hopes and aspirations. Without these great vital principles, we are but puppets responding to whim and fancy, failing entirely to grasp the hidden meaning of it all. We must readdress ourselves to these questions which press for answer and solution. The issue cannot be avoided. There they stand. It is upon you—and you—and yet even upon me that the yoke of responsibility falls.

"What, then, is our duty? Shall we continue to drift? No! With all the emphasis of my being I hurl back the message, No! Drifting must stop. We must press onward and upward toward the ultimate good to which all must aspire. But I cannot conclude my remarks, dear friends, without touching briefly upon a subject which I know is steeped in your very consciousness. I refer to that spirit which gleams from the eyes of the new-born babe; that animates the toiling masses; that sways all the hosts of humanity past and present. Without this energizing principle, all commerce, trade, and industry are hushed and will perish from this earth as surely as the crimson sunset follows the golden sunshine. Mark you, I do not seek to unduly alarm or distress the mothers, fathers, sons, and daughters gathered before me in this vast assemblage, but I would indeed be recreant to a high resolve which I made as a youth if I did not at this time and in this place and with the full realizing sense of responsibility which I assume, publicly declare and affirm my dedication and my concentration to the eternal principles and receipts of simple, ordinary, commonplace justice.

"For what, in the last analysis, is justice? Whence does it come? Where does it go? Is it tangible? It is not. Is it ponderable? It is not. Justice is none of these, and yet, on the other hand, in a sense it is all of those things combined. Although I cannot tell you what justice is, this much I can tell you: That without the encircling arms of justice, without her shield, without her guardianship, the ship of state will sail through uncharted seas, narrowly avoiding rocks and shoals, headed inevitably to the harbor of calamity.

"Justice! Justice! Justice! To thee we pay homage. To

thee we dedicate our laurels of hope. Before thee we kneel in adoration, mindful of thy great power, mute before thy inscrutable destiny!"

At first glance this speech may seem to be full of "language." Not much examination is necessary, however, to discover that the speaker really has said nothing. His language is so vague and general that it produces no mutual understanding. In such a case, the listener makes the language mean whatever he wants it to mean.

Just as in other aspects of oral communication, it is important to remember that language is used by one person to transmit messages to the minds of other persons. Therefore, the language of oral communication must be adapted not only to the receiver but to the transmitter as well. The speaker has a habitual code of communication. He uses certain words and he uses them in certain combinations. His linguistic code is uniquely his own. He should, of course, seek to improve and modify his use of the code, but he should not seek to substitute another code for his own. It is senseless for you to attempt to impersonate the oral style of Winston Churchill or Abraham Lincoln or Franklin Delano Roosevelt, laudable as these styles may be. The simple fact is that you are not Churchill, Lincoln, or Roosevelt. You are you, and your use of language is your own. You must express your ideas in the symbols with which you encode them, not in someone else's code. You should constantly strive to improve your language code, not to adopt another one.

Language that is well suited to the speaker may not necessarily be well suited to the receiver. The transmitter must not only encode in symbols that are meaningful to him; he must also choose symbols that convey meaning to his receivers. The experience, education, and background that a speaker shares with his audience makes it easier for him to use more understandable language. The lack of mutual experience, education, and background makes it more difficult for the speaker to use understandable language. We understand, of course, that a large proportion of our code is common to almost all speakers of English. Nevertheless, we recognize that we will have less difficulty using language that is clear to classmates than with almost any other group. If you were to speak to an audience of college professors, for example, you might raise the level of your language. If you speak to an audience of fourth-graders, you might lower the level of your language.

Once certain terms have been assimilated into our communicative code, many of us tend to use them as if they have universal meaning. This happens particularly often in the case of technical terms. All of us know a number of technical terms that we share with only a relatively small number of people. Those terms may be derived from occupations, hobbies, education, and other sources. The physician has his own technical code, which is understood mostly by other doctors. The lawyer, the teacher, the farmer, the football player, the actor, the skier, the lumberjack, the automobile mechanic— all have their own technical terms. Those terms are precise and meaningful if a receiver understands them, but they are only gibberish if they are not part of the receivers' linguistic code. The moral of this discussion is: do not use such terms as "nasal-pharyngitis," "tort," "oedipal," "double-team," "flat," "slalom," "green chain," "compression-ratio" unless you are fairly positive that your audience knows them. If you must use technical or unusual words, which your audience may not know, be sure you define them in language that is clear to your audience.

Since you will be engaged in oral communication, make sure that your language is oral. Keep in mind the differences between written and spoken language that we outlined earlier. Use language that is simple enough and clear enough so that it is understandable at once. Use sentences that are short enough so that their meaning is immediately clear. Use words that you ordinarily utilize in speaking—not those which are in your written vocabulary. Use language that is personal and direct. The speaker, in contrast to the writer, will make use of personal pronouns. His speech will be liberally sprinkled with "you," "I," "me," "we," "us." Above all, avoid the kinds of terms that reveal instantly that your language is literary and not oral. Such terms include "the following," "the former," "the latter," "as cited above," "as noted below." The speaker will use direct discourse. He will speak directly to his listener. He will make use of questions. He will ask, "What are the causes of our difficulty?" more often than he will say, "the causes of our difficulty bear examination."

To this point, we have devoted our discussion to improving the clarity of language. We have done so because we feel strongly that the first responsibility of the speaker, in using language, is to transmit his ideas as lucidly as possible. If a student has learned something about improving the clarity of his communication, that is a very great accomplishment indeed. Only after the lessons of clarity have been learned should the student speaker become concerned about the vividness of his language. Nevertheless, we offer some brief suggestions about how vividness may be increased.

It goes without saying that not all human beings are able to use language vividly. The simple truth is that many of us do not think vividly. It is as impossible to encode dull thoughts in vivid language as it is to encode murky thoughts in clear language. Unless one thinks in terms of figures of speech, it is almost hopeless to think that any profit may be gained from learning various figures of speech. Every element of your language is your own. If your language is clear but not very decorative, you have succeeded in attaining the most important part of the mastery of language. But there are some things almost anyone can do that may help increase, at least a little, the vividness of language.

One way to increase vividness is to find new ways of saying old things. In great measure, the new ways involve the use of figurative language. Winston Churchill could have said, "The Russians have isolated Eastern Europe." Instead he said, "From Stettin in the Baltic to Trieste in the Adriatic, an Iron Curtain has descended across the Continent." He could have said, "I have nothing to offer but death, work, and sorrow." Instead he said, "I have nothing to offer but blood, toil, tears, and sweat." Franklin Delano Roosevelt could have said, "This nation's greatest concern is its own internal anxiety." Instead he said, "We have nothing to fear but fear itself." William Jennings Bryan could have said, "You capitalists shall not persecute labor." Instead he said, "You shall not press down upon the brow of labor this crown of thorns; you shall not crucify mankind upon a cross of gold."

There are two major dangers in using figurative language. The first is that a speaker will "reach" for figurative speech and the result will be labored, obvious, and ludicrous. Unless figurative language suggests itself to you rather readily, it is advisable not to search too long in hopes of inventing a new expression.

The second danger is that a speaker will use figurative language that has become trite. Many of our clichés were once fresh and novel ways of expressing ideas. Their very aptness and resultant popularity has sapped them of the strength and vigor they once had. The following phrases, once effective figures of speech, are now so threadbare that they call unfavorable attention to themselves: "birds of a feather," "blind as a bat," "bolt from the blue," "budding genius," "busy as a bee," "dead as a doornail," "diamond in the rough," "die is cast," "hard as nails," "hook, line and sinker," "lock, stock and barrel," "mountains out of molehills," "sleep like a log," "tired to death." Even many of our proverbs have become clichés; consider, "a rolling stone gathers no moss," and "don't count your chickens before they are hatched." Other terms, such as, "last but not least," "coast-to-coast," "too numerous to mention," "proudly presents," "few and far between," "after all is said and done," "breathe a sigh of relief," and "better late than never," are also very trite.

We have already discussed one means of increasing vividness in the preceding chapter. The use of specific supporting material, which is well adapted to you and your receivers, will add life to your speech and to its language. Examples phrased in terms the audience understands contribute directly to vividness. Analogies, authority, comparison—all play their role in contributing to interest by making the images, in the minds of your listeners, more vivid, more real, and more interesting.

Before we close this chapter, it should be noted that clarity and vividness contribute to one another. A speech in which language is not clear cannot hold the attention of listeners, no matter how figurative the language. On the other hand, if well-chosen, figurative language is used, the increased attention of the audience will re-enforce the strength of a message encoded in clear language.

There are several principles about language that are well worth remembering:

(1) Meanings are in people, not in language.
(2) All words are arbitrary, and are culturally determined.
(3) No word has exactly the same meaning to receiver and transmitter.
(4) We never say exactly what we mean.
(5) Words are assigned both denotative and connotative meanings.
(6) Oral language is different from written language.
(7) English is a versatile, simple, and flexible language.

SUPPLEMENTARY READING:

_____

BROWN, ROGER. *Words and Things.* New York: The Free Press of Glencoe, Inc., 1958.

GRAY, GILES WILKESON AND WISE, CLAUDE MERTON. *The Bases of Speech,* 3rd ed. New York: Harper and Brothers, 1959, Chapters VI and IX.

JESPERSEN, OTTO. *Growth and Structure of the English Language,* 9th ed. Garden City: Doubleday and Company, 1955.

LAIRD, CHARLTON. *The Miracle of Language.* Greenwich, Conn.: Fawcett Publications, Inc., 1957.

SAPIR, EDWARD. *Language: An Introduction to the Study of Speech.* New York: Harcourt, Brace and Company, 1949.

## INAUGURAL ADDRESS

### BY JOHN F. KENNEDY

*Delivered by President Kennedy at the Capitol, Washington, D. C., January 20, 1961.*

My Fellow Citizens:

We observe today not a victory of party but a celebration of freedom—symbolizing an end as well as a beginning —signifying renewal as well as change. For I have sworn before you and Almighty God the same solemn oath our forebears prescribed nearly a century and three quarters ago.

The world is very different now. For man holds in his mortal hands the power to abolish all form of human poverty and to abolish all form of human life. And yet, the same revolutionary beliefs for which our forebears fought are still at issue around the globe—the belief that the rights of man come not from the generosity of the state but from the hand of God.

We dare not forget today that we are the heirs of that first revolution. Let the word go forth from this time and

**1 5 7**

place, to friend and foe alike, that the torch has been passed to a new generation of Americans—born in this century, tempered by war, disciplined by a cold and bitter peace, proud of our ancient heritage—and unwilling to witness or permit the slow undoing of those human rights to which this nation has always been committed, and to which we are committed today.

Let every nation know, whether it wish us well or ill, that we shall pay any price, bear any burden, meet any hardship, support any friend or oppose any foe in order to assure the survival and success of liberty.

This much we pledge—and more.

To those old allies whose cultural and spiritual origins we share, we pledge the loyalty of faithful friends. United, there is little we cannot do in a host of new co-operative ventures. Divided, there is little we can do—for we dare not meet a powerful challenge at odds and split asunder.

To those new states whom we now welcome to the ranks of the free, we pledge our word that one form of colonial control shall not have passed merely to be replaced by a far more iron tyranny. We shall not always expect to find them supporting our every view. But we shall always hope to find them strongly supporting their own freedom—and to remember that, in the past, those who foolishly sought to find power by riding on the tiger's back inevitably ended up inside.

To those peoples in the huts and villages of half the globe struggling to break the bonds of mass misery, we pledge our best efforts to help them help themselves, for whatever period is required—not because the Communists are doing it, not because we seek their votes, but because it is right. If the free society cannot help the many who are poor, it can never save the few who are rich.

To our sister republics south of our border, we offer a special pledge—to convert our good words into good deeds, in a new alliance for progress; to assist free men and free Governments in casting off the chains of poverty. But this

**1 5 8**

peaceful revolution of hope cannot become the prey of hostile powers. Let all our neighbors know that we shall join with them to oppose aggression or subversion anywhere in the Americas. And let every other power know that this hemisphere intends to remain the master of its own house.

To that world assembly of sovereign states, the United Nations, our last best hope in an age where the instruments of war have far outpaced the instruments of peace, we renew our pledge of support—to prevent its becoming merely a forum for invective, to strengthen its shield of the new and the weak, and to enlarge the area to which its writ may run.

Finally, to those nations who would make themselves our adversary, we offer not a pledge but a request: that both sides begin anew the quest for peace, before the dark powers of destruction unleashed by science engulf all humanity in planned or accidental self-destruction.

We dare not tempt them with weakness. For only when our arms are sufficient beyond doubt can we be certain beyond doubt that they will never be employed.

But neither can two great and powerful groups of nations take comfort from their present course—both sides overburdened by the cost of modern weapons, both rightly alarmed by the steady spread of the deadly atom, yet both racing to alter that uncertain balance of terror that stays the hand of mankind's final war.

So let us begin anew—remembering on both sides that civility is not a sign of weakness and sincerity is always subject to proof. Let us never negotiate out of fear. But let us never fear to negotiate.

Let both sides explore what problems unite us instead of belaboring the problems that divide us.

Let both sides, for the first time, formulate serious and precise proposals for the inspection and control of arms—and bring the absolute power to destroy other nations under the absolute control of all nations.

Let both sides join to invoke the wonders of science instead of its terrors. Together let us explore the stars, conquer the deserts, eradicate disease, tap the ocean depths, and encourage the arts and commerce.

Let both sides unite to heed in all corners of the earth the command of Isaiah—to "undo the heavy burdens . . . [and] let the oppressed go free."

And if a beachhead of co-operation can be made in the jungles of suspicion, let both sides join in the next task: creating, not a new balance of power, but a new world of law, where the strong are just and the weak secure and the peace preserved forever.

All this will not be finished in the first one hundred days. Nor will it be finished in the first one thousand days, nor in the life of this Administration, nor even perhaps in our lifetime on this planet. But let us begin.

In your hands, my fellow citizens, more than in mine, will rest the final success or failure of our course. Since this country was founded, each generation has been summoned to give testimony to its national loyalty. The graves of young Americans who answered that call encircle the globe.

Now the trumpet summons us again—not as a call to bear arms, though arms we need; not as a call to battle, though embattled we are; but a call to bear the burden of a long twilight struggle, year in and year out, "rejoicing in hope, patient in tribulation"—a struggle against the common enemies of man: tyranny, poverty, disease, and war itself.

Can we forge against these enemies a grand and global alliance, north and south, east and west, that can assure a more fruitful life for all mankind? Will you join in that historic effort?

In the long history of the world, only a few generations have been granted the role of defending freedom in its hour of maximum danger. I do not shrink from this responsibility —I welcome it. I do not believe that any of us would exchange places with any other people or any other generation. The energy, the faith, and the devotion which we bring to this endeavor will light our country and all who serve it— and the glow from that fire can truly light the world.

**1 6 0**

And so, my fellow Americans: Ask not what your country will do for you—ask what you can do for your country.

My fellow citizens of the world: Ask not what America will do for you, but what together we can do for the freedom of man.

Finally, whether you are citizens of America or of the world, ask of us the same high standards of strength and sacrifice that we shall ask of you. With a good conscience our only sure reward, with history the final judge of our deeds, let us go forth to lead the land we love, asking His blessing and His help, but knowing that here on earth God's work must truly be our own.

CHAPTER VIII

# The Visible Aspects of Speech

T HE INEXPERIENCED TEACHER's first instruction and the beginning speaker's first questions revolve about the problem of one's physical appearance and behavior. "How do I look? What shall I do with my hands? What types of gestures shall I use? When shall I move and where?" are typical questions. Some teachers tell their students to stand erect, to keep their arms at their sides except when gesturing, to move at certain transitional points in the speech, and then give detailed and elaborate instructions on the various types of gestures and the thoughts and moods which they should acompany, as well as specific formulas for moving forward and backward as a means of emphasis.

The sum and substance of modern psychology, however, suggest that gesture and movement are natural impulses of a communicating organism, and that they will occur naturally in proportion as the speaker has developed a sincere and un-inhibited desire to speak his thoughts to others.

What shall the student do, then? Shall he study the characteristics of effective posture, gesture, and movement, and consciously work to acquire skill in their performance? Or shall he attend first to the content and form of his message, to understanding himself and his audience, to developing a proper attitude toward the whole process of communication, hoping that appropriate visible behavior will develop as naturally as green leaves come out in spring?

Obviously, those who recommend study of bodily expression as the first step in speech instruction stand at the opposite pole from those who believe that all else should be studied first, and that, in due season, action will suit itself to the word.

Perhaps some further analysis will give the student a better basis for judgment. At least five major theories have held vogue at some time or other.

The first of these is now commonly called *elocution*. Although it once properly implied the "style or manner of speaking," it has gradually come to connote a studied or artificial manner, and has become more and more associated in our minds with the physical behavior of speaking. The main objective of teachers of elocution for many decades was to teach precise control of voice and body, and to give little or no attention to speech composition or audience analysis. This procedure, along with various other unknown causes, led to a highly artificial style of delivery against which the general reaction was so strong that it has been very difficult for sounder instruction to regain academic respectability and public acceptance. But, in fairness, it should be said that the practice of elocution preceded modern psychology and our present understanding of human nature.

Early in the present century, the behaviorist psychologists claimed not only that enforced gesture and movement were conducive to developing a feeling of naturalness, but also that the assumption of certain bodily actions and movements could create corresponding attitudes of mind and emotional tones. Although these theories have not been proven invalid, they have lost some of their popularity.

The opposite of the principles of elocution is the theory that the only prerequisite to effective physical performance is a clear concept of the message to be delivered. This school of thought, therefore, requires its students to read models of good composition, teaches outlining, forms and sources of evidence, types of reasoning—in fact, everything except delivery—and assumes that, once the mind has freed itself from clutter and confusion, the body and the vocal mechanism will perform adequately if not artistically.

Another point of view is that inexperienced speakers assume awkward stances, make ludicrous gestures, shuffle and slouch and lean and pace, speak in monotones and whispers, and otherwise perform badly because they are possessed by fear. Therefore early assignments for students ask self-study, an analysis of why one is afraid. These teachers reason that once the student is aware of the reason for his fearing an audience, he will no longer be afraid. He will also presumably do none of the extraneous things he did because of fear, and now that his mind and emotions are free and undisturbed, he will be peaceful and poised, graceful and effective.

More recently, gestalt psychology, emphasizing the organismic nature of man, the integration of mind, body, and emotion, has lent credence to the concept that mental and emotional poise are essential concomitants, even prerequisites, of physical poise and grace. It also assumes that to the degree the individual stands, walks, and talks expressively in social situations in which he feels at home, he will also exhibit those performance characteristics in a public speaking or reading situation to the degree he has come to feel at home in it.

Each of these theories is probably valid to some degree. The latest concepts are presumably more valid than the earlier ones, because they are based on a more profound understanding of human nature. It is recommended, therefore, that you hold all these practices and beliefs in mind, noting the ways in which they overlap and agree with each other, as well as the differences between them. You will probably conclude that there is no one right way to develop effective delivery, but at least several, and that probably the most effective for you is a combination of the best of these.

The authors, believing this too, encourage you to think through and try out at least some of the more recent theories. In the main, however, we subscribe to the belief that genuine poise, controlled movement, and effective gestures are not only, as we said earlier, the natural impulses and consequences of a communicating organism that has developed an uninhibited desire to speak his thoughts to others, but also that it is hardly reasonable to expect effective and convincing physical behavior from any but a mentally and emotionally poised person. We suggest, therefore, that in general the following order of emphasis be given: (1) attention to the message to be communicated—i.e., ideas, materials of development, organization, language, study of self and of the audience; (2) practice in speech-making without concern for bodily action; (3) attention to voice and articulation; (4) speech-making in which blackboard sketching and display of object-type visual aids are employed; (5) specific attention to movement and gesture.

In short, we believe that bodily action should spring from within rather than be imposed or superimposed from without. We believe that giving a beginning speaker detailed instruction in bodily action before he has come to feel somewhat at home in speaking to classroom and other audiences is likely to result in stiff, unnatural, elocutionary speech rather than its opposite.

The use of objects and sketching on the blackboard will give much of the natural release desired; the rest must wait for adjustment and the urge to convey a message. In the beginning, a speaker should feel free to lean, sit, put his hands behind him or into his pockets, or to do whatever puts him most at ease. These liberties need not lead to bad habits; the speaker can very soon abandon them as he comes to feel at home. He should not, however, allow himself to violate interminably the laws of poise and purposive action. The point is that the beginner should concern himself little with bodily behavior during early weeks, and also that the usual taboos against informal behavior are hangovers from elocutionism and the days of pedantic oratory. Modern attitudes demand freedom, individuality, greater informality.

Eventually one ought consciously to control his behavior so that he will avoid slouching, undue pacing, excess gesticulation, leaning heavily upon a stand or table, indulging in annoying and distracting mannerisms. He may even go so far as to study the principles of gesture and movement. He will plan to suit the formality of his behavior to the dignity of the occasion. He will realize that amount and types of action should be dependent on personality. For example, tall men usually maintain more reserve than short men, and men should be free and forceful as opposed to the reserve and charm of women.

In many instances, more important than behavior is one's dress. The well-groomed man and the carefully dressed woman inspire confidence; untidy appearance, baggy knees, open neck, and flashy dress destroy it.

The real tests of appropriateness of bodily behavior are: Does it make the speaker feel comfortable, at ease? Does it do the same for the audience? Beyond these basic tests we ask whether it is purposive, expressive, natural, excessive or deficient, free or stiff, descriptive or suggestive, forceful or weak, graceful or awkward. But for the beginner, our forceful admonition is to disabuse your mind of the importance of "correct" behavior. Forget about *yourself* as much as possible; concentrate upon your message. Give spontaneous action an opportunity to grow. Let it develop. Then you may give your attention to refining your platform conduct in accordance with principles instead of in conformity to stereotyped rules.

Assuming, however, that you have finally reached the place where you feel relatively uninhibited, or at least have passed through the stage of not being able to speak for shaking, to where you can speak and shake at the same time, and yet you know that from a physical standpoint you are not expressive, a few specific suggestions may be helpful.

Assuredly there is some validity in the theory that whereas an individual will begin to gesture when his inhibitions are replaced by positive motivation, it is also true that forcing himself to gesture and move about may in turn hasten the removal of inhibitions. Thus, while conducting his "experiments" in speaking, the intelligent learner will force himself to try a few gestures now and then, and to move about from place to place. His first attempts may result in weak, half-hearted, partial gestures, and dragging, uncertain steps. But both can improve rapidly if the beginner will persist and if he will give conscious study to the problem. One should stand before a mirror and experiment with gesture, posture, and movement, noting the unconvincing effect of an unfinished or too short movement of the hand, undue spreading of the fingers, excessive repetition of the same gesture or movement, failure of a gesture to involve the whole body, so that it seems detached and mechanical, and the lack of dynamic vigor in a slouching or bent-at-the-knees position.

Conversely, some speakers, as soon as they lose their inhibitions, unconsciously fall into habits of superfluous gesticulation and aimless pacing. In their enthusiasm to convey their ideas, they seemingly try to express physically what they are unable to convey verbally. Mirrors and candid friends will quickly tell one whether he gestures too much, and whether he paces like a caged panther, so that the audience wishes he would either stand still or go some place.

As short, useful exercises, memorize brief passages from famous speeches, and try different patterns of gesture and movement while speaking these before a mirror. In general, your own judgment will tell you whether your action is appropriate. However, bear specifically in mind that one rarely points to himself, especially to specific parts of his anatomy; gestures should seldom call for the full extending of a limb; mere nodding or shaking of the head may be as effective as an arm movement; an idea may be conveyed equally well by several different types of gestures; rarely should a gesture attempt to depict literally, but should confine itself to the sphere of suggestion; and ordinarily a gesture gets under way before the idea it is to assist has actually been uttered, that is, it is in the process of formation as the idea nears expression, so that its completion coincides with the high point of the idea to be emphasized by this physical supplement.

The following sentences may be helpful in studying bodily behavior, either with or without the aid of a mirror:

There is one way and one way only to solve this problem.

Why did the people vote against our proposal? Why did they reject it when it was designed to aid them?

I will fight against this action as long as I can raise a hand! (The appropriate gesture will not be the raising of the hand!)

These tactics will divide the people, divide the money, and divide the benefits; but they will not separate an honest man's actions from his convictions.

Where in the whole country will you find another like it?

I will accept it if the majority demand it; I will cooperate in its enforcement if it is made law; but I will *not* vote for it!

Originally at the extreme left, he has swung as far to the right as a man can go.

What did I do? What could one do?

This is one point I must make clear.

But wait! Where will he find help?

One specific problem confronts all beginners and plagues even the experienced: How can one walk some distance in view of a waiting audience, take his place in a chair on a platform or stage and sit comfortably, or turn and face his audience and begin to speak without appearing awkward and feeling self-conscious? The first and most honest answer is that most people cannot do either. The second answer is that the mere admonition to be natural is not enough. The true solution lies in three procedures: (1) Recognizing that by the very nature of the situation any intelligent person will feel self-conscious. If he feels self-conscious, that is in itself some indication that he is normal—though not absolute proof! (2) Reminding oneself that he will not be permanently ruined if he does not appear to be the exemplification of dignity and self-possession. To allow oneself to be unduly self-conscious is to place too great emphasis on one's own importance. After all, other people are not particularly concerned with how we behave in such circumstances, unless we do something obviously ludicrous. (3) Carefully observing the behavior of others, and using common sense. If one has opportunity to look ahead, he can anticipate what will be the proper behavior for him. If not, he can be guided by the actions of those who have reason to know who sits where, when to stand, what is the logically best position from which to speak, and how formally to conduct oneself. When the time comes to speak, the poised person knows before he has risen where he is going—and goes there! When he gets there, he stops without any flourishes, looks at his audience long enough to "take possession of them," but not long enough to make them wonder why he is waiting, and begins to speak.

When one is seated "on public display," no chair seems comfortable. Certainly no chair *looks* comfortable if its occupant sits like a poker, one foot bearing southwest forty-seven degrees, and the other bearing slightly east of south. The best way to appear relaxed is to relax, consciously to force oneself to release the tension which has accumulated. This does not mean that he should slouch down in his chair far enough to abandon the dignity appropriate to the formality of the occasion. One should sit straight but not stiffly so; he should not lapse into unconventional positions, but neither should his posture seem studied; he should change his position often enough to let those who see him know that he is alive, but not often enough to be guilty of fidgeting.

All in all, the factors which contribute to poise in the public speaking situation are those which give poise in all social life: experience; common sense; *feeling* at home; careful observation; and, eventually, a degree of conscious control.

It should, perhaps, be re-emphasized that the ideal for visible and audible behavior, for language, for analysis and synthesis of subject matter, in fact, for everything that goes into human communication, is essentially the same for drawing room and public platform. True, public situations usually demand more restraint and formality, and public speaking is a one-sided affair in some respects; but the governing *principles* of appropriate behavior are the same for both situations. No student should study any aspect of human speech without seeking perspective of the whole range of activity between conversation and formal address; and nowhere is this guiding dictum more valid than in the realm of bodily action.

# CHAPTER IX

# The Audible Aspects of Speech

ALTHOUGH OUR EVERYDAY use of speech is so commonplace that we look upon the process as relatively simple, a full understanding of what speech sounds are and how we produce them is in reality exceedingly difficult. Much confusion exists in the mind of the average person as to what constitutes good speech and its component elements: vowels, consonants, voice, rhythm, pronunciation, articulation, enunciation, resonance, quality, modulation. Yet in spite of the prevailing chaos, this body of knowledge is now relatively well standardized, and rests upon a relatively scientific foundation. This section presents in simple form the basic concepts of speech sounds as they relate to a desirable standard of speech performance.

## THE PROBLEM OF A STANDARD

The inevitable question raised by students and often discussed by teachers is, "What is a reliable 'standard' toward which one may strive?" Some teachers have gone so far as to attempt the phonetic description of such a standard and try to teach their students to acquire it. The main objection to such a procedure is that those who have chosen to lead the way have often prescribed a "standard" now used by a given region or group, but largely foreign to many localities and populations. The result has been that the young man or woman going away to college and acquiring to some extent such a "standard" of speech, has returned to his own community feeling conspicuous and artificial because of his *difference* after having conformed to a *standard*!

Contrast this outcome with the insistence that *the best speech is that which everywhere calls least attention to itself.* It is free from local or group peculiarities; it is pleasing, yet gives no hint that special care is being exercised to make it pleasant; it is so natural in its effect that the listener thinks not of the speaker's speech, but gives his whole attention to *what* the speaker is expressing. This standard, then, involves *the minimizing of differences, the omission of peculiarities, the achievement of* distinct and pleasing utterance without the appearance of special effort or care.

If you wish an example of this latter standard, we refer you to the leading TV newscasters and commentators, and to the voices of most of the spoken commercials. Please do not confuse these groups with leading personalities in special programs. One of the latter individuals may possess a distinct, sometimes a *distinctive,* characteristic of speech wholly compatible with the practice in his community or region, but not to be emulated as a standard by young people who have acquired their speech patterns in other environments.

Between 1920 and 1950, roughly speaking, our people developed a kind of self-consciousness about their speech habits. On the one hand, the automobile increased the mobility of our population, bringing Westerners, Southerners, and

New Englanders into more frequent contact with each other and consequently with "strange" speech patterns. This was in contrast to the occasional traveler of earlier years who was himself immediately conspicuous on entering a "foreign" community but did not disturb the self-satisfied equanimity of the natives. Then came radio, with its golden-throated announcers of East, West, North, and South, each making his speech impressions on the millions who listened, and each adding to the speech consciousness and eventually the self-consciousness of all. The increasing popularity and prevalence of sound motion-pictures added, if not to the confusion of tongues, at least to the confusion of ears.

Thus, in these years, speech students and speech teachers gave much thought, time, and talk to standards. After 1950, the addition of one or more television sets to almost every home brought a kaleidoscope of interesting if not always attractive faces into the household, and along with them an even greater variety of speech characteristics. To some degree, the attention to speech as such was lessened, because the visual image, so consistently absent from radio, now played its part again as a medium of expression, and took some attention away from voice. Simultaneously, however, as unselected faces and voices and articulation patterns appeared in increasing numbers on quiz shows, interviews, political campaigns, investigating agencies—in fact, the entire gamut of the social milieu—watchers became increasingly aware that American life presents a wide variety, if not a hodgepodge, of speech patterns: some regional, some personal, some arising from the influence of another language having been learned first.

And so the melting and melding processes continue. The fact that speech as an acquired tool of both society and the individual is dynamic, and therefore in the constant process of mutation and change, subject to vagaries of taste and circumstance, makes us, and should make us, tolerant of its individuality, but also aware that the reduction of conspicuous differences should be our goal. *Conspicuous* differences not only reduce the efficiency of communication through distraction and distortion, but they also are inimical to the desired aesthetic result. This assertion assumes that educated persons are interested in both clarity of speech (for practical purposes) and pleasantness of speech (for aesthetic reasons). Thus, to repeat our definition of a standard—it is speech that calls least attention to itself.

Assuming that the general characteristics of good speech have now been satisfactorily delineated, we can proceed to analyze the particulars on which students may broaden and deepen their understanding and thus lay specific foundations for self-improvement.

## THE PROCESS OF ARTICULATION

Although voice seems to occur constantly during speech, and articulation appears also to occur continually, it is well to make an arbitrary separation of the two for purposes of practical discussion at this point. Eventually we must view them again as one process in synthesized, natural speech.

Strictly speaking, *articulation* denotes connection or contact of two structures, and connotes further a functional, or acting-with-purpose, relationship between the parts. In the field of speech, it is used frequently to imply the production of consonant sounds, and occasionally to mean the formation of both consonant and vowel sounds.

*Enunciation* sometimes is employed to denote only vowel formulation, but frequently applies to both consonant and vowel sounds, and so becomes often synonymous with articulation.

*Pronunciation* denotes production of both consonant and

vowel sounds in conformity with a given standard (usually a dictionary standard), together with appropriate syllabic stress. It usually connotes, however, the utterance of a single word, whereas articulation and enunciation, in their various connotations, apply to continuous speech.

*Diction,* meaning originally the choice of one's words, has gained a usage in speech terminology which implies all that is intended by the other three terms discussed, with the additional significance of individuality or peculiarity or clarity of the whole pattern of utterance, sometimes including the elements of rhythm, pitch changes, loudness variation, and voice quality.

In our discussion, *articulation* has been chosen for use in the broader sense, connoting the general process of speech sound formation. If other terms are used, care will be exercised to make their signification in the specific case clear through sentence context.

In breaking down the complex pattern of fluent speech into its component parts, exclusive of voice, we must consider three elements: the *consonant,* the *vowel,* and *syllabic stress.* And in this approach our first hurdle lies in a full appreciation of the fact that the usual classification of vowels and consonants is of little or no value. For example, we have learned that the vowels are *a, e, i, o, u.* Accurately speaking, the first and third, as ordinarily pronounced, are diphthongs, the second and fourth are true vowels, and the fifth is a consonant-vowel combination. Similarly, the consonants as named by most people are not true consonants, but combinations of consonants and vowels; e.g., the letter *b* is actually pronounced like the word *bee,* the letter *c,* like *see,* etc. Even when these so-called consonants are given sound values as they appear in words, we must not fail to note their inconsistency of phonetic sound. For example, *c,* as used in *cat, face,* and *perch,* has three different values; *s,* as employed in *sea, fuse,* and *fuchsia,* has three; *k,* as pronounced in *knife, ankle,* and *polka,* three. Because we cannot depend upon the system by which we learn the sound of a word in terms of the sight of it, and because a consideration of the phonetic character of speech sharpens one's sense of speech sound differences, it is well for any student who desires to improve his accuracy in utterance of speech sounds to learn the phonetic consonants and vowels, and to attempt some phonetic transcription.

A study of the anatomical adjustments for production of the various sounds will reveal that the true vowels are characterized by a relatively open-mouth cavity, each vowel achieving its character by the position of the tongue in the floor of the mouth,[1] and by the degree and type of the lip opening. The soft palate is lowered to some degree for each normal vowel, so that the nasal cavity may contribute its resonance potentialities. Too great or small a degree of opening into the nasal chambers does not destroy recognizability of the vowel, but distorts the quality of the voice, as will be seen in the discussion of that item. It should be borne in mind that all vowels are characterized by voice, except when whispered. Even then they necessitate the production of a fricative (or whispered) sound at the point of the vocal cords. A diphthong results from a continuous change from one vowel position to another, frequently accompanied by a change in pitch and stress.

Consonants, on the other hand, may result from: (1) obstructing escape of the breath stream momentarily, and then releasing it suddenly with a mild puff or expulsive action as in *p, t, k, b, d, g,*[2] (2) impedance of the breath stream, so

---

[1] Note that in forming vowels the tongue never makes contact with the hard or soft palate or upper teeth, and only incidentally with the lower teeth.

[2] See phonetic key, p. 197-198 for sound values of symbols hereafter employed to signify phonetic concepts.

**1 7 6**

that it is emitted with a hissing sound as in *s, h, ʃ, f. v,* θ, *z;* (3) combinations of the two actions just named, as in *tʃ;* (4) adjustment of the tongue to the hard palate so as to modify the vocal sound only slightly, as in *l, r;* (5) sudden changes in position of lips or tongue, as in *w, ɱ;* (6) direction of the vocal stream through the nasal cavity, as in *m, n,* ŋ. These last three groups are not true consonants, but are sometimes classified as semiconsonants, and more often as semivowels. They lie somewhere between true vowels and true consonants, though they are classified usually in the consonant group.

One more concept should be clarified before dismissing our consideration of the consonants: some are voiced and some are voiceless. That is, although in every consonant some sound is present, the sound known as voice is present in only about half of them. For example, compare *p* and *b, f* and *v.* It will be readily discerned that in each of these pairs the second sound differs from the first almost solely through the addition of voice.

The most common fault of articulation is the occasional inaccurate formation of vowels and consonants in fluent speech. That is, no one sound is consistently produced incorrectly; but one sound in this word, and two sounds in the next word, etc., because of inactive tongue or jaw or lips, are produced so indistinctly that the listener must exert effort to understand what the speaker says. The remedy lies in being more careful and in becoming more sensitive to speech accuracy or inaccuracy. A less common but more obvious fault is the omission of consonants, and sometimes both vowels and consonants, as in *gunna* and *whatcha.* A less easily discernible fault is in vowel distortion, as in *becuz, fer, doug, dook.* For both of these faults the remedy is the same as that prescribed for general carelessness and inactivity.

Errors of syllabic stress mean simply placing the empha-

**1 7 7**

sis, or stress, on the wrong syllable, and are infrequent except in the speech of foreigners who have acquired our language after having learned their own. For most of us, the problem is confined to a few specific words such as *abdomen, alias, armistice, detail, illustrate, research, finance, perfume.*

## VOICE

Since voice exists in all vowel sounds and is present in many of the consonants, the student may well wonder how we may speak of voice and characterize it as if it existed apart from other aspects of speech. The answer is that in spite of the intermittent character of voice, as well as its production simultaneously with other sounds, it does nevertheless achieve an identity quite distinct from other elements of the total pattern of speech. Interestingly, it derives this identity almost solely, if not wholly, from its appearance during the production of vowels and diphthongs. The explanation lies in the fact that it is (1) during this time free from the noise characteristics present when it appears in some voiced consonants; (2) that it here reaches its greatest intensity, or loudness; and (3) that the vowels constitute the majority of total audible speaking time.

The human voice, or any other sound for that matter, manifests four attributes, or definable and measurable characteristics. These *attributes* are to a large degree mutually exclusive and independent of each other; that is, one may change without affecting the other three, though usually a change in one does change the character of one or more of the others. The important consideration is that if one learns to recognize and describe the nature of each attribute separately, he has laid the basis for an analytical characterization of any voice. Instead of thinking and speaking in vague terms, he can be accurate and exact; and he can understand

and be understood by others in any discussion of his own or another person's voice.

*Pitch*  /  One of the most readily recognizable attributes of voice is *pitch*. Although the physicist may choose the term "frequency," we must bear in mind that frequency, or the rate at which the sound source vibrates, is rather the determinant of the psychological experience of pitch. The terms "high" and "low" are frequently employed to describe the pitch of a voice, but the more accurate description is to indicate its place upon the musical scale. In other words, pitch might well be defined as the position, or changing position, of a sound in relation to the musical scale. With this concept well in hand, the terms "high" and "low" may be appropriately used to indicate whether a voice is too high or low in pitch to be pleasing to the ear. In general, a voice of medium or low pitch is most pleasant, though much depends upon the voice instrument of the individual concerned. In some cases, a relatively high pitch may give the best total result, if the resonance cavities of the voice apparatus are small and better attuned to high frequencies. Interestingly, women's voices are on the average pitched almost an octave higher than men's, for women's vocal cords are only a little more than half as long as men's. Yet this circumstance is probably fortunate, because women's resonance cavities are usually much smaller than those of men.

Whereas a common error of pitch may lie in its general level's being too high or too low, an equally grave fault is in the failure of pitch to change easily and naturally from its normal level through all the phases of its potential range. That is, it lacks variation, or flexibility; it is monotonous. Or, while it may appear to achieve considerable variation, it may vary so consistently according to the same pattern that it becomes monotonous in its mode of variation. A less serious habit is the tendency to end sentences on a rising inflection.

The correction of faulty pitch level is not difficult if the fault is simply the result of habit. Mere recognition of the problem, and constant attention for a few weeks to the controlling of pitch, may be all that is necessary. Sometimes the assistance of a piano or other instrument to enable one to determine his pitch level will be desirable. Frequently, supervised drill is imperative. If the fault lies, however, in inadequate or too great length of the vocal cords, or in some defect of the musculature which controls them, a revision of pitch habits is often difficult or impossible. In such cases, it is well for the subject to have the assistance of a clinician to guide him toward the most effective use of the mechanism which he has. If the fault is derived from deficiency in pitch discrimination, that is, inability to hear pitch differences as accurately as the average person, again the clinician may assist the subject in improving his powers of discrimination. If the fault is pitch monotony, either of level or of pattern, the problem is again one of developing the power to hear what occurs. Clinical drill in reading, courses in reading aloud, constant attention to the sound of one's voice will usually remedy the deficiency. The same applies to the habit of rising inflection.

*Loudness* / An attribute sometimes more easily identified than pitch is *loudness,* or *intensity.* Intensity is accurately used by both the physicist and the psychologist. To the physicist it means the energy expended by the vibrating source or moving through the atmosphere; to the psychologist it means the magnitude of the stimulus or the intensity of the auditory experience.[3] But for practical purposes, loudness is an acceptable term.

[3] The term "experience" is an attempt to divorce our psychological reactions from the physical conditions which cause them. For example, a blow causes you pain. The blow is physical; the pain is a psychological experience. Likewise, sound waves are physical, but sound is an *experience.*

A few voices are too loud most of the time, but a far greater number are too weak. If one varies his pitch appropriately, his loudness variations will usually be adequate also. Some people are guilty of decreasing loudness at the termination of phrases or sentences, so that we fail to hear the last few words of the group. Of such a person we often say that he "drops" his voice or his final words. If a departure from normal in the matter of loudness is purely habit, then the general prescriptions for remedy of pitch will apply. If the fault lies in the vibrator, a clinician may be of some assistance. Rarely is the problem one of breathing. In most cases one needs simply to talk a little louder or not so loud.

*Duration* / A more difficult attribute to understand clearly is that of *duration*. In its simplest meaning it denotes for both physicist and psychologist the length of time a sound endures. It is short or long, or somewhere in between. But in the voice aspect of speech, its significance is more complex. Strictly speaking, it is not a characteristic of voice, but of the voiced portions of speech in relation to the unvoiced units. Going one step further, it is probably best to consider the duration of the vowels as opposed to the consonants. If one tends to attack his consonants vigorously and to shorten or omit the vowels, his speech is characterized by the musical term "staccato." If he inclines to lengthen his vowels beyond normal usage, so that he produces a drawling or lazy effect, his speech is identified by the recently employed phrase "tonal perseveration." That is, he perseveres in the tonal aspects (vowels) of his speech. A departure in either of these two directions, if firmly fixed as a habit, is invariably stubborn of remedy. Its improvement is accomplished through expert supervision and through increased sensitiveness to speech sounds. Organic contribution to staccato speech or to tonal perseveration may be either glandular or neurological, but the discussion of remedy under such conditions is better reserved for speech pathology.

*Quality* / Although the attribute of *quality* gives rise to more confusion than any other, recent investigation in this area has contributed much to standardization of concept, if not to uniformity of terminology. Quality is sometimes described as that element of voice which makes one voice recognizably different from another, or which makes it possible for us, upon hearing a voice, to say to whom it belongs. Such a description is particularly valid if we think of the other three attributes as being the same in any circumstance of comparison. It will be readily recognized that pitch and loudness could well be the same for two voices; duration is usually not a point of distinction, though upon occasion it may be the major point of difference. Quality, however, is never the same for two people. It may be similar, is usually quite different, but never the same for two people.

TONE COMPLEXITY / The physical correlative of *quality* is *tone complexity*. That is, quality, like pitch, is an *experience,* a psychological term; complexity, like frequency, is the physicist's view of the tone as it is produced by the vibrating source and by modifying resonators, or as it exists in the atmosphere through which it is transmitted from its source of origin to the human ear—or, more accurately, to the human brain. We know that most sounds are highly complex. That is, they are combinations of what might be a great number of individual sounds, all occurring simultaneously. This is true of a single tone from a violin or piano, or of a simple vowel uttered by a human being. In this combination, we may think of one sound as being the *fundamental,* or foundation tone, and of the others as being *overtones,* or multiples of the fundamental. They occur two, three, four, five, etc., times as often each second as does the fundamental. A given sound may be composed of two or three overtones, or it may embody a great number. The *quality* of the sound we hear depends primarily upon four factors: (1) the number of overtones present; (2) which overtones of those that theoretically could be present actually are present, e. g., whether one, two, seven, and nine exist, or whether three, four, six, and eight are present; (3) the relative energy possessed by each overtone present; (4) whether or not those overtones present are exact multiples of the fundamental or fractional multiples of it. The more the overtones are exact multiples of the fundamental, the more they are in harmony with it and produce what we call harmonious sounds or *tones*. If the overtones tend to be fractional multiples of the fundamental, the result is inharmonious, or what we call *noise*. It will be readily evident that the degree to which a given sound resembles either tone or noise is purely relative. Most tones, including the human voice, possess some noise; most noises contain some elements of tone.

RESONANCE / The concept of *resonance* needs brief comment before we are ready to discuss quality as it relates to the human voice. Briefly, resonance is the power of cavities of certain sizes and shapes to select from a given complex tone passing by or through them certain overtones for resonance, or re-sounding, with the result that they are made prominent in our perception of the sound. Through this process of resonance the quality of a sound may be changed, or determined. It is important to an understanding of human voice to realize that resonance chambers do not ordinarily affect the degree of noise in a sound. They may re-sound inharmonics already present, but they do not introduce them. Consequently, when we describe a voice as possessing noise characteristics, we must ascribe the cause to the vibrating source (the vocal cords), not to the resonance chambers. At the same time, we must recognize that resonance does play a large part in determining the ultimate quality of the voice. The fact that people's mouth and nose and throat cavities differ in size and shape is in itself sufficient to cause their voices all to be different in quality. When we add the fact that no two people would use even the same set of resonators in just the same way, we have additional explanation of differences in human voice quality.

TERMINOLOGY IS DIFFICULT  /  The adjectives which are employed to describe these differences in quality are so numerous as to be highly confusing. Since no two voices are quite alike, we need an adjective for each person, and since no one adjective often adequately describes even one aspect of the peculiar quality of a given voice, we really need a great number of adjectives. And yet the fact that we take an adjective from a field of usage in which it has become relatively stable in denotation and connotation, and attempt to apply it on the basis of analogy in an entirely different field, invariably results in a degree of misconception on the part of the listener or reader. However, there are some relatively standard bases on which to rest a classification of voice quality; and it is in terms of such bases that the following classification is given. They are "standard" partly because they convey the same meaning to different persons, partly because they indicate the anatomical adjustments or sources responsible for the observed quality or in some other way refer to some stable concept or condition, and partly because they signify general groups into which voice qualities tend to fall.

GOOD QUALITY  /  Three justifiable terms may be used to give description to the *desirable* characteristics of voice quality: rich, or resonant; balanced resonance; and melodious, or harmonious.

The rich voice is one which is rich in, or possesses an abundance of, overtones. It is sometimes referred to as resonant because it is assumed that resonance contributes to richness. And this is partly true. If your head were cut off just above the vocal cords, your voice would sound flat indeed— if you could produce one. One should remember, though, that resonance is only one determinant of richness. The vibrator itself may send out a great number of overtones from which the resonators may select their groups for emphasis, or prominence; or the vibrator may send out few overtones on which the resonators may operate selectively. Thus richness is originally determined at the point of the vocal cords, and secondarily affected by way of the resonators. The important concept is that some voices do seem to have more overtones than others, and such voices sound rich and resonant (*resonant*).

It is important, however, that the resonators be adjusted in such proportion and in such relation to each other as to avoid an unbalance of overtone selection. We shall note in the following paragraphs that some quality abnormalities are the result of improper balance between resonators. A voice which is free from such evidence of unbalance is said to possess the character of balanced resonance.

We have listed the adjectives "melodious" and "harmonious" because they imply the absence of inharmonious, or noise, elements. A pleasant voice is usually relatively free from noise characteristics. If a more accurate term than either of those listed could be found to imply the absence of noise, such a term would be desirable to use.

UNDESIRABLE QUALITY / *Resonance faults.* Beyond these positive terms are a few which possess some stability in indicating *undesirable* voice qualities. First are the group which derive their significance from the resonance chambers. Of these the *nasal* and the *denasal* are most easily identified. Nasal quality occurs from too large an opening at the point of the soft palate into the nasal chambers. The result is that too much resonance energy is contributed by the nasal chambers; or, in other words, those overtones selected by the nasal resonators contain a disproportionate amount of the total sound energy, so that a disbalance between nasal and oral resonance obtains. When the opposite condition prevails, the voice may be described as denasal, or deficient in nasal contributions. Nasal quality gives the impression that one is "talking through one's nose"; denasal suggests that one has a serious head cold, so that no sound can pass through the nasal cavities. In reality, a person may possess either quality to an unhappy extreme when all anatomical and physiological conditions are normal; he may exhibit either quality as the result of a cold; he may possess either of them through inactive or paralyzed palate, through deviated septum, swollen turbinates or other nasal obstructions; he may be nasal because of a cleft palate. And in rare cases, an effect which we would characterize as nasal may be contributed by a peculiar adjustment of the epiglottis or by some unusual cavity created by an operation or growth.

The second direction of deviation determined by the resonators is toward the opposite extremes of what has been widely termed in recent years the *metallic* and the *muffled*. Synonyms for *metallic* are "bright," "high-frequency," "ee-ness." That is, the sound exhibits that "brilliance" contributed by the high frequencies. On the other hand, the terms "dull," "hollow," "low-frequency," and "oo-ness" are synonymous with *muffled* quality. The cause of these extremes lies in the adjustment of the oral and pharyngeal cavities. The metallic extreme obtains when adjustment approximates that for production of the phonetic $i$ (ee); the muffled extreme occurs when adjustment resembles that for producing the phonetic $u$ (oo). Such abnormalities thus are nearly always a matter of habit rather than organic faults.

VOCAL CORD FAULTS / Another source of voice quality deviations lies in the vocal cords themselves. These irregularities are invariably characterized by the element of noise. Descriptive terms most frequently employed are "harsh," "hoarse," "husky," "breathy." These terms are not synonymous, nor do they represent opposite conditions as in the quality abnormalities originating in the resonators. Rather,

"harshness" is an unusual evidence of inharmonics; "huski-
ness" and "hoarseness" are derived from analogous qualities
prevailing during a cold or physical strain; "breathiness" suggests unnecessary escape of the air stream during the production of voice. Such terms are not wholly accurate, but they
are consistently suggestive; and as a group they at once signify the source of difficulty. Such eccentricities of voice are
sometimes caused by growths on the cords, broken or irregu-
lar cord edges, muscle paralysis, inflammation of the cords
through colds, laryngitis, sinusitis, asthma, and smoking. In
the great majority of instances, however, such unpleasant
qualities are solely the result of improper use of a perfectly
normal mechanism, i. e., habit.

It should be emphasized that any abnormality arising at
the point of the vocal cords may exist in combination with
one derived from resonance unbalance; and nasal unbalance
in either direction may combine with either muffled or metallic quality, though antithetical qualities naturally do not
exist concomitantly. The fact is, however, that quality abnormalities nearly always exist in combinations rather than
singly. The point is that some qualities will combine; others
will not. Descriptive terminology should be in terms of analysis rather than upon a basis of combination.

Remedy for defects of quality should be sought through
consultation with a specialist in speech. The general approach is fundamentally the same as that for remedy of the
other discrepancies of voice, though in some cases surgery
or special treatment or drill is necessary. In any case, the
subject should be diagnosed before attempting remedy on his
own part. With a few exceptions he may be able to do much
good for himself; but without qualified advice he may do
harm.

*Flexibility*  /  We have emphasized the separateness of
the attributes of voice, for analysis demands separation. But

it must be borne in mind that when voice is produced, pitch, intensity, duration, and quality all occur simultaneously. They are aspects, or *attributes,* of the sound produced. Some may be changed while others remain constant, or all may be changed. In normal speech all four are constantly changing, each in relation to the other, depending upon the thought or mood to be expressed. It is this changing pattern, appropriately suited to thought and mood and the personality expressing itself, which makes speech expressive, alive, vibrant, sometimes even beautiful. To achieve such results the voice must be flexible, and the ear must be keen in order to control purposively, or to modulate, the flexibility. Thus it is appropriate that we add the feature of *flexibility* or *modulation* as a functional characteristic of the four attributes of voice in action.

One's voice may conceivably be reasonably good in each of the four attributes if these inherent characteristics are studied separately and without regard to their conveyance of meaning or emotion, yet be quite lacking in expressiveness because it fails to vary the four in a properly changing pattern of significant relation to each other. The well-modulated voice not only refrains from unpleasant or conspicuous traits in any of its attributes, but it also nicely adjusts each and all of them to the maximum expression of thought and feeling. It is *flexible*; it varies easily, readily, pleasantly, and naturally —neither calling attention to its inadequacies nor giving evidence that the owner is consciously trying to be expressive.

**When Is a Voice Good?** / All in all, the good voice is, first, one which, as was said of good speech (of which voice is a part), *calls least attention to itself*. It is so suited to the personality and his thought and mood of the moment, and to the situation in which he speaks, that no hint of incongruity exists. It is an instrument of expression, not a thing to be noticed for itself.

Secondly, its *pitch level is usually medium or low, and its range is wide*. Women's normal pitch is around middle *C* or slightly below, which is about 256 d. v. An appropriate pitch for men is about an octave lower. However, both men and women may vary from this "medium" and still manifest acceptable pitch level if the chosen pitch seems consistent with physique and bearing, and if other aspects of voice are satisfactory. The usual pitch *range* for an expressive voice under normal circumstances of conversation is about an octave.

Thirdly, the *loudness of a person's voice should suit his personality and the situation*. It should be loud enough to be easily heard, but not loud enough to make listeners aware of its loudness as such or to be offensive. At the same time, it should be congruent with the personality it represents. A large man with a high-pitched or weak voice "surprises" those who hear him for the first time. Similarly, a small man with a "big" voice immediately calls attention to himself. After a time, listeners adjust their responses to these ostensible incongruities, and the voices and persons no longer seem incompatible. On radio, of course, where the speaker is only heard and not seen, the criterion of congruency with physical sizes does not apply.

Fourthly, the *quality of the voice should be characterized by freedom from harshness or inharmonic elements, and should manifest none of the resonance unbalances: namely, nasal, denasal, metallic, muffled.*

Fifthly, it should be *legato* rather than drawling on the one hand and too vigorously sharp in its syllabic attacks on the other.

## RHYTHM

When we combine voice and articulation in all their aspects, we have a fairly complete picture of the audible aspects of speech except for the difficult concept of *rhythm*.

Although everyday speech manifests no such obvious pattern of rhythm as poetry and some types of prose, it nevertheless exhibits certain ebbs and flows of time and consistencies of time relationships as to give rise to use of the term "rhythm" as a means of signifying the appropriateness or indisposition of this relationship. Fluent, easy speech is said to have good rhythm. Jerky, uneven speech is poor in rhythm. The stutterer is afflicted with a pathology of rhythm. Analysis reveals that the component parts of rhythm in speech are primarily the length of the syllable, the pitch change at the beginning and within the syllable, and the intensity changes between and within syllables. But for our purposes, good rhythm is fluency, or controlled timing, while poor rhythm is its opposite.

## THE INSTRUMENT OF SPEECH

The attempt thus far has been to give a picture of the nature of speech as it is received by the listener, with only occasional reference to the mechanism which produces both voice and articulated sounds. It may therefore help somewhat to give a very elementary picture of the operation of the physical speech machinery, that is, of what is known as the "peripheral" mechanism. Speech really begins in the frontal lobe of the brain, and many complicated processes occur before the diaphragm and other bodily structures begin to act toward the actual physical production of speech sounds. But we shall concern ourselves only with that portion of the anatomy borrowed from respiration and from the digestive functions for the purposes of speech.

Basically there are four major parts to this sound-producing instrument: the *pump*, the *vocal vibrator*, the *resonators*, and the *articulation-vibrators*.

The pump is essentially the breathing instrument. It is

the means by which air is brought into and forced out of the organism. It consists of the diaphragm, the abdominal muscles and the organs of the abdomen against which they play, the rib cage and the muscles which move its walls in an outward-upward motion and back again, and the lung sacs themselves. The diaphragm is a hill-shaped, muscular structure which cuts the body literally in two, thus separating it into abdomen and thorax. The thorax is made up of the lungs (including the trachea), the heart, and the ribs which enclose them. The abdomen is made up of stomach, liver, and intestines, enclosed by the diaphragm as roof, the pelvic bones as floor, the rigid back bone as one wall, and the flexible "belly" muscles as its forward wall.

The increase and decrease of the volume of the thorax by means of the muscles and structures thus far mentioned constitute the cause of intake and outgo of air.

Briefly, when the diaphragm responds to the nerve stimulus to contract its muscles, its consequent movement means that the floor of the thorax (the roof of the abdomen) moves downward, thus expanding the thoracic cavity in a vertical direction and causing the forward abdominal wall to "push out" as a result of the viscera being forced against it. At the same time, the ribs are usually lifted up and out so as to increase the chest volume in a horizontal direction. The lungs, being elastic tissue, follow this expanding wall and floor in much the same fashion as the lining of a bellows would follow its expanding walls as air rushes in from the outer world in response to the greater space available. The important principle to remember in this sequence of action is that the incoming air does *not push the chest boundaries out, but that the atmospheric pressure of the outside causes air to move through the nose or mouth and down the trachea into the space made available.*

Expiration involves essentially the opposite action of

inspiration, except that the diaphragm moves upward, not by its own power (except for a certain elasticity inherent in its having "worked" to move itself and other structures out of their resting position), but by power applied by contraction of the abdominal muscles against the viscera, and so indirectly against the diaphragm. Too, the weight of the ribs causes them to return to their original position ordinarily without the employment of muscle action. The consequent decrease in chest volume from both vertical and horizontal directions causes the air to be forced out of the lungs, and so provides the air-power for speech-sound production.

Thus it will be seen that the diaphragm and the abdominal muscles antagonize each other, that is, each does work only in the direction opposite the other; and two more complicated networks of muscles antagonize each other to accomplish expansion and diminution of the thorax. Because these two pairs of action work more or less separately, we arbitrarily speak of "chest" and "abdominal" breathing as though they were two separate types, one good and one bad. In reality, either type may consciously be used quite exclusive of the other; but under normal circumstances the two work co-operatively. Abdominal action, being more efficient because of the flexibility of structures used, usually takes precedence in function, especially in men, and in sleep may do all the work of respiration. Usually, however, chest action will begin at whatever point some movement of the cumbersome rib-cage is more efficient than more extended action of the abdominal structures. Thus the type of breathing is usually a relative matter, depending on the depth of inspiration and the desired force of expiration.

The main consideration from the standpoint of producing speech sounds is that breath constitutes the power-supply. Only indirectly does the manner of breathing affect the character of the sounds produced, except in the case of loudness,

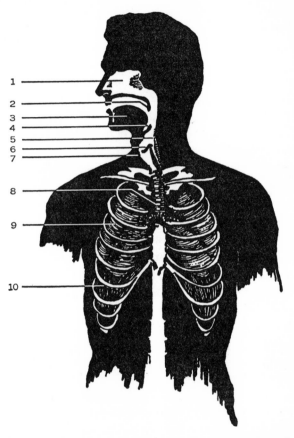

A sagittal view of (1) nasal chambers, (2) soft palate, (3) tongue, (4) epiglottis, (5) esophagus, (6) vocal folds, (7) "Adam's apple;" and a frontal view of the (8) trachea, (9) lungs, and (10) diaphragm.

where the force applied is the first of three factors determining how loud the sound shall be. The second determinant is the responsiveness of the vibrator (vocal cords, or articulation point), and the third is resonance (*re*-sounding).

The second part of the sound-producing instrument, the *vocal vibrator,* or vocal cords, consists of a valve-like pair of membranes anchored in a horizontal plane in a complicated structure known as the larynx, the forward portion of which is often called the "Adam's apple."

These thin membranes, less than an inch long, are so anchored that their edges may be moved close together so as to impede the passage of air or so as to prevent it altogether. At the same time, their tension may be delicately adjusted so that they are very thin and tight, or so that they are thicker and more loose. When they only impede the air stream, the passing of air over their edges sets them into motion in a more or less regular pattern of oscillation, or "vibration," which gives rise to the sound known as *voice*. So much could be said about this whole structure and its operation and consequent determination of sound that it is perhaps best to stop with only this very sketchy picture.

This much may be said. The pitch of the voice will depend on three factors: (1) length of the cords—the longer the cords the lower the pitch, all else being equal; (2) weight or mass—the more heavy the cords the lower the pitch, and vice versa; (3) tension—the more loose the cords the lower the pitch. Furthermore, the total manner in which the cords are adjusted will determine whether they respond in a natural swing or are "forced" in their vibration, the former resulting in a "harmonious" sound, the latter in a "noisy" or inharmonic type of sound. Also, volume, or loudness, really depends upon how far the vocal folds move from their position of rest as the result of pressure of the breath stream.

The *resonators* of the sound set up by vibration of the cords are the trachea, the laryngeal cavity itself, the pharynx, the mouth or oral cavity, and the nasal cavity. The sinuses are sometimes named as resonators, but their participation in resonance is doubtful. In any case, because of their inability to change either their sizes or shapes, they must for all practical purposes be considered no more than adjuncts of the nasal cavity, and so are not given separate consideration.

The trachea is quite invariable in character; the nasal cavity participates only to the degree in which it is turned on and off by the soft palate, or "swinging door" at the back of the oral cavity, and by change of its character through colds or nasal injuries or growths; the larynx is modified in shape somewhat by the angle of the epiglottis; the pharynx is capable of considerable adjustment by action of its muscular walls and by the position of the back of the tongue; the oral cavity is highly changeable in form because of the ability of the tongue to move into so many different positions within it.

The resonators contribute loudness to voice through their function of *re-sounding* the original air waves, but they perform two other distinctive functions. First, they modify voice quality through their "selective" *re-sonance,* e. g., nasal, denasal, metallic, and muffled qualities. Secondly, they so greatly and so consistently modify the vocal tone beyond the mere realm of voice quality that they *actually create the various vowels.*

The fourth aspect of the "peripheral" speech mechanism is a group of parts known as the *articulators.* Chief of these is the tongue, aided by the lips, teeth, hard palate, soft palate, and in one instance by the vocal cords.

These parts create and modify sound in three ways. First, they simply redirect or "cloud" tones emanating from the cords, e. g., *m, n,* ŋ, *l, r.* The *m* would be a vowel, except that the lips prevent emission of the tone from the oral cavity and *reroute* it through the nasal resonator. The *l* results from simply raising the tip of the tongue to the roof of the mouth so as to make a potential vowel flow around the sides of it—which is in reality only a changing of the shape of the oral resonator.

Secondly, when the vocal cords are idle, the articulators may impede escape of the air stream, or stop it temporarily and release it suddenly, so that a series of minute repercussions or "eddies" are set up, which constitute a kind of vibration themselves. Thus the term "articulation-vibrators." The articulators do not actually vibrate, as do the vocal cords, but they give rise to atmospheric pressure variations that are sound. The *s* sound in "hiss," the *t* in "tip," and the *p* in "pony" are good examples of this type of sound creation. The group of sounds made in this fashion are known as *voiceless* consonants: that is, they are produced without the use of voice, or "vocal" action.

Thirdly, vocal sounds and this latter group are combined in what are known as *voiced* consonants, e. g., *z, d, b*. The difference between the *s* and the *z* is the addition of voice to the first to create the latter. In like manner *t* becomes *d* and *p* becomes *b*.

Thus all vowels are voiced; about one-third of the consonants are characterized by voiceless sounds; and the other two-thirds are a combining of the voice with the voiceless elements.

All in all, fluent speech is a complex pattern of starting and stopping of the pump, vocal cord movement into and out of position for brief moments of vibration, momentary obstructions of the breath stream and redirecting of the sound initiated at the cords by means of quick tongue and lip action or a swinging up or down of the soft palate. This latter organ moves into a different position for every sound uttered, or a minimum of 375 times per minute, yet most of us are not even conscious of its action—or even of its existence! The time the vocal cords remain in position to vibrate even a single vowel in a word like "hospitable" is measured in tenths or hundredths of a second, and nine separate and distinct combinations of adjustment of many separate parts are necessary for utterance of the whole word. No wonder that speech is a more complex subject of study than most people realize.

## *KEY TO PHONETIC SYMBOLS*

| PRINTED SYMBOL | SCRIPT SYMBOL | KEY WORDS INDICATING PHONETIC SYMBOL VALUES |
|---|---|---|
| i | *i* | *ease, feet, feat, retreat, be, bee, Caesar, receive, believe.* |
| ɪ | *ɪ* | *it, sit* |
| e | *e* | *apex, favor, caisson, coupe, obeisance, neighbor, bouquet, tray* |
| ɛ | *ɛ* | *efferent, set, pleasant* |
| æ | *æ* | *atom, flat* |
| a | *a* | *ask, grass* |
| ɑ | *ɑ* | *ah, obstreperous, father* |
| ɔ | *ɔ* | *awkward, all, paw, gloss, clause* |
| o | *o* | *obese, notary, halo* |
| ʊ | *ʊ* | *pull, book* |
| u | *u* | *zoo, flu, flew, through, blue, who, bouquet* |
| ʌ | *ʌ* | *up, cup* |
| ɘ̂ | *ɘ̂* | *adult, incandescent, arbitrary, iconoclast, the, sofa* |
| m | *m* | *my, amend, am, comb, come* |
| n | *n* | *no, anew, nun, none* |
| ŋ | *ŋ* | *singing, pancreas, anger* |
| *p | *p* | *pay, apart, flop, ape* |
| †b | *b* | *be, about, fib* |
| *t | *t* | *tie, atone, at* |
| †d | *d* | *do, ado, did* |
| *k | *k* | *kit, cat, quip, chaos, akin, actor, ache, equine, block, poke* |
| †g | *g* | *go, ago, ghost, aghast, gag* |
| r | *r* | *rip, writ, bring, flower* |

| PRINTED SYMBOL | SCRIPT SYMBOL | KEY WORDS INDICATING PHONETIC SYMBOL VALUES |
|---|---|---|
| l | ℓ | *l*it, a*l*ight, pu*ll* |
| *f | f | *f*it, *ph*armacist, a*ff*able, a*ph*asia, cou*gh* |
| †v | v | *v*ery, a*v*ow, ha*v*e, ha*lv*e |
| *θ | θ | *th*in, a*th*wart, slo*th* |
| †ð | ᵹ | *th*is, ei*th*er, loa*the* |
| *s | s | *s*o, *sc*ion, *sch*ism, *c*ease, al*s*o, a*ss*ist, a*c*etate, hi*ss*, win*c*e |
| †z | z | *z*oo, free*z*ing, u*s*able, di*sc*ern, ra*sp*berry, gla*z*e, fill*s*, no*s*e |
| *ʃ | ʃ | *sh*ow, *Ch*icago, *s*ure, a*sh*ore, nau*s*ea, addi*ti*on, gra*ci*ous, ma*ch*ine, gna*sh*, gau*ch*e |
| †ʒ | ʒ | a*z*ure, gara*g*e |
| *h | h | *h*e, *wh*o, a*h*a |
| ʍ | ʍ or h | *wh*ere, a*wh*ile |
| †w | w | *w*e, a*w*ait |
| j | ȷ | *y*et, *u*niform, fo*y*er, f*ew*, j*u*ice, bea*u*ty, c*u*te |
| *tʃ | tʃ | *ch*alk, i*tch*ing, ha*tch*, *ch*urch |
| †dʒ | dʒ | *g*em, *j*et, indi*g*ent, *j*udge, *G*eorge |

* These sounds are all unvoiced, i.e., the vocal cords do not vibrate to produce them.

† Vocal cord action is added to the unvoiced symbol immediately above each of these consonants to create its distinguishing character, e. g., *s* and *z*. All remaining consonants and all vowels are produced by cord tones and the addition of resonance, without any contributory "friction" or "plosive" element.

Only the more commonly used and easily discernible symbols are listed here. Diphthongs, closer vowel distinctions, and rare consonants have been omitted in an attempt to hold to the salient principle of this book: to present basic and practical information, but to avoid minutiae and technicalities that confuse the beginner.

# CHAPTER X

# Group Communication

I N THE EARLIER SECTIONS of this book, we have discussed oral communication largely from the point of view of public speaking. We seem to have assumed that a single speaker communicates to one or more receivers. The principles we have discussed, however, are as applicable to other forms of oral communication as they are to public speaking. As we pointed out in Chapter II, the general theory of communication applies equally to all forms of communication: for they all involve an understanding of the process of communication; and they all must be organized, developed, encoded in language, and presented vocally and physically. Therefore, what we have written to this point applies equally to what follows.

We have stated, earlier in this book, that all communication is bilateral or multilateral. That is, one transmitter may communicate with one receiver, as in public speaking, or, at various times, a particular person may be either a receiver or transmitter, as in group discussion and parliamentary procedure. In this chapter, we intend to focus our attention on those aspects of multilateral communication that distinguish it from bilateral communication. Since multilateral communication is concerned with communicative interaction within groups, we shall adopt the more convenient synonym *group communication,* rather than multilateral communication.

If we are to understand the operation of group communication, it is first necessary to examine the characteristics of groups with a view to determining how the process of communication within groups is different from bilateral communication. Further, since every member in group communication is both a transmission source and a receiver, we will need to look closely at the way in which personal interaction takes place.

In order to clarify some of the problems we have posed, we first need to be very clear about what we mean by the term "group." When we say "group," we do not mean a random collection of individuals. Although the people found on Main Street at 11 A.M. on Thursday are not ordinarily a group, the whittlers on the courthouse square probably are. Under usual conditions, however, the Main Street pedestrians could become a group. If a serious automobile accident were to occur and the passers-by actively engaged in a common effort to call an ambulance, summon a doctor, or administer first aid, they would now be a group. They would be considered a group because they have assumed some of the characteristics that differentiate groups from collections of people. They have agreed, tacitly or openly, to accept a common goal. More importantly, they have begun to interact with each other.

These are two very important characteristics of groups, but we must list some others in our brief treatment. A group is aware of its identity as a group. A group sets up patterns of internal communication. Group members are dependent on each other. Groups know the identity of their members. Each member has a reason for being a member of a group. Each group develops its own status hierarchy or "pecking order." Groups develop their own standards for admission and rejection of members. If you consider groups, formal or informal, to which you belong, you will notice that they have most of these characteristics.

Each group determines for itself what the behavior of its members shall be. In each group to which you belong, there are certain things you must do, certain things you must not do, and certain things that you may do. Sometimes these behavior norms are explicitly stated; at other times, they are tacitly understood by the group. A school teacher, for example, *must* maintain order in the classroom. She *must not* smoke and drink in the classroom. She *may* wear a sweater and skirt, a suit or a dress. In any group, those persons whose behavior does not conform to the norms of the group are likely to be expelled from the group. Generally speaking, the more autocratic groups have more *musts* and *must nots* than democratic groups. In the Soviet Union, for instance, there are more things that citizens are required to do and more things they are prevented from doing than in a society like ours, where there is a great middle ground of permissive behavior.

As a social system increases in complexity, it develops a greater number of groups. In a primitive society, the loyalties of persons are directed almost entirely to family and tribal groups. In a social system such as ours, almost everyone enjoys membership in a multitude of groups. In each of these groups, each member plays a somewhat different role. He may have high status in one group and lower status in another. A college student may have high status as president of his fraternity and low status as a busboy in a restaurant. In each of the many groups to which we belong, we are aware of our positions on the "pecking order," and our communication patterns conform to the roles we play.

The groups to which a person belongs may represent a variety of types. Some of them, such as fraternities, religious organizations, lodges, clubs, and service organizations, may be permanent. Others may be more temporary, such as committees, conferences, and public meetings. Groups will also vary in the formality of their structure—from that of the Senate of the United States to that of a cocktail party or a golf foursome. As indicated earlier, there may also be considerable variation in the permissiveness of the groups. Some groups may have explicitly prescribed norms; in others, the norms may be more permissive.

To this point, we have focused our attention on the characteristics of groups, but something needs to be said about the members of groups. It is as much a mistake to assume that a group member will lose his personal identity as an individual as it is to assume that a group is merely a collection of individual personalities. Actually, the truth probably lies somewhere between these two extremes. Each person brings his total personality to the group, but some modification occurs due to the interaction with other members of the group. In short, the success or failure of group communication may often be attributed to the interpersonal relations between group members. All too often, however, interpersonal conflict is not immediately evident and the failure of the group process is blamed on some other factor. A group discussion which, for example, seems not "to get off the ground" because of lack of interest in the subject may, in reality, find its deficiencies in the fear and anxiety of the members.

A chapter in a general oral-communications textbook is

not the place to present a systematic discussion of the intricate field of personal interaction in group communication. Nevertheless, it is possible, at least, to point out some of the interpersonal factors that affect the fidelity of the group communication process.

In the group process, communication flows more easily and with higher fidelity when members of the group like each other. Furthermore, within the group, we communicate more freely and more effectively with those persons whom we like and who seem to like us. Although there are real and substantive differences between the Soviet Union and the United States, and between labor and management, blame for the failure of negotiation between those groups must, to a considerable extent, be attributed to existing hostility.

As we have pointed out elsewhere, communication is more successful with people we know well, as opposed to people with whom we are barely acquainted or whom we do not know at all. We share common experiences and are likely to have a much higher degree of mutual feedback. High feedback allows communication to take place with less anxiety and higher sensitivity.

The group process operates most effectively when felt differences in status among group members are minimized. Conversely when the members are sensitized to their status, communication is likely to become inhibited or distorted. A "bull-session" among college students will be more frank and free than if the college president and the dean of men were also to participate in the discussion. The barriers of status are reduced, however, when those higher in the order do not seek to make other members aware of the status differences. Nevertheless, we tend to show deference in the face of power and status, and our communication shows it. We must recognize that those with power and prestige influence the behavior of groups.

The factor of status is closely related to that of threat. If a member of a group feels that his contributions will cause consequences that may be unfavorable to him, his communication will likely be inhibited. If a member feels that his self-respect, his ego, his esteem, his prestige will suffer, he will be reluctant to participate freely and fully. On the other hand, if there is a minimum of threat in a group, if ideas are dissociated, as much as possible, from the communicator, thoughts will be presented with greater frankness and less inhibition.

## *GROUP DISCUSSION*

Perhaps the most common form of group communication is the group discussion. The term "group discussion" is so general as to need definition. For our purposes, we do not regard random "bull-sessions," coffee-break conversations, or general comments about the weather as being group discussion. These are, to be sure, varieties of group communication. They are too diffuse and unstructured, however, to be considered genuine group discussions. For the purposes of this brief and general treatment, let us consider group discussion to be "the systematic, purposeful attempt of an interacting group to reach common conclusions about matters of mutual concern." If we accept such a definition, it should be clear that the kind of discussion where the subject drifts haphazardly from sports-cars to football games to the weather is not really a group discussion. It is neither systematic nor purposeful, and there is no desire to reach any kind of conclusion about things that concern the group.

It might be helpful at this point to distinguish between "group discussion" and "debate." When a group is unable to reach common conclusions, it may often happen that one or more members lose their group orientation and seek to persuade others to their point of view. They have become advocates for their cause. In many cases, debate becomes institutionalized, as in the case of parliamentary procedure, and some groups choose the method of debate as their form of communication. For group discussion to continue, however, the members of the group must co-operate rather than compete with each other, as in debate. Later in this chapter, we will discuss parliamentary procedure as a form of group communication in which the tools of debate are utilized.

Group discussion, like other forms of communication, may deal with almost any subject. Since it deals with the search for mutual agreement, however, it is helpful to think of the subjects of group discussion as questions to which the group seeks answers. In order to understand the objectives of a given group, it is convenient to classify the kinds of questions with which groups deal. These may be classified as questions of *fact, value,* or *policy.*

*Questions of fact* have to do with providing and sharing information: that is, the assumption of the question is either true or false. If a group wanted to determine whether the Germans are more militaristic today than they were at the end of World War II, they would be embarking on the discussion of a question of fact. Similarly, a discussion of "What is existentialist philosophy?" would be a question of fact. So would "What is the ideology of the Republican Party?"

We should avoid discussing questions of fact that are easily answered, such as "What is the population of San Francisco?" and "How many cars pass the corner of 18th and Main every day?" Discussable questions of fact involve the sharing of facts between the members of a group. Each member of the group may have his own interpretation of the facts. It is by no means certain that all members of a group will give the same answer to a question of fact, even though they all possess the same data.

It is interesting to note that the kinds of questions treated in law courts are almost always questions of fact. Such questions are asked as: "Did Jones murder Smith?" "Did Mrs. Brown drive recklessly?" and "Was Mr. Johnson mentally cruel to Mrs. Johnson?"

*Questions of value* superficially resemble questions of fact —but only superficially. Questions of value deal with attitudes, feelings, and sometimes with subjective judgments. They resemble questions of fact in that they are often answered "yes" or "no." The following questions are examples of questions of value:

> Do labor unions benefit society?
> Is capital punishment justified?
> Was Eisenhower a better president than Truman?
> Do fraternities and sororities have a beneficial effect on college students?

Questions of value obviously depend on facts for the determination of answers, but the facts are not an end in themselves. The objective is not to determine facts but to arrive at a common attitude or feeling.

Some questions of value are not really very discussable because they are so subjective that no data may be found to support a common conclusion. It does not make much sense to ask, "Is blue a better color than green?" or "Was Marilyn Monroe more beautiful than Elizabeth Taylor?" For there are no dependable criteria for answering such questions.

Even with facts available, questions of value are always answered in terms of the values of the group and its members. Questions of value must involve personal and group considerations of beauty, morality, goodness, and other subjective factors.

*Questions of policy* always have their focus in the future. In effect, they do not ask, "What are the facts?" or "What do we feel about this problem?" but "What should we do?"

Deliberative bodies ranging from high-school student councils to the Security Council of the United Nations find it necessary to answer questions of policy:

> Should our school district organize a junior college?
> Should the reciprocal trade treaty be extended?
> Should fraternities and sororities be abolished?
> Should India be censured for the invasion of Goa?
> Should capital punishment be abolished?

Note that some of these questions are related to previously cited questions of value. Often a group, after deciding what its feelings are, may decide to investigate the question of what action, if any, it should undertake.

It is important for a group to know what kind of a question it is they have before them. They must know whether the result of their discussion should be information, attitude, or action. It is probably clear to you by now that there is a relationship between the three kinds of questions. Determination of group attitude is often based on a previous question of fact, and determination of group action is often based on a previous question of value.

Just as there is structure in all forms of bilateral communication, so there is structure in group discussion also. Since the structural pattern in group discussion is directed by all members of the group, it is sometimes not so evident and often more difficult to control. Nevertheless, the necessity for moving logically to conclusions is perhaps even more important in group discussions than in public speaking. A disorganized or unorganized group discussion is even more chaotic and disordered than if it were a speech. In group discussion, all communicators can contribute irrelevancies, digressions, and confusion. A well-planned and thoroughly developed outline is as important in group discussion as in public speaking. The important difference between the two kinds of outlines is that the outline for a group discussion includes only mainheads and subheads. The developmental material, however, is ordinarily provided by the individual members of the group.

The same standards for the selection of structural patterns, discussed in Chapters IV and V, also apply for the selection of patterns for group discussion. The group must decide for itself which pattern is best suited to the question under consideration. Almost all of the patterns described earlier will, at some time or other, be suitable for group discussion.

In the case of a question of policy, however, there is a pattern uniquely suited to problem solving. It is a structural scheme based on man's solution of problems, from his first awareness of a difficulty to his implementation of a proposed solution. In some ways, this pattern of *reflective thinking* bears some superficial resemblance to the motivated sequence discussed earlier. The steps of a reflective thinking sequence may be specified as follows:

1. The awareness of a felt difficulty.
2. Description and definition of the problem.
3. Determination of the causes of the problem.
4. Formulation of possible solutions to the problem.
5. Selection of the best solution or combination of solutions.
6. Implementation of the chosen solution.

In the first step, the group is aware, more or less vaguely, that something is wrong in a particular area. It is not until the second step that the group undertakes to find out specifically what the trouble is by describing the situation as completely and as precisely as it can. The second step ordinarily involves considerable research, investigation, and contemplation in order to determine the exact nature of the problem. After the problem has been delineated, the group must ask itself, "How did this problem come into being?" or,

"What are the causes of our difficulty?" This third step is essential, because any proposed solution to a problem must not only alleviate the surface symptoms, but must, if possible, eradicate the underlying causes as well. Once the causes have been described, it becomes the responsibility of the group members to suggest possible solutions to the problems. The solutions must, of course, relate directly to the problem and its causes. After all possible solutions have been proposed, the group must then agree upon which solution or which combination of solutions is *most* effective in relieving the felt difficulty. Finally, the group must make a decision as to how the solution will be implemented or put into action.

In a sense, this pattern resembles the way in which a physician might undertake a diagnosis and treatment. A patient may appear at the doctor's office complaining of a stomach-ache. The doctor, however, does not begin treatment based on the simple complaint of a stomach-ache. Most of us would be quite dissatisfied with a physician who, upon hearing that we had a stomach-ache, merely said, "Take these pills," and sent us on our way. Rather, the doctor would attempt to determine the symptoms as exactly and as accurately as possible. He would try to find the location of the pain, the nature of the pain, the duration of the pain, and other symptoms that accompany the pain. Having located and described the problem, the physician might undertake, perhaps by further examinations and tests, to find the cause of such symptoms. If the doctor is satisfied that an ulcer is causing the difficulty, he must think of solutions that will alleviate the cause and its resultant pain. He might consider a special diet, surgery, bed-rest or psychotherapy, for example. After considering the various solutions, he must choose that procedure or combination of procedures that will be most effective in that case. Finally, he will implement his solution by beginning his treatment and by instructing his patient. Although this example deals with reflective thinking used as a problem-solving pattern by an individual, it should readily be seen that it is equally applicable to the group process.

We mentioned that the reflective thinking pattern is, at least superficially, similar to the motivated sequence. Although they both deal with problem solving and with movement from a felt difficulty to implemented action, there is one profound difference that should be noted. The motivated sequence has as its goal persuasion, whereas reflective thinking has as its objective co-operation through agreement.

The reader should not be left with the impression that this pattern always moves easily from the first step to the last. The success of reflective thinking is dependent upon agreement at every step of the discussion. If a group cannot agree upon the nature of a problem, it does not offer much hope to determine the cause. If a group cannot agree upon the cause of the problem, it does not make much sense to propose solutions. If a group cannot agree upon a solution, there is nothing to implement. Thus, at any stage in the process, discussion, as we have defined it, may cease and debate may begin or purposeful communication may stop altogether.

Because of the importance of interpersonal factors in group discussion, the participant must, at all times, be aware of the way he interacts with other members of the group. There are some suggestions that might prove helpful for the participant in group discussion.

First of all, the participant should approach the problem with an open-minded point of view. That is not to say that he should have no opinions about the subject. That is hardly possible. He should not, however, have made up his mind in advance. He should be receptive to new ideas. He should be willing to discard his notions in favor of those that seem superior. He should be willing to engage in compromise and conciliation. He should recognize his own biases and motives and try to minimize their influence on his own communication.

At the same time that the participant is objective about himself, he should also be as objective as possible about other participants and their ideas. He should seek to examine ideas on their merit rather than being influenced by his favorable or unfavorable biases toward his fellow communicators.

Closely related to the participant's objectivity is his sense of co-operation. He should always be aware that his objective is not to persuade others to his beliefs but rather to seek a mutually satisfactory solution to a common problem. The ideal discussion participant sublimates his personal interest in the interests of the group. He seeks to advance group goals rather than his own goals.

The participant should also be tactful and courteous. He should not avoid the honest presentation of his views, in the interests of sweetness and light, but he should seek to present his views without offending other members of the group. He should be able to disagree without incurring animosity, threatening others, or offending feelings.

It should be the responsibility of the group member to see that his contributions are relevant, not only to the discussion question but to the point immediately under consideration. Since discussion is a group effort, it should be the responsibility of each member to see that the discussion adheres to its structural pattern and does not wander off into side-roads.

The group member must tread carefully the line between underparticipation and overparticipation. The participant should neither be so dominant that he tends to monopolize discussion, nor so inhibited that his point of view is not expressed. A good rule to follow is: Talk when you have a relevant contribution to make, but make sure you do not deprive others of their opportunity to contribute. It seems almost unnecessary to add that the discussion participant should be as well informed as possible on the question under discussion. Even when a group member already has some knowledge of the question, he will often find it helpful to supplement it with further research and investigation.

In almost every discussion group, someone will be selected or designated as the leader or chairman of the group. Since it is his responsibility to direct the discussion, the role he plays is probably more important than that of any other participant. He should follow all the suggestions listed for the participants. In addition, there are some suggestions that apply uniquely to the role of discussion leader.

Some responsibilities almost automatically become those of the discussion leader. Although all members of the group should participate in the framing and wording of the discussion question and the preparation of a group outline, the ultimate responsibility for the formulation of a question and an outline will, ordinarily, fall to the discussion leader.

The preparation and presentation of an introduction to the discussion is also his responsibility. In its essentials, the introduction to a group discussion does not differ substantially from that of a speech. The standards for developing an introduction have been outlined in Chapter IV.

In addition to the assigned tasks of the leader, there are some personal characteristics he should possess or develop. First of all, he should know as much—or more—about the question as any other member of the group. A leader who is deficient in knowledge of the subject cannot hope to guide or direct a discussion. How could he know if contributions are irrelevant or when a point has been exhausted?

The discussion leader should be as impartial as possible. If any member of the group senses that the leader shows partiality towards any other participant, the hopes of the leader's exercising the function of conciliator or moderator may well be diminished. The history of negotiations is replete with examples of meetings that have disintegrated because one side or the other accused a chairman of bias.

The discussion leader should have a sense of structure of the discussion. He should be able to recognize when contributions are irrelevant or tangential. He should be able to recognize when a point has been adequately covered. He should then summarize that point, and, through the use of transition, move on to the next point.

Another important role the discussion leader should play is that of clarifying the discussion. When a participant makes a contribution that is not completely clear, it should be the leader's responsibility to restate the remark so it is clear, or to question the participant tactfully to clarify the meaning.

The leader should seek to regulate the amount of discussion contributed by group members. He should try to achieve approximately equal participation, which means that he should encourage the inhibited member to participate, perhaps by directing questions to him. He should see to it that other members do not dominate the discussion by excessive contributions. He should be careful, however, not to offend any participant in working toward equitable participation.

The discussion leader should have some skills that enable him to resolve conflict. At any point in the discussion, when productive communication seems to be blocked by disagreement, he should make a sincere attempt to keep the discussion moving by suggesting a compromise that might be acceptable to all group members. If it is not possible to resolve the conflict, he should state the various points of view as clearly as possible so that the exact nature of the differences are evident to all members.

In general, it should be the responsibility of the discussion leader to keep the discussion moving. He should ask the proper questions and make the proper statements that allow the discussion to proceed from point to point. Finally, when the discussion has gone as far as it can go, he should summarize the conclusions of the group and indicate which issues are still unresolved.

Before we close our examination of group discussion, it should be noted that a group discussion may be either *internally oriented* or *externally oriented*. That is, the discussion may be carried on entirely for the benefit of the participants, or it may be presented before, and for the benefit of, the public audience. All of the points made in this section apply as much to an externally oriented group as to an internally oriented group. The participants, however, will always be aware of the presence of an audience and will recognize that the development of the discussion must be adapted to the general listeners as well as to the participants. The term *public discussion* is often used to describe the externally oriented group process.

There are two types of public discussion that are made use of frequently. Perhaps the most common is the *panel discussion,* which is a group discussion as we have described it in this chapter except that it is carried on for the benefit of an audience. Many of the discussion programs seen and heard on radio and television are of this type.

Another commonly used form of public discussion is the *open forum.* The open forum may appear by itself or it may follow some other form of bilateral or multilateral communication. Open forums can be conducted as question-and-answer sessions following a speech, at which time members of the audience or members of a selected panel may direct questions to the speaker. Panel discussions are often followed by open forums in which the audience is allowed to engage in general discussion with the primary participants. When two or more speakers appear together in a symposium, the opportunity is often provided for them to discuss and question the ideas that have been developed.

## PARLIAMENTARY COMMUNICATION

When group discussion is not feasible, practical, or desirable, parliamentary communication is the most common form of group communication. Although parliamentary communication is multilateral and depends on personal interaction, to some degree its uses and its underlying assumptions are quite different from those of group discussion. Parliamentary procedure is used when the group is too large to work its problems out through the more intimate and personal procedure of group discussion. The parliamentary method is often used when a group has been unable to reach agreement through discussion. When agreement is not reached in discussion, the participants frequently turn to debate, and parliamentary communication is a form of debate. The questions with which parliamentary communication deals are almost always questions of policy.

Since parliamentary procedure is a type of debate, the assumptions on which it is based are quite different from those of group discussion. Where group discussion assumes that decision-making will occur through mutual co-operation and agreement, parliamentary procedures assume that decision-making will occur through persuasion and the majority vote. Parliamentary procedure does not assume that all members of the group should accede to the decisions of the group.

Although parliamentary communication and group discussion operate on different sets of assumptions and make use of different methodologies, their orientations are very much alike. Both forms of communication are democratic in their outlook. Both agree that all voices should be heard, that the rights of both the majority and minority will be protected, and that all members of the group have equal opportunity to participate in the decision-making process. Parliamentary communication is more formal and more institutionalized than group discussion, and makes use of public speaking as its primary communicative tool.

Parliamentary communication is probably more familiar to readers than is group discussion. At every level of our society, from the election of the president of the third-grade class to the deliberations of the United States Senate, parliamentary procedure is used as a means of making decisions. We have all made use of parliamentary procedure, at one time or another, in clubs, classes, fraternities, church groups, and other organizations. Unfortunately, parliamentary communication is sometimes so inept that it impedes rather than assists the process of decision-making.

The view is often held that parliamentary procedure is a means of frustrating the will of the individual by hedging him in with a complicated set of rules. It is, unfortunately, true that something like that happens when there are great discrepancies in skill at parliamentary procedure among members of a group. It therefore should be the responsibility of all members of a group to have at least minimal knowledge of the rules of parliamentary communication so that business may proceed smoothly. At the same time, group members should avoid becoming infatuated with procedure for its own sake. Members of deliberative groups should not get involved in playing parliamentary games; their aim is to conduct serious business. Furthermore, a group should not use a set of rules that is needlessly complicated. Such organizations as the United States Senate, the House of Representatives, and the United Nations need sets of rules that, in their published form, are several inches thick. It would be foolish for the Ladies' Garden Club, however, to make use of a detailed and complex set of rules. If a group is fairly informal, its parliamentary rules may be treated in the same way. There is no need for members of groups to memorize *Robert's Rules of Order* or some other code, and to insist upon applying it exactly under all circumstances. It should be kept in mind that the function of parliamentary communication is to make it easier, not harder, to reach decisions.

Group members should know some of the simple rules of parliamentary law in order to conduct business in an orderly manner, to assure that the will of the majority predominates, and to protect the rights of the minority. Rules of parliamentary procedure are derived from centuries of observation and experimentation that have made relatively evident certain principles that should guide human beings in their conduct when courses of action are decided by groups rather than by individuals. These rules are man-made, but by many men over many centuries, rather than being "made up" at one time by a single individual.

*Four basic principles should govern all group action:* expediency, or the efficient disposition of business; courtesy and consideration toward all; rule of the majority; and protection of the minority.

*Expediency* demands that only one thing at a time should be considered, or "before the house." If this "one thing" has parts or modifications, or if the will of the group is to be tested on any phase of it, such as change of wording or limiting of debate, these parts should be so arranged that they will be subsidiary in nature. Logically, each of them should, depending on its nature, have a place in the order of precedence, and should be acted upon only in that order. All subsidiary matters should find their way in systematic order back to the main problem, or thesis. Business should not lag, but should always move forward.

*Courtesy* is a governing rule and principle of human conduct everywhere. It has no more cause to be ignored in group legislation than elsewhere. Every act and every word should be considered in the light of its conforming to courteous conduct. This is true not only in the interest of consideration for others, but also on the purely selfish basis of getting results. The speaker who fails to be courteous will offend and antagonize other members of the group so that they refuse to support him even when he is right. If he is courteous, he will receive support.

*Rule of the majority* is an accepted principle of the democratic way of life. That majority may be described for special reasons as simple (one more than half), two-thirds, or three-quarters. It is nevertheless a majority. And upon subscription to this principle depends true democracy. It is easy enough for us to accept this philosophy when we are one of the majority, but not so easy when we are in the minority. A member of the minority may feel that he is so utterly right in his view that only a very foolish group of persons could hold opposite opinions. He may be right—or he may be wrong in spite of the strength of his conviction. In any case, if he is to act in accordance with democratic principles, he will accept the will of the majority as gracefully as possible and abide by it— at least until he can make the majority as wise as he and so cause them to change their will. Parliamentary rules are formulated on this principle; be conscious of it always.

Equally important, though not so widely recognized, is the principle of *protection of the minority*. The minority must yield; but it must also be considered and protected. The will of the majority may be in terms of the special interests of members of the majority group; and such interests may be destructive of the welfare of the minority members. True democracy may be said to be that state in which both parties receive full consideration; but in which, all else being equal, the majority desire prevails. Rules that are designed to protect the minority, as well as to accomplish other ends, are: right of amendment; referring to committee; postponement of consideration; vote by roll call; two-thirds or three-quarters majority for passage.

These four principles should guide every chairman of a meeting in making his decisions and applying his remarks, but they should be of equal force in governing the conduct of all members. If both parties will temper their awareness of these principles with good taste and sound judgment, and if both will familiarize themselves with the main governing rules, parliamentary procedure will comply with its proper intent and function: the efficient and just determination of courses of action.

Since we neither presume nor desire to do more in this chapter than make the reader aware of the principles and practical, everyday rules of procedure, we intentionally list only those rules most commonly used. Those who expect to find themselves in situations where more intricate combinations of rules will be applied can easily find them listed in other sources.

The normal order of procedure in business meetings is:

Reading of minutes
Reports of officers and committees
Unfinished business from preceding meetings
New business

*The purpose of reading minutes* is to bring before the assembly a record of their proceedings of the preceding meeting. Since this record is subject to error, it is brought before the main body for their approval. Either in its original form or as corrected by them, it then becomes a record to which they may refer at any later time for proof of action.

*Reports of officers and committees* are for the purpose of establishing the present state of the organization and determining progress made on problems referred to committees.

The treasurer gives his financial report, including amounts on hand and disbursed, income, uncollected dues, or need for more funds for specific obligations. The vice-president or the program chairman (frequently one and the same person) reports on plans for future meetings or events. A committee may have been appointed to investigate some matter of concern to the organization, perhaps even only the availability and cost of a place to hold a class dance or banquet. It makes its report at this point in the meeting. Officers and committees constitute a kind of administrative staff for any organization, and it is proper for them to render reports early in every meeting so that futher "business" or "work" of the organization may proceed intelligently from the status quo to things desired.

*Unfinished business* naturally should be completed before new problems are considered.

"Unfinished" literally means *unfinished*. That is, such business represents projects attempted and not finished at some previous meeting. Lack of time or of information may have prevented final action, so that the matter was "postponed indefinitely" or "laid on the table till the next meeting." Such business is taken out of its "postponement" either by the chair or by motion from a member.

*New business* ordinarily assumes the form of bringing forward problems, discussing them, and proposing action. Sometimes proposed action is the first step; but very often a problem will receive broad statement by the chairman or a member, be discussed in general before specific action is proposed, then crystallize into the offering of motions.

Since business in parliamentary groups is largely conducted through the presentation of motions that are voted on, it is helpful to consider the various classes of motions and the way in which they are used. It is useful to think of motions in terms of the *main motions* and the *secondary motions*. The main motion is the motion dealing with the substance of the proposal for action. "I move that the Student Council donate $500 to the Foreign Student Fund," is a *general main motion* in that it proposes an action to be undertaken by the group. A motion to reconsider a previously proposed course of action is a *specific main motion.* It may be applied to any proposal but it deals with the actual substance of the proposal. Less commonly used specific main motions are the motions to rescind, to resume consideration, and to create orders.

The secondary motions represent actions that may be taken to dispose of the main motion. There are three classes of secondary motions: *privileged motions, incidental motions,* and *subsidiary motions.* The privileged motions concern themselves with the privileges of members. They must be decided before the main question is disposed of. The most common forms of privileged motions are the *motion to adjourn,* whose purpose is to terminate the meeting; *motion to recess,* whose purpose is to permit an interlude in the meeting; and the *question of privilege,* whose purpose is to secure immediate action on a matter that concerns the privileges and conveniences of the group or its individual members. A request that the chairman speak more loudly is a question of privilege. Privileged motions have precedence over main motions. *Precedence* means that any privileged motion may be made while a main motion is being considered.

*Incidental motions* are higher in precedence than main motions, but lower than privileged motions. Incidental motions arise out of the proposed action but are only incidentally related. There are many kinds of incidental motions. The most common, however, are an *appeal from the decision of the chairman,* a *point of order,* which occurs when a member wishes to note any question of procedure; a *parliamentary inquiry,* which is really a request for information; and a *motion to withdraw a motion.*

*Subsidiary motions* have the lowest order of precedence, except for main motions. Subsidiary motions are applied to other motions in order to modify them, to dispose of them

| ORDER OF PRECEDENCE | CAN IN-TERRUPT SPEAKER? | REQUIRES A SECOND? | DEBAT-ABLE? |
|---|---|---|---|
| *I. Privileged Motions* | | | |
| 1. Adjourn | no | yes | no |
| 2. Recess | no | yes | no |
| 3. Question of Privilege | yes | no | no |
| *II. Subsidiary Motions* | | | |
| 4. Postpone Temporarily (Lay on the table) | no | yes | no |
| 5. Vote Immediately (Previous question) | no | yes | no |
| 6. Limit Debate | no | yes | no |
| 7. Postpone Definitely | no | yes | yes$^2$ |
| 8. Refer to Committee | no | yes | yes$^2$ |
| 9. Amend | no | yes | yes |
| 10. Postpone Indefinitely | no | yes | yes |
| *III. Main Motions* | | | |
| 11. (a) A General Main Motion | no | yes | yes |
| (b) Specific Main Motions | | | |
| Reconsider | yes | yes | yes |

$^2$ Restricted.
$^3$ After change in parliamentary situation.

## Governing Motions

| Amendable? | Vote Required? | Applies to What Motions? | Motion Can Have What Applied to It (in Addition to Withdraw?) | Can Be Renewed |
|---|---|---|---|---|
| no | majority | no other motion | no other motion | yes³ |
| yes² | majority | no other motion | amend² | yes³ |
| no | no vote | no other motion | no other motion | yes³ |
| no | majority | main, amend, appeal | no other motion | yes³ |
| no | two-thirds | debatable motions | no other motion | yes³ |
| yes² | two-thirds | debatable motions | amend² | yes³ |
| yes² | majority | main motion | amend,² vote immediately, limit debate | yes³ |
| yes² | majority | main, amend | vote immediately, limit debate | yes³ |
| yes | majority | variable in form | subsidiary motions, reconsider | no |
| no | majority | main motion | vote immediately, limit debate | no |
| yes | majority | no motion | specific main, subsidiary, object to consideration | no |
| no | majority | main, amend, appeal | vote immediately, limit debate, postpone definitely | no |

| ORDER OF PRECEDENCE | CAN IN-TERRUPT SPEAKER? | REQUIRES A SECOND? | DEBAT-ABLE? |
|---|---|---|---|
| *Specific Main Motions (Cont.)* | | | |
| Rescind | no | yes | yes |
| Resume Consideration | no | yes | no |
| Create Orders | no | yes | yes[2] |
| **IV.** *Incidental Motions* | | | |
| Appeal | yes | yes | yes |
| Point of Order | yes | no | no |
| Parliamentary Inquiry | yes | no | no |
| Withdraw a Motion | no | no | no |
| Suspend Rules | no | yes | no |
| Object to Consideration | yes | no | no |
| Division of a Question | no | no | no |
| Division of Assembly | yes | no | no |

[2] Restricted.

# Governing Motions

| Amendable? | Vote Required? | Applies to What Motions? | Motion Can Have What Applied to It (in Addition to Withdraw?) | Can Be Renewed |
|---|---|---|---|---|
| no | majority | main motion | all subsidiary motions | no |
| no | majority | main, amend, appeal | no other motion | yes[3] |
| yes[2] | majority | main motion | amend | yes[3] |
| no | tie or majority | decision of chair | reconsider, limit debate, vote immediately, postpone temporarily or definitely | no |
| no | no vote | any error | no other motion | no |
| no | no vote | no motion | no other motion | no |
| no | no vote | all motions | none | yes[3] |
| no | two-thirds | no motion | no other motion | no |
| no | two-thirds neg. | main motion | no other motion | yes[3] |
| no | no vote | main, amend | no other motion | no |
| no | no vote | voice votes | no other motion | no |

[3] After change in parliamentary situation.

without voting, or to move immediately to a vote. Frequently used subsidiary motions include motions *to postpone temporarily* (lay on the table), *to vote immediately* (previous question), *to limit debate,* and *to refer to committee.*

The *motion to amend* is a subsidiary motion that is sometimes vexing for beginning parliamentarians. It is useful to remember that only one amendment to a motion may be before a group at any time. No more than one amendment to an amendment may be before a group at any time. Amendments to motions are sometimes called *first-order amendments* and amendments to amendments are called *second-order amendments.* Only one first-order and one second-order amendment may be on the floor at one time. After a first-order or second-order amendment has been accepted or rejected, another may be considered. There is no limit to the number of amendments that may be considered in succession. Second-order amendments must be voted on before first-order amendments. First-order amendments must be voted on before the main motion. If the amendment is rejected, there is no change in the motion. If the amendment is accepted, the main motion must be voted on *as amended.*

With a knowledge of the simpler rules of parliamentary communication, it should be possible for students of group communication to engage in purposeful decision-making. Our objective has not been to present a detailed guide to parliamentary law. Instead, it is our hope that these suggestions will be helpful to you in participating in parliamentary communication.

*The Principal Rules Governing Motions,* reprinted above, will be helpful to you when questions about parliamentary procedure arise.[1]

[1] Alice F. Sturgis, *Sturgis Standard Code of Parliamentary Procedure* (New York: McGraw-Hill, Inc., 1950). Reprinted with the permission of the publisher.

BARNLUND, DEAN C., AND HAIMAN, FRANKLYN S. *The Dynamics of Discussion.* Boston: Houghton Mifflin Company, 1960.

BRADEN, WALDO W., AND BRADENBURG, EARNEST. *Oral Decision-Making.* New York: Harper & Brothers, 1955, Parts I and II.

GULLEY, HALBERT E. *Discussion, Conference, and Group Process.* New York: Henry Holt & Company, 1960.

KELTNER, JOHN W. *Group Discussion Processes.* New York: Longman Green & Co., 1957.

ROBERT, H. M. *Robert's Rules of Order.* Chicago: Scott, Foresman & Company, 1951.

STURGIS, ALICE F. *Sturgis Standard Code of Parliamentary Procedure.* New York: McGraw-Hill Book Company, Inc., 1950.

————. *Learning Parliamentary Procedure.* New York: McGraw-Hill Book Company, Inc., 1953.

# CHAPTER XI

# Special Forms of Speech

T HE PURPOSE OF THIS CHAPTER is to present selected prac- tical suggestions for some special forms of oral com- munication. All the theoretical materials and instructional materials, presented in earlier chapters, are completely ap- plicable to any of the forms of communication that will be discussed here. We have, however, singled out some of the more common kinds of speeches you might be called upon to present. Most of them are "special" in the sense that they are not quite like the longer, more detailed speeches we have referred to earlier and that they tend to be presented on "special" occasions. If you have mastered the fundamentals of general oral communication, these special forms of speech should pose no problem for you.

## SPEECHES OF INTRODUCTION

Perhaps you will prepare and present speeches of intro- duction more frequently than any other type of speech. Most persons are more often called on to introduce other speakers than they are to speak themselves. Although the speech of introduction is common, it is often badly done. An unsatisfactory introduction, unfortunately, creates a difficult situation for the speaker who follows. Although most introductions are fairly brief, they should not be presented in a routine and off-hand manner. They deserve special consideration.

The obligation of anyone introducing a speaker is first of all to secure the attention of the audience. He is the "goat," as it were, who stands and waits for a noisy audience to come to order, for stragglers to find their places and become quiet, for extra chairs to be brought in so that all may be seated, for those dozen last-minute adjustments that someone should have made hours earlier but overlooked. He is the one who must consume time by being jovial, and possibly funny, while late-comers continue to rattle doors and clump down the aisles, until such time as, in his judgment, he has before him the approximate totality of the group, and until he has from them at least an outward show of respectful attention.

His next task, after he is sure the attention is actual, is to create a unity of attitude. He may do this by one ingenious stroke of humor, by making reference to the purpose of their gathering, by polite banter, and by numerous other means.

Assuming the audience is relatively unified and attentive, he must then proceed to establish the integrity of the speaker. Whatever confidence he may have secured in himself is to some degree a recommendation for whomever he introduces, for every act of introduction, public or private, is basically a seal of approval. Beyond this are the more directly active agents of referring to occupation, hobby, rank, works, reputation, and special attributes of the person to speak. The task may be done obviously and awkwardly, or it may be done adroitly. The latter quality is achieved through weaving select information about the speaker into a pattern of dramatic interest, perhaps including humor, which causes the audience to empathize with him through his life experiences and qualities, rather than simply listing his qualities and achievements perfunctorily as if it were the thing to do and that were your only reason for doing it. The audience must feel in the introducer a sincere interest in and enthusiasm for the person introduced.

Although the person doing the introducing should do all in his power to give the speaker every advantage that his ability warrants, he ought to be equally cautious not to give the speaker a reputation that he cannot exemplify in performance. This may best be avoided if the introducer will emphasize the speaker's knowledge in a given field, his distinctive work, his fame—anything but his speaking ability! If a speaker cannot fulfill what the audience has been led to expect of him, then the introduction has done him positive harm. It is a point of fine judgment to be able to give a speaker the "build-up" he deserves, but not to build him up to an audience "let-down."

If you tell jokes about the speaker, or relate humorous incidents of which he has been a part, be sure they establish a friendly feeling toward him rather than an attitude of laughing at him. Humor of a personal nature, if well chosen, is one of the subtlest and most effective means of elevating a speaker; but error of choice is one of the most certain and devastating roads to his derogation.

Do not infringe on your guest's time. He is giving the speech, not you. The time you consume will be determined by the period necessary to secure audience attention and unity, by the opportunity and necessity of giving information about the speaker, and by the relative leisure of the occasion. One of the authors once heard a pompous gentleman show off for fifteen minutes before presenting a well-known and highly respected speaker to an audience. Two or three minutes would have been in far better taste.

Do not trespass on the speaker's subject. He has his own plan of attack (we hope!) and any violation of his territory may upset his plans. Better by far to shun his subject than to mar it for him. Whether you announce his subject, title, or thesis should depend upon his preference. Ask him.

Suit your own relative formality of behavior to what you may expect of him and to the probable spirit of his remarks. Be always friendly, usually jovial, rarely undignified, invariably gracious; but never, if you can avoid it, put the audience into a mood contrary to that which his remarks would stimulate.

Subordinate yourself to the speaker in every way. That is, you, as we said before, are the "goat." Just as you must endure the discomfort of awkward waiting and adjustments, so does courtesy demand that you refrain from stealing the show from your guest. He is the main actor; yours is a bit part. Even though you may be a much better speaker than he, you should not allow the audience to become conscious of the fact. Such a restriction does not mean that you should deliberately speak poorly or give an unfortunate impression of yourself. It means that the power you possess should not be used to make yourself the center of the picture, but to turn all attention upon the speaker.

Outline your main remarks. The entire introductory procedure ought to be highly flexible, but the liberty of adjustment is derived from the restraint of having a plan and a definiteness of purpose. Unless your words are exceedingly brief, plan three or four main headings to act as points of dependence; and adhere to the general movement of what you have prepared.

*Present* the speaker. All too often a chairman will do reasonably good work up to the point of actually yielding the floor, but sits down without uttering the final sentence that signifies he has finished and that the speaker may begin. In lacking a concluding sentence, he fails to be gracious. One should not employ stereotyped phrases; but if he is pleased to introduce the speaker, he ought to say so.

## ANNOUNCEMENTS

A form of public speaking that the average person is sure to find occasion to use frequently throughout life is the making of announcements. Basically, there is no essential difference between the announcement and other organized efforts of oral communication. It is an attempt to convey an idea or to secure belief or action from listeners. It is distinguished from other forms solely by its brevity. But this difference, and the force it has in modifying normal procedures, is sufficient to warrant special consideration of it.

If brevity is the distinguishing feature of the announcement speech, the foremost admonition is, "Be brief." If there is one occasion which more than any other demands absolute adherence to the time allotted you, it is that on which you are permitted to announce some event or opportunity. It is "so very easy" to use "only a few extra minutes"; and it is also *"so very exasperating"* to a chairman or master of ceremonies to have several persons do that on the same day so that the real purpose of the meeting, or program, is spoiled by having to be forced into only half the time it should be given. Therefore, plan your remarks and control them to suit your time allotment.

However, some matters are so important, or of such a nature, that too great stress on brevity may not allow justice to be done. Consider carefully how much time your announcement needs and deserves. If it can be done in a single sentence, and be done well, do not use two. For example, "I just want to remind the members of the Executive Council that our regular monthly meeting is here, next Thursday evening, at 7:30." If it requires the giving of detailed information, perhaps also the persuasion to come, buy, give, support, or sell, then it is a matter of taste, judgment, and ingenuity to so arrange and develop the thought and material as to accomplish your end without exceeding either the time allotted or the patience of your hearers.

Most of these procedures will ordinarily assume the form of mainheads and general processes, for other materials of development would consume too much time. However, instances, statistics, and quotations may be used frequently if special care is taken to make them brief, pointed, and interesting. Detailed illustrations should rarely be used. Mainheads, though, should invariably be present in longer announcements, as should consciousness of, and eventual statement or implication of, thesis. The leading points of emphasis are the mainheads; the purpose is the thesis.

Thus it will be evident that the outline of an announcement speech may resemble the general form of that for any other speech. The basic modification is made in reduction of materials. What one is denied in the way of "cumulation," however, he accomplishes through heightened attention, clarity, and repetition.

All in all, the announcement is a streamlined model of a regular speech. It must be brief; it must emphasize clarity; it must have definiteness of purpose; it must be organized.

## SPEECHES OF WELCOME, RESPONSE, AND ACCEPTANCE

You may often be called upon to welcome a person or a group. We have all seen and heard speeches of response presented at high, ceremonial state occasions such as a speech by the President of the United States welcoming the President of France. However, speeches of welcome are heard on much humbler occasions. The president of a student council may welcome a group of visiting high-school students to a college or university campus. As a member of a club, you may be asked to extend a welcome to a visiting dignitary on behalf of your group. No matter what the level of the meeting or the dignity of the occasion, a speech of welcome should express cordiality and a spirit of genuine hospitality and welcome. It should make reference to the special nature of the occasion. If possible, sincere praise should be directed to the accomplishments and the status of the guests. Above all, it should make the guests feel glad to be there.

Speeches of response are sometimes presented by a guest, or representative of a group, after a speech of welcome has been given. In a speech of response, the recipient must tread a thin line between what might seem to be conceit and what might seem to be undue modesty. He must seem worthy of the praise extended in a speech of welcome, but he should not seem to applaud himself and the group he represents. He should not, however, be so deferential as to seem to be undeserving of the praise extended him. If at all possible, the speech of response should convey the same tone, dignity, or informality of humor or seriousness as the speech of welcome.

Many persons are called upon to speak when special honors, gifts, or awards are given them. The occasions for speeches of acceptance range from the election-night speech of a new President of the United States to a speech accepting a going-away gift. Above all, such speeches should indicate the speaker's gratitude and appreciation. If other persons have been involved in the enterprise for which the recipient is being honored, he should recognize their contributions and thank them for the part they have played. A speech of acceptance should be simple, brief, and sincere.

## RADIO AND TELEVISION SPEAKING

*(This section was prepared especially for this edition
by John R. Shepherd, University of Oregon.)*

The general principles of good speech apply equally to the special conditions that exist in speaking on radio or television. The best advice that can be given to the speaker upon his arrival in the studio is to "forget about the medium and concentrate on what you have to say." This does not mean, of course, that the same performer would not have been more effective if he had understood some of the particular attributes of the mass media.

With these ideas in mind, we have a clear statement of the objectives of this section—to help you understand broadcasting a little better in order for you to take full advantage of the skills you already possess. Rather than make an attempt to list numbers of "do's and don'ts," we will consider the matter from the standpoint of principles, and articulate those which make it possible for you to capitalize on your personal assets, as well as those of the medium in which you work.

Let us begin by recognizing that radio *is* different from television. It is not, as some seem to suggest, television without pictures! Similarly, radio and television are both different from the platform. It is because of the similarities of these media that the good principles of one are applicable to the other. The question that is of prime concern to us here is what do we have to do in order to make allowances for the *differences* that do exist?

*Principle One: When speaking on the radio, it is essential to increase the intensity of delivery.* Good broadcasters learn early in their experience that the intensity with which they deliver their ideas has much to do with the amount that is communicated. Very probably you have had experience with tape recordings of your voice that demonstrated that, whereas you thought you were making adequate use of variety and emphasis, the recording, when played back, showed your voice sounded curiously flat and atonal. You have demonstrated that verbal communication, without visual cues to stimulate and direct you, calls for what might ordinarily be judged excessive intensity in the delivery. Although "intensity," as used here, relates directly to vocal emphasis, it should be understood that this is not achieved solely through stress, but also is a function of the way in which you group ideas. The combination of more vocal emphasis, with attention to the comprehension and vocal grouping of ideas, results in a kind of intensity that is reflected directly in the delivery. It is this intensity—*conviction* if you wish—which seems to be one of the most important factors in effective performance on the radio.

*Principle Two: In speaking on the radio or on television, it is imperative to consider the fact that your audience is not committed.* When a person enters a hall to hear a public lecture, he has committed himself to remain at least until an opportunity is presented for him to escape! But the situation in the home gives complete freedom of movement to the audience. Your listener or viewer is not constrained in any way to listen to you, unless it be through the compelling ideas you present. This peculiar freedom of action means that you must make each of your ideas perfectly clear, and keep organization essentially simple. The complex weaving of ideas that might succeed in a platform presentation could be deadly to your cause on radio or television. In the conventional speaking situation, about the only result you might get from bemusing your audience with a complex statement would be that the listener could begin to examine the ridiculous hat of the lady sitting in front. In the case of broadcasting that same statement, however, the result could be that some members of your audience might decide this is the opportunity to check the icebox. As every broadcaster knows, once the viewer or listener has broken his relationship with the receiver, he is potentially lost as an audience.

Related to this problem of how the broadcast message is received, we must consider the fact that there is little opportunity for the audience to *verify* information put forth by the broadcast speaker. In the case of the platform speech, the audience ordinarily feels it has some opportunity of either questioning or talking with the speaker, but with the broadcast message it is most unusual that such an opportunity exists. The speaker is continuously inaccessible to the television and radio audience. The kind of verification demanded by the audience gives rise to the observation that no single device is more helpful to a speaker utilizing the mass media than the use of restatement and repetition, keeping the ideas always clear and concrete.

*Principle Three: The television camera is additive, and tends to enlarge and amplify all that it sees.* What this means is that you will find the camera will amplify all aspects of the total performance, regardless of what this may be, desirable or not. The classic example observed by those who first perform on television is the realization of how sensitive the camera is to the lack of eye contact. We have all had the uncomfortable experience of watching a performer read from a teleprompter, and it is a naive person indeed who believes that he can fool the sophisticated audiences of today. The very slight angle required to use the teleprompter *is* communicated—and this is a function of the additive nature of the camera. (Although of less immediate importance to the speaker, but still a good demonstration of the principle, relatively short distances between objects, people, and visual aids become chasms of yawning space on the air.) If the performer attempts surreptitiously to use his notes, the camera will catch this and enlarge it accordingly. If he uses as much emphasis and intensity on television as he would on radio, the result is very likely to be an obvious and stilted kind of performance. Aristotle's classical admonition, "Great art conceals art," is a practical rule for the television speaker to observe.

Look on the other side of the coin, and think how this characteristic of television is so beautifully adapted to help the speaker who is really observing the principles of good speech. A good speaker may approach the medium with complete confidence, knowing that because of the characteristics we have been discussing, he can expect even his most subtle mood or emotion to be communicated to his audience.

*Principle Four: The camera is selective and can therefore direct the audience.* Related to the consideration of the additive function of the camera, we should also consider the fact that the camera is selective; it can become a kind of extension of the audience and control that audience through movement. What does the platform speaker do when he is anxious to get into closer contact with his audience? He may lean forward, or perhaps step from behind the lectern to the front of it. But the distance that remains is still great, and at best he remains a small figure, high up on a platform, dislocated in space from the audience. On television, however, there is no reason why each person in the audience cannot be brought to a face-to-face relationship with the speaker. If, before the performance, the speaker indicates there is a point he would like to emphasize, it is a simple matter for the director either to move the camera or to change the lens in order to meet these requirements.

*Principle Five: Since television is a visual medium itself, "visual aids" must be integrated and not overlaid.* In connection with any discussion of techniques, we should note the use of visual materials on television. In platform speaking, we have become accustomed to the idea that "visual aids" are to be used as illustrative of points made in the talk. In a sense, the use of a chart or graph requires some kind of break between the speaker and the audience in order to introduce the visual presentation. In television presentation, however, it is a waste of the potentialities of the medium to let the screen simply become a kind of static stand onto which illustrations are flashed. This will occur if we approach the use of visuals on television in the same way we use them on the platform. In television speaking, we have the singular opportunity to do two things at once—to weld the auditory and the visual image, moving from speaker to visual image to visual image to speaker without interruption or disturbance to the communicative structure. On television, by means of a number of technical devices and procedures, a speaker can present immediate analysis of information contained on a chart or graph, even while that visual is being developed on the screen before the eyes of the audience. If you think for a moment of the difficulties of using motion pictures in a platform presentation, and then contrast this with how easy they are to use on television for the same purpose, one begins to see the potential offered by the medium. It is the wise speaker who discusses the problem of visual treatment of his subject with the producer of the program well in advance of final planning. You will find that the personnel of the station will be pleased to help you with your preparation—after all, it makes their work easier and your performance better, both of which are their primary objectives.

*Principle Six: When performing on television or radio, one speaks to individuals.* We need to consider what the relationship of a radio or television speaker is to his *real* audience. Note that we have stressed the "real" in contrast to what is often assumed to be the audience for these media. We glibly speak of "mass media" and "mass audiences," thereby indoctrinating performers into thinking of their audiences in this

2 3 9

way. The fact is that nothing could be further from the truth. Put this idea to test this evening while you are watching television or listening to the radio. Ask yourself if you really are a "mass audience" and what you will find is that what is erroneously thought to be "mass" is, in fact, nothing more than multiples of "you"! The realization of the one-to-one relationship of the performer to his audience has always been the secret of success for the best performers in broadcasting, and it is of particular importance to the public speaker. In spite of how obvious this may be to you now, you will find yourself slipping into old ideas about your audience the moment you see the camera lights come on or the technician give the cue that you are on the air. Keep in mind constantly that you are talking with that good, warm, interested, and personal friend, *the audience*—a single viewer, or at most, a handful of viewers. And although he may be multiplied hundreds, or thousands of times over, you *are* talking to him *individually* and *personally*.

Research and demonstration in recent years have made abundantly clear that broadcast media are effective persuasive devices. We have known for centuries what "the good man speaking well" is capable of doing. When the two are brought together, each capitalizing on the potentialities of the other, we have made possible a kind of performing situation that could produce results of untold value to the human race.

CHAPTER **XII**

# *Reading Aloud*

"**J**OHNNY CAN'T READ" is a complaint against American education full of too much truth for comfort. Although it probably is not true that modern educational methods are producing a higher percentage of poor readers than the methods of "the good old days," it is true that many young people have not put forth the effort to develop skills necessary for reading with either speed or a high degree of comprehension. Blame the students, blame the teachers, blame the methods, blame all three; the fact is that no one has found the solution for developing a high percentage of skilled, silent readers.

Those who can read aloud effectively are still fewer. It is axiomatic that unless a person can read well silently, he will not read well aloud. But it is also true that some of our best artists in reading aloud have not developed the special skills for reading rapidly and at high comprehension silently. In fact, experience indicates that many of those subject to oral-reading exercises early in their training have difficulty in avoiding a kind of subvocalizing of words in their normal silent reading, and are thus slowed down in rate even though their comprehension may be high. This means not only that oral and silent reading are sufficiently different from each other that a reader may have skill in one and not in the other, but also that they have many elements in common, so that improvement in one may enhance one's ability in the other. Certainly the desirable state of affairs is to be proficient in both.

Our concern in this chapter, of course, is guidance in achieving competency, even artistry, in reading aloud. At its best, reading aloud may justifiably be called an *art of interpretation;* for, in the larger sense, anything done well is an art, and the particular process of understanding fully the printed page, and, through the medium of voice and body, conveying that meaning and an appropriate degree of feeling to others, is assuredly an interpretative art, a highly creative one. Somewhere short of the artistic level of interpretative performance is a practical level of respectable competency, which every person who has the intelligence to strive for probably has the inherent potential to achieve. The only reason that so few attain even this practical modicum is that few put forth diligent and systematic effort to do so. Many persons wish in a general way that they might read well; but most of them possess no strong desire to acquire the skill and no clear concept of how to proceed if they did.

Yet the importance of reading well, silently or aloud, is so self-evident as to warrant no argument or special exhortation. How to improve, should the burning desire be present, is not so apparent, but even that is patently clear to those who have taught long in the field, especially the improvement of oral expression if one has already attained the normal minimum in silent reading.

Although writers of recent decades have disagreed on some particulars, they are virtually unanimous on the basic points of view expressed in the remainder of this chapter.

First of all, the initial reading of the printed page is for the reader's understanding of the writer's message; but the oral reading of such a page is for a listener's understanding of the writer's message *as conveyed by the oral reader.* Four opportunities for error occur: first, the writer's failure to employ the proper word combinations for conveying his thought; second, the reader's failure to grasp the full thought, however well or poorly expressed; third, the reader's failure to employ the appropriate timing, voice, articulation, and bodily expression to convey to the listener what the interpreter intends; fourth, the failure of the listener to receive and interpret accurately the audible and visible symbols the oral reader has used for him. Conversely, a good interpreter can, by use of a lively imagination "read into" a writer's product much more than was intended, and, by employing skill in voice and action, pass on to the listener a much deeper, richer, and more beautiful message than the writer alone created. Calling your attention to this multi-loss or gain chain of communication has a twofold purpose: first, to cause you to be conscious of the vagaries and imperfections of the processes; and, second, to establish a perspective of the place of the oral reader in the sequence of writer, reader, and listener.

We oversimplified the process of the reader's understanding of the writer's writings when we referred to the proper understanding of "word combinations." True, the writer's words may be the reader's initial and ultimate clues to meaning. But there are many others between the "initial" and the "ultimate." A single word may be charged with a thousand different auras or connotations beyond its normal denotation, depending on what the reader knows of the writer's life and times, and of the circumstances out of which a particular piece of writing grew.

For example, consider the following lines from Shakespeare's *Merchant of Venice*:

> SIGNIOR ANTONIO, many a time and oft
> In the Rialto you have rated me
> About my moneys and my usances.
> Still have I borne it with a patient shrug,
> For sufferance is the badge of all our tribe.
> You call me misbeliever, cut-throat dog,
> And spit upon my Jewish gaberdine,
> And all for use of that which is mine own.
> Well then, it now appears you need my help.
> Go to then! You come to me, and you say,
> "Shylock, we would have moneys;" you say so—
> You, that did void your rheum upon my beard
> And foot me as you spurn a stranger cur
> Over your threshold; moneys is your suit.
> What should I say to you? Should I not say,
> "Hath a dog money? Is it possible
> A cur can lend three thousand ducats?" Or
> Shall I bend low and in a bondman's key,
> With bated breath and whispering humbleness,
> Say this:
> "Fair sir, you spat on me on Wednesday last;
> You spurned me such a day; another time
> You call'd me dog; and for these courtesies
> I'll lend you thus much moneys?"

Remember, first, that Shakespeare's Shylock was intended as the main object in a comedy, but through the centuries has come to be played more often as the leading subject in a tragedy. If the reader interprets him as a modern clown designed to give rise to humor and dramatic interest, the lines will have one meaning. If he is visualized as the epitome of Jewish suffering through the centuries, faithfully exemplifying the tribulations of a buffeted people, and is looked upon as bargaining with Antonio as a deliberate means of compensating in a very real way for the repeated insults he has suffered at the hands of an unfeeling majority, the lines take on quite different meaning.

In either case, the following words are worth noting because of their denotation and connotation, and in particular because of their difference in value today, in normal contexts, as opposed to their value as used in Shakespeare's time: *rated, usances, sufferance, badge, tribe.*

In our eagerness to make a point, we have mentioned both background and specific words. To be logical, we should perhaps structure our approach somewhat as follows:

Know the background of the writing. First of all, know the author. *When* was he? In what times did he live? What was the influence of these times upon him? *Who* was he? Out of what did he grow, and how did he develop? Who and what were his parents, brothers, sisters, other relatives, neighbors, friends, enemies, community, country, etc.? *What* was he? Catholic, Protestant, Jew, Buddhist, atheist, Democrat, Republican, Communist, socialist, thief, introvert, pervert, idealist, etc.?

Know the writer's purpose—generally and specifically. Was he genuine artist or cunning propagandist? Was he social reformer, political protagonist, detached philosopher, or religious idealist? You probably can put Plato, Henrik Ibsen, Eugene O'Neill, Thomas Paine, and Harriet Beecher Stowe easily and quickly into one of these categories; but O. Henry, Mark Twain, Tolstoy, Charles Dickens, T. S. Eliot, Robert Frost, Ernest Hemingway, and Ralph Waldo Emerson are probably not so easily pigeonholed. Some analysts suggest that the most common purposes for writing are *to inform, to persuade,* and *to dramatize.* These *purposes* do not contradict the *forms* of prose, poetry, drama, essay, fiction, exposition, description, narration, comedy, tragedy, prose-drama, dramatic poetry, lyric poetry, poetic prose, and drama written in poetic form. In fact, the purpose of "dramatizing" may be done more effectively sometimes in prose form or poetry than through the drama. In any case, the student-analyst should learn to distinguish between form and purpose, and should at least make an attempt to identify the writer's purpose, whether he be entirely successful in this aim or not. The more he knows about the purpose, form, motivation, and total background of what he reads, in short, the better he understands what he is to interpret to others, the better he can interpret it.

Know the writer's sources. Where did the writer get the idea for what he wrote? Did his materials arise from reading history, from observing his neighbors, from a study of literary prototypes, from imagination, from intensive research, or from a combination of these?

Know where the writing stands among writings of its time, and also its place among all the writings in the total scope of literature. This is a big order; and the student's success, therefore, will be limited. Nevertheless, one should know that the ultimate in artistry imposes this requirement, and that to the degree he falls short of this knowledge, to a commensurate degree is he likely to miss the level of true art in interpretation.

A few illustrations of the importance of knowing the background of selections to be interpreted may be helpful. Sam Walter Foss' famous poem, "The House by the Side of the Road," has only very general meaning until one realizes that it grew out of an experience he had one warm day. Trudging wearily along a dusty road, he found a bench in the shade that had on it a written invitation to linger and rest, a bucket of apples and the request to eat of them, and a sign directing him to cool, pure water. His curiosity led him to discover that these conveniences were his, or anyone's, through the generous courtesy of an elderly couple who lived in a little "house by the side of the road" and showed their friendship "to man" in this fashion.

Knowing that William Henley wrote his "Invictus" after years of agonizing pain from tuberculosis of the bone, amputation of his leg, and months of weariness in a hospital in the days before anaesthesia was successful—these facts allow one to understand the true meaning of his poem.

The following lines from Tennyson's "In Memoriam" become much richer in meaning and feeling when one reads them with the realization that they were written in a mood of pensive sadness over the loss of a close friend.

### IN MEMORIAM

STRONG SON OF GOD, immortal Love,
    Whom we, that have not seen thy face,
    By faith, and faith alone, embrace,
Believing where we cannot prove;

Thine are these orbs of light and shade;
    Thou madest Life in man and brute;
    Thou madest Death; and lo, thy foot
Is on the skull which thou hast made.

Thou wilt not leave us in the dust;
    Thou madest man, he knows not why,
    He thinks he was not made to die;
And thou hast made him; thou art just.

Thou seemest human and divine,
    The highest, holiest manhood, thou.
    Our wills are ours, we know not how;
Our wills are ours, to make them thine.

Our little systems have their day;
    They have their day and cease to be;
    They are but broken lights of thee,
And Thou, O Lord, art more than they.

Browning's "Prospice" is richer, too, when one reads it knowing that it refers to his anticipated reunion in heaven with his so deeply loved, departed wife, Elizabeth.

## PROSPICE

FEAR DEATH? to feel the fog in my throat,
    The mist in my face,
When the snows begin, and the blasts denote
    I am nearing the place,
The power of the night, the press of the storm,
    The post of the foe;
Where He stands, the Arch Fear in a visible form,
    Yet the strong man must go:
For the journey is done and the summit attained,
    And the barriers fall,
Though a battle's to fight ere the guerdon be gained,
    The reward of it all.
I was ever a fighter, so—one fight more,
    The best and the last!
I would hate that death bandaged my eyes, and forbore,
    And bade me creep past.
No! let me taste the whole of it, fare like my peers
    The heroes of old,
Bear the brunt, in a minute pay glad life's arrears
    Of pain, darkness and cold.
For sudden the worst turns the best to the brave,
    The black minute's at end,
And the elements' rage, the fiend-voices that rave,
    Shall dwindle, shall blend,
Shall change, shall become first a peace out of pain,
    Then a light, then thy breast,
O thou soul of my soul! I shall clasp thee again,
    And with God be the rest!

Similarly, knowing the fact of John Milton's blindness, and in particular being familiar with his well-known poem

"On His Blindness," places the interpreter in a favorable position to appreciate the mood, intent, and particulars of Leonard Bacon's attempt to dramatize an imagined segment of life from the Milton household.

## AN AFTERNOON IN ARTILLERY WALK
### (*Mary Milton loquitur*)

I THINK IT IS his blindness makes him so.
He is so angry, and so querulous,
Yes, Father! I will look in Scaliger.
Yes, Cousin Phillips took the notes—I think—
May all the evil angels fly away
With Cousin Phillips to the Serbonian Bog
Wherever that may be. And here am I
Locked in with him the livelong afternoon.
There's Anne gone limping with that love of hers,
Her master-carpenter, and Deborah
Stolen away. Yes, Father, 'tis an aleph
But the Greek glose on't in the Septuagint
Is something that I cannot quite make out.
The letter's rubbed.

Oh, thus to wear away
My soul and body with this dry-as-dust
This tearer-up of words, this plaguey seeker
After the things that no man understands.
'Tis April. I am seventeen years old,
And Abram Clark will come a-courting me.
Ah, what a Hell a midday house can be!
Dusty and bright and dumb and shadowless,
Full of this sunshot dryness, like the soul
Of this old pedant here. I will not bear
Longer this tyranny of death in life
That drains my spirit like a succubus.
I am too full of blood and life for this—
This dull soul-gnawing discipline he sets

Upon our shoulders, the sad characters,
Chapter on chapter, blank and meaningless.
Now by the May-pole merry-makers run,
And the music throbs and pulses in light limbs,
And the girls' kirtles are lifted to the knee.
Ah would that I were blowsy with the heat,
Being bussed by some tall fellow, and kissing him
On his hot red lips—some bully royalist
With gold in's purse and lace about his throat
And a long rapier for the Puritans.
Or I would wander by some cool yew-hedge,
Dallying with my lover all the afternoon,
And then to cards and supper—cinnamon,
Some delicate pastry, and an amber wine
Burning on these lips that I know a year-long lent.
Then to the theatre, and Mistress Nell
That the King's fond of. Mayhap gentlemen
About would praise me, and I should hear them buzz,
And feel my cheek grow warm beneath my mask,
And glance most kindly—
I was in a muse
I have the paper, father, and the pens.
Now for the damnable dictation. So!
"High—on a throne—of royal state—which far
Outshone—the wealth of 'Ormus'—S or Z,
How should I know the letter?—"and of Ind.
Or where—the gorgeous East—with richest hand
Showers—on her kings—barbaric—pearl and gold,
Satan exalted sate."

In addition to knowing general background, the would-be
interpreter needs to know particulars. Some of these particulars, such as dates, places, names, persons, and events, become known to him as he studies the general background.
Even some word meanings are attached to specific historical
events. But others lie in denotations, connotations, and se-

mantic implications that inhere in the writer's artistic devices. The student's need, therefore, is to become word-conscious. He must know not only the distinction between *denotation* (the face-value of a word) and *connotation* (the implicative or even insinuative value of a word), but also the place of allusion, or indirect reference, in artistic writing, and likewise the distinction between literal and figurative language. Beyond these awarenesses, he needs to increase his consciousness—as the whole world has in recent years—of the fact that words at best are only "signs" for objects and ideas, and thus subject to vagaries of value from person to person and time to time.

And so one might continue listing what a student must know in order to be a good interpreter, until the conscientious student might well despair of even trying, for fear of becoming like the centipede that ran speedily and easily until it began to think about the order in which it moved its legs, then became so confused about which leg was which that it soon lay helpless in a ditch.

Therefore, let us hope that we have opened the door of opportunity to better interpretation through increasing the student's awareness that understanding is important, and that we have not instead opened a Pandora's box (a literary allusion!) of troubles to plague him. Suffice it to say that the importance of understanding individual word meanings cannot be overemphasized. In fact, the reader must understand the "language" or meaning of the whole if he is to interpret it to others.

Hamlet's famous soliloquy has been often misinterpreted by high-school and college students who lacked full realization of the meaning behind the Prince's words. Consider that Hamlet was presumed to be deeply Catholic, and that through his mind ran many thoughts of hell, purgatory, and final judgment. Many interpret his "power-of-action-lost-in-the-energy-of-resolve" complex as being a hesitation to seek earthly revenge for the misdeeds against him and his father because he feared the consequences in after-life if he accepted less than vengeance. Consider the distinction between "revenge" and "vengeance," then read the following lines of Hamlet's speech, keeping the thought in mind of his probable religious thinking. Note how it changes your concept of many of the terms used.

> To BE, or not to be: that is the question.
> Whether 't is nobler in the mind to suffer
> The slings and arrows of outrageous fortune,
> Or to take arms against a sea of troubles,
> And by opposing end them. To die; to sleep;
> No more; and by a sleep to say we end
> The heartache and the thousand natural shocks
> That flesh is heir to. 'T is a consummation
> Devoutly to be wish'd. To die; to sleep;—
> To sleep? Perchance to dream! Ay, there's the rub;
> For in that sleep of death what dreams may come,
> When we have shuffl'd off this mortal coil,
> Must give us pause. There's the respect
> That makes calamity of so long life.
> For who would bear the whips and scorns of time,
> The oppressor's wrong, the proud man's contumely,
> The pangs of despiz'd love, the law's delay,
> The insolence of office, and the spurns
> That patient merit of the unworthy takes,
> When he himself might his quietus make
> With a bare bodkin? Who would fardels bear,
> To grunt and sweat under a weary life,
> But that the dread of something after death,
> The undiscovered country from whose bourne
> No traveller returns, puzzles the will
> And makes us rather bear those ills we have

Than fly to others that we know not of?
Thus conscience does make cowards of us all;
And thus the native hue of resolution
Is sicklied o'er with the pale cast of thought,
And enterprises of great pith and moment
With this regard their currents turn awry,
And lose the name of action.

Not only are the general meaning and feeling of Longfellow's "The Cross of Snow" enhanced by knowledge that it was written in memory of his wife, who died as the result of burns suffered when her lacy gown caught fire from candles burning in celebration of their wedding anniversary, but both the connotation and denotation of numerous words within the poem are also dependent upon this fact.

## The Cross of Snow

In the long, sleepless watches of the night,
    A gentle face—the face of one long dead—
    Looks at me from the wall, where round its head
    The night-lamp casts a halo of pure light.
Here in this room she died; and soul more white
    Never through martyrdom of fire was led
    To its repose; nor can in books be read
    The legend of a life more benedight.
There is a mountain in the distant West
    That, sun-defying, in its deep ravines
    Displays a cross of snow upon its side.
Such is the cross I wear upon my breast
    These eighteen years, through all the changing scenes
    And seasons, changeless since the day she died.

One more subject, however, needs mention in the category of what we will call "impression" as we close this section —namely, *mood.* This intangible quality permeates and pervades a selection, instead of riding on or near the surface, as does meaning. It is felt rather than defined, though such words as "melancholy," "foreboding," "boisterous," "pensive," "philosophical," "unhappy," "sprightly," "gay," "grave," may be highly suggestive. But in spite of its airy nature, mood must be sensed, even analyzed, by the interpreter if he is to give the totality of any piece of literature to his listeners.

Consider that Macbeth has run his course of ambition, treachery, and murder, and has at last come to full realization of the folly of it all upon hearing of his wife's death; then note how the emotional tone of the following lines is dependent entirely upon that factual background.

> SHE SHOULD HAVE DIED hereafter;
> There would have been a time for such a word.
> To-morrow, and to-morrow, and to-morrow,
> Creeps in this petty pace from day to day
> To the last syllable of recorded time;
> And all our yesterdays have lighted fools
> The way to dusty death. Out, out, brief candle!
> Life's but a walking shadow, a poor player
> That struts and frets his hour upon the stage
> And then is heard no more. It is a tale
> Told by an idiot, full of sound and fury
> Signifying nothing.

Similarly, Browning's "Prospice" and Shylock's speeches, already quoted, become much more filled with feeling as well as with meaning when one gains the power to emphasize with the author's mood directly or through one of his characters as a visualized human being.

Eugene Field's "Little Boy Blue" is only a sentimental little jingle until one views it as arising from the heart of a man whose anguish over the loss of his child is assuaged only by his unwavering faith in God and an after-life. To get fully into the mood of the poem one should try singing it, for it has been effectively set to music. A girl who once read the poem without either meaning or feeling was asked to secure the music and to try reading the poem as she played her own xylophone accompaniment. She then read it with such feeling that she placed third among more than a thousand contestants in the reading of poetry of their own choice.

A person may move still more fully into the poem's mood if he will read other sadly reflective writings from Field's collection under the title *Poems of Childhood*. Especially helpful is the companion poem, "Pittypat and Tippytoe."

All we have said thus far is directed to the oral reader's understanding, or appreciation, of what he reads in preparation for the actual reading, or interpreting, of it to listeners. Although from the teacher's standpoint this preparation is the essential pre-ingredient of effective performance, students are probably impatient to "get on with the show." Even intensely interested students are so concerned about the personal aspects of performance that they have difficulty accepting what the teacher is so sure is good for them. They are more concerned with voice, gesture, posture, movement, with themselves as performing personalities possessing feelings of fear, even panic, and disappointment, elation, satisfaction, embarrassment. Do not misunderstand: your teachers have experienced all of these emotions, not once but often. Out of their happy and unhappy experiences, they may not have found the wisdom that enables them to know everything that is good for you; but they have learned through bitter experience that some first things ought to be first, and that if they are, many other things will work out much more satisfactorily.

One of these is that effective expression must be preceded by effective understanding, as we have said before. The other is that man is a naturally expressive creature, and that, once filled with something to say, he will express himself effectively—*unless he is inhibited by fear or is limited by poor vocal and/or physical habits or other basic inadequacies.* You may well answer that you are limited by one or all of these; therefore why fill yourself with so much to express when your fears and inadequacies will not let you express it? The answer to your combination answer-question is that, by being prepared, you have a chance; but without your being properly equipped in advance, the certain outcome is failure. Even more important is the psychological concept stressed earlier in this book, that action suits itself to the word: i.e., that action *follows* thought, that only confused action can follow confused thought, but that co-ordinated action will follow organized, clear, and coherent thought. This principle and concept—that spontaneous and appropriate action will follow "something to express" as inevitably and naturally as night follows day—is immeasurably important in a student's attitude toward developing satisfactory skills in interpretation.

Whether or not you have been won to this point of view, a few specific suggestions on the techniques of *ex*pressing the *im*pressions you have been developing may be helpful.

First, read to your audience, not to the book. If you are interpreting *for* them, you must read *to* them. The reader should be so familiar with his material that he can look most of the time at his hearers, making only occasional reference to the page. With practice, he will be able to grasp a whole sentence or more at a glance, giving practically all of his eye-contact to people before him.

Next, observe the limiting principle of *suggestion.* Oral reading lies between the direct discourse of speaking and the detached spectacle of acting. The speaker is his own agent; the actor is a character out of another world, assuming as completely as possible all the characteristics of the personality painted by the author, and the audience looks through a window, as it were, at him. The reader stands before his listeners and stimulates their imaginations with the words from the printed page. Thus the reader is neither actor nor speaker. The audience does not empathize[1] with *him*, but with the pictures created by the words he reads. He must therefore be careful not to put so much of his own personality into the picture that he breaks the illusion created by the author. He should not make movements that are inconsistent with the imaginative patterns created in the minds of the audience. Thus, bodily action for oral reading should be stringently limited, confining itself purely to suggestion, and never demonstrating directly. The audible aspects of reading, however, do not give rise so readily to anomalies of perception. One may run the gamut of pitch, quality, loudness, and time, without fear of incongruity, for voice changes and diction patterns are basically only suggestive; they do not depict directly as bodily movements sometimes do. One exception to this generalization should be observed, and that concerns the rendering of dialect. If a reader reproduces accurately the eccentricities of a foreigner's use of English speech, he usually sacrifices intelligibility. Consequently, he must confine himself to *suggesting* the salient characteristics of the dialect. This is usually sufficient, for most listeners respond through general impression rather than through anaylsis of detail.[2]

Differentiation between characters, and between dialogue and general exposition, is frequently not well done. Some readers employ the same tones and rates for all passages, whereas others make the changes so extreme that the effect of naturalness is lost. The first fault leaves an audience unresponsive and unable to follow easily; the second error makes them squirm in embarrassment for the reader. Both results may be avoided if the potential reader will study

[1] Empathy means "feeling into" a situation without feeling in it. You experience the anger or excitement of an actor in a play while at the same time you feel a detachment from him and his situation.

[2] Charlotte Lee, *Oral Interpretation*. Boston: Houghton Mifflin, 1959, p. 5.

carefully the normal differences in pitch between men and women, and between individuals of both sexes; if he will likewise observe studiously differences in loudness, quality, and time; if he will avoid the falsetto; if he will study articulation patterns; and if he will clearly delineate in his own mind every character who speaks, and attempt in his speech pattern to suggest significant characteristics of each. The last precaution will automatically differentiate between dialogue and regular narrative.

Above all, the reader's task is to give the effect of naturalness. In his effort to articulate distinctly and to make his voice carrry to all parts of the room, he must not resort to a "ready" tone or to artificial articulation. He must not make unnatural approaches by uttering stock, trite remarks or by failing to give any sort of introduction. He ought to plan preliminary remarks that will put the audience into a receptive mood, either by acquainting them with the author or with the motivation (cause for writing) of the piece, or by relating some incident that makes them empathize with the reader or with the idea of the selection. He should maintain an attitude appropriate to the spirit of what he reads. If it is humorous, he should smile at the high points. If it is grave, he should be generally serious, though always friendly. He is in a sense the confidant of the audience. They get their cues from the twinkle in his eyes and the play of his smile or the clouding of his mien, as well as from his voice and the author's words.

In summary, effective oral reading depends upon two factors: adequate *im*pressions and skillful *ex*pression. But that is too brief a story even for a summary. The *im*pression process must be viewed from long-range and from short-range objectives; likewise must the skills of *ex*pression. If "Rome was not built in a day," neither are profound and incisive insights into literary forms and values. Years of study are necessary for the development of superior skills in literary analysis and appreciation, and for the cultivation of refined literary taste. Hours of study of a given selection are a part of such a long-range program, even though the immediate objective may be better performance in tomorrow's assignment. Similarly, the cultivation of a well-modulated voice and controlled posture and movement requires years; but today's exercise before the class will contribute its part to the ultimate.

A third factor should be in every student's mind: namely, that writings vary greatly in being easy or difficult to interpret, in both the *im*pression and the *ex*pression categories. As with music, skating, swimming, golf, and many other activities in life, some things are simpler and therefore easier than others. Thus the wise student will climb the ladder of interpretation skills and insights gradually, step by step. He will choose first those things that are easy to understand and to convey, that are suited to his personality and experience, and are easy for an audience to enjoy. As he gains skill and confidence, he will select increasingly difficult "experiments."

The authors are convinced that although numerous excellent texts on oral interpretation have been written in recent years, none has presented the student with a satisfactory collection of materials of graduated difficulty. Especially has the beginner been neglected. One of the reasons that no collections of such materials has been made is that costs of permission to reprint are prohibitive. Accordingly, a special feature of this chapter is the listing of suggested readings, identified in categories of increasing difficulty, and selected with special attention to their "oral readability." Comments are designed to help the student find "laboratory" materials appropriate to his level of skills and taste, and also to insure his maximum success in eliciting a satisfying audience response.

In general, it is safe to assume that narrative prose containing little dialogue is easiest to read well. Next in difficulty, perhaps, is prose monologue, followed by narrative prose with considerable amounts of dialogue. Third is narrative poetry. Fourth is the poetic dramatic monologue (e.g., Browning's "My Last Duchess," or his "Soliloquy in a Spanish Cloister"). Fifth is drama, and sixth poetic drama. Dialect is a problem all its own, and ordinarily increases the difficulty of any of the other types or forms, though sometimes it is the key to unlocking one's inhibitions and releasing one's insights and powers of expression. These distinctions and gradations are admittedly arbitrary, and are dependent on many, many internal factors such as style, simplicity of structure, subtlety of plot or character delineation, excitement of plot, or humor of treatment. Ordinarily, a student feels the best response from his audience when what he reads evokes frequent laughter. The response may arise from the irresistible humor of what he reads rather than from any skill in his reading of it; but it is a response that both he and his respondents identify with him, so that both parties feel he has been "successful." It is also true that overt laughter may *seem* a better response than deep quiet, and is thus misleading, though nonetheless satisfying.

It is suggested that the student "experiment" with a wide variety of selections as he explores the development of increasingly sound reading habits. The suggested order of difficulty and the arrangement of selected references are only general guides for students in general, and not specific formulas for any one student in particular. No selection is included, however, which has not survived the test of repeated success with classroom audiences.

The mark of (1) indicates easy reading; (2) a little more difficult; and so on to (5), the most difficult.

Many of the suggested selections have interesting stories behind them. If these backgrounds are investigated, and if they are employed as introductions to the "experiments in reading aloud," they can add much to an audience's response.

Grouping the selections according to narrative prose, dramatic dialogue, and so on, was seriously considered but finally discarded in favor of a simple listing by authors. The student will find his best guide in the marks that indicate the degree of difficulty in interpretation that each selection offers.

Anonymous:
   *Courtship of Miles Standish, The.* The old story in Swedish dialect. (3)
Bacon, Leonard:
   *An Afternoon in Artillery Walk.* An imaginary scene between John Milton and his daughter Mary. For advanced experiments, but outstanding in interpretative demands and opportunities. (5)

Beck, Allen
   *What is a Boy?* (1)
Benét, Stephen Vincent:
   *Devil and Daniel Webster, The* (3)
   *John Brown's Body.* Selected portions (3)
   *Mountain Whippoorwill, The* (2)
Blanding, Don:
   *Bluebeard Speaks to His 'Steenth Wife* (2)
   *Cornfield Romance* (1)
   *Dog and a Cockleburr* (1)
Bradford, Roark:
   *Adam Bomb, The* (2)
   *How Come Christmas?* Negro dialect. (2)
Brown, John Mason:
   *We Have With Us Tonight* (1)
Browne, Porter Emerson:
   *The Bad Man.* Found in greatly condensed form in the Burns-Mantle collection of best plays. (5)
Browning, Robert:
   *Bishop Orders His Tomb, The* (4)
   *Fra Lippo Lippi* (4)
   *Incident of the French Camp* (2)

*My Last Duchess* (4)
*Porphyria's Lover* (4)
*Soliloquy of the Spanish Cloister* (4)
Carroll, Lewis:
*Jabberwocky, The* (2)
*Walrus and the Carpenter, The* (2)
Connelly, Mark:
*Green Pastures.* Selected cuttings make excellent reading: For example, the scene in which God gives Noah instructions on preparing for the flood; and the scene in which Gabriel reports on problems of horn blowing. (2)

Cook, Edmund Vance:
*Hen, The* (2)
*Moo Cow Moo, The* (1)
Daly, T. A.:
*Mia Carlotta* (3)
Dickens, Charles:
*Christmas Carol, A* (1)
Disney, Walt:
*Happy Valley.* A modern Disney treatment of the old story of Jack and the Beanstalk. (2)

Dunbar, Paul Lawrence:
*Delinquent, The* (2)
*In De Mawnin'* (3)
*When Malindy Sings* (2)
Field, Eugene:
*Duel, The* (2)
*Sugar Plum Tree, The* (2)
Frost, Robert:
*Death of the Hired Man* (2)
*Departmental* (2)
*Fear, The* (3)
*Home Burial* (3)
*Mountain Tragedy* (3)

Graham, Al:
*Casey's Daughter at the Bat*. A sequel to *Casey at the Bat*. (2)

Gross, Milt:
*Ferry Tail from King Mitas*. Found in Boardman, Gail, *Oral Communication of Literature*, p. 420 (3)

Halsey, Margaret:
*With Malice Toward Some* (2)
Johnson, James Weldon:
*Creation, The* (2)
Leacock, Stephen:
Many of his humorous prose selections are excellent because they read easily and are entertaining. Among the best are:
*Behind the Beyond, A Modern Problem Play*. 40 minutes. (2)
*Hoodoo McFiggin's Christmas* (1)
Lowell, Amy:
*Patterns* (3)
Magee, John G., Jr.:
*High Flight* (2)
Markham, Edwin:
*Man with the Hoe, The*. (2)
Milne, A. A.:
*Winnie the Pooh* (2)
Nash, Ogden:
*Adventures of Isabelle* (1)
*My Future Son-in-Law* (1)
Noyes, Alfred:
*Highwayman, The* (2)
O. Henry:
*Jack the Giant Killer* (1)
*Ransom of Red Chief, The* (1)

Patrick, Luther:
  *Sleepin' at the Foot o' the Bed* (1)
Poe, Edgar Allen:
  *Annabel Lee* (3)
  *Cask of Amontillado, The* (2)
  *Raven, The* (2)
  *Telltale Heart, The* (2)
Riley, James Whitcomb:
  *Bear Story, The* (1)
  *Liz Town Humorist, The* (3)
Sandburg, Carl:
  *Chicago* (3)
Service, Robert:
  *Cremation of Sam Magee, The.* Familiar, but always welcome. (2)
  *Face on the Bar Room Floor, The* (2)
  *Fleurette.* Serious and dramatic. (4)
  *Shooting of Dan McGrew, The* (2)
Sill, Edward Roland:
  *Fool's Prayer, The* (3)
Smith, Gerald:
  *Herbert and the Electricity* (1)
Tazewell, C.:
  *Littlest Angel, The* (1)
Tennyson, Alfred:
  *Crossing the Bar* (2)
Thayer, Ernest Lawrence:
  *Casey at the Bat.* A worn-out bit of cheap verse—until you look into the story behind it. (2)

Thurber, James:
  *Mr. Preeble Gets Rid of His Wife* (2)
  *Night the Bed Fell, The* (2)
  *What Do You Mean, It's Brillig?* (2)
Twain, Mark:
  Many, many of Twain's writings are good reading. But portions especially recommended are:

*Why the French Speak French.* A scene from Huckle-berry Finn. Nigger Jim and Huck philosophize on this subject as their boat rests on the Mississippi.

Other scenes are Tom Sawyer's fence-painting salesmanship and the drama of a presumably drowned and greatly mourned boy hiding under the bed listening to the lamentations of his elders.

Wôlo:
  *Amanda* (2)
  *Friendship Valley* (2)
  *Sir Archibald* (2)
  *Tweedles Be Brave* (2)
Wood, Clement:
  *Glory Road, The* (2)

# Index

# Index

# Index